K. Hannah Holtschneider

German Protestants Remember the Holocaust

RELIGION – GESCHICHTE – GESELLSCHAFT
Fundamentaltheologische Studien

herausgegeben von

Johann Baptist Metz (Münster / Wien)
Johann Reikerstorfer (Wien)
Jürgen Werbick (Münster)

Band 24

LIT

K. Hannah Holtschneider

German Protestants Remember the Holocaust

Theology and the Construction of Collective Memory

LIT

Die Deutsche Bibliothek – CIP-Einheitsaufnahme

Holtschneider, K. Hannah:
German Protestants Remember the Holocaust : Theology and the Construction of
Collective Memory / K. Hannah Holtschneider. – Münster : LIT, 2001
   (Religion - Geschichte - Gesellschaft ; 24.)
   Zugl.: Birmingham, Univ., Diss., 2000
   ISBN 3-8258-5539-2

© LIT VERLAG Münster – Hamburg – London
   Grevener Str. 179   48159 Münster   Tel. 0251-23 50 91   Fax 0251-23 19 72

Distributed in North America by:

Transaction Publishers
New Brunswick (U.S.A.) and London (U.K.)

Transaction Publishers
Rutgers University
35 Berrue Circle
Piscataway, NJ 08854

Tel.: (732) 445 - 2280
Fax: (732) 445 - 3138
for orders (U. S. only):
toll free (888) 999 - 6778

Table of Contents

Acknowledgements

I am indebted to several people and institutions who were instrumental in making this book possible.

The research for this book could not have been completed without the financial assistance of the Futures of Theology Initiative of the University of Birmingham. The Centre for Jewish-Christian Relations in Cambridge provided me with time to transform my doctoral dissertation into this book.

I am grateful for the advice of my supervisor Isabel Wollaston. I could not have done without the critical suggestions of Werner Ustorf and Björn Krondorfer. I thank Jürgen Manemann and Johann Baptist Metz who supported this publication, as well as Michael Rainer and Michael Heimann at Lit. Verlag.

I am grateful to Birgit Spörl, Anja Behrens, Desmond Bell and Petra Cremer for their hospitality and friendship during my research trips to Germany. A source of encouragement during my work on this project and beyond is the friendship of Claudia Wild, Peter Kevern, Sarah Fishwick and George Wilkes. I am indebted to my parents and my brother without whose generous support none of this would have been possible.

Abbreviations

CCJ	The Council of Christians and Jews
DP	Displaced Person
EKD	Evangelical Church in Germany
EKiR	Evangelical Church in the Rhineland
FAZ	*Frankfurter Allgemeine Zeitung*
FRG	Federal Republic of Germany
GDR	German Democratic Republic
ICCJ	The International Council of Christians and Jews
NS	National Socialism/st
RCC	Roman Catholic Church
SS	*Schutzstaffel* (NS protection squad, NS elite troops)
UK	United Kingdom
USA	United States of America
USHMM	United States Holocaust Memorial Museum
WCC	World Council of Churches
WDR	*Westdeutscher Rundfunk*

Introduction

> In this country [FRG] the collective memory remains tied to National Socialism – be it as remembrance of guilt, be it as defence. Either way: without any outside assistance the collective memory is fixed to this past and, thus conveyed, it paradoxically constitutes belonging. The condition of membership in the collective of Germans, defined in a racist ethnical way by National Socialism, constitutes now, as morally justified connection of guilt, a significant feature of substantial belonging to the ethnic community defined as collective memory. Thus the historically aware retreat to the connection of guilt, caused by National Socialism, in particular becomes a fundamental pillar of the collective "We".[1]

This study examines how Protestants in Germany interpret their self-understanding as part of this community which is defined by its connection to NS by analysing representations of the Holocaust and Jews in three exemplary theological texts. Theories of collective memory suggest that interpretations of the Holocaust and Jews as part of Protestant theological reflection inform the self-definition of Christians in Germany. Hence the narratives on the Holocaust and Jews presented in Protestant discourses inform the narratives of collective memory of the church. Representations of Jews[2] are part of all Christian theological texts that reflect on Christian-Jewish encounters in Germany and their meaning for Christian-Jewish relations. Located in the cultural context of post-Holocaust Germany Christian-Jewish encounters, and the Christian theological reflection upon these encounters, are arguably defined by their relation to the Holocaust.

At a time when the communicative memory of NS and the Holocaust ceases and the culturally defined memory on communal and national levels becomes dominant, the third generation of Germans after the Holocaust assumes increasing importance in shaping the narratives of NS and Holocaust memory.[3] This study intends to understand the extent to which theologies developed by the second generation of Germans after the Holocaust facilitate the articulation of issues of Holocaust remembrance pertaining to the third generation.[4]

---

[1] Diner 1995, 118. Translations from German publications which were not available in English while writing this study are mine. Unless otherwise indicated emphases are original.

[2] Theological texts in particular often use Jews, Jewish people, Israel, G-d's people, or chosen people interchangeably. I prefer Jews and Jewish people, and use Israel only in conjunction with the State of Israel. Cf. also the discussion in chapters I. and III. I follow Jewish tradition and hyphenate all words which contain the name of the creator. Direct quotations and translations, however, reflect the spelling of their author.

[3] Regarding the distinction between communicative and cultural memory cf. Assmann 1988, 9-19.

[4] For a definition of generations cf. chapter IV.

This study builds on the efforts of the previous generation to formulate responsible answers to the Holocaust. Without their courage, my analysis would not be possible. While appreciating their pioneering work, changes in the social-historical situation and a generational change in German society suggest that a renewed reflection on the challenges the memory of NS and the Holocaust poses to Germans is warranted. In particular, paradigms generated by Christian reflection on the Holocaust and Jews and their consequences for the contemporary situation of Christian-Jewish relations in Germany will be addressed in this study.

In the analyses presented in this study I am guided by two concerns. Firstly, I am concerned about the ways in which Jewish tradition and Jewish memories of the Holocaust are appropriated in these Protestant theologies. However, I am conscious of the efforts made by German Protestants, whose faith has been challenged through the impact of events of the Holocaust and their memory, to renew Christian faith and theology in such a way that these exclude antisemitism[5] and are morally defensible after the Holocaust. Secondly, I am occupied with issues particular to the third generation of non-Jewish/Christian Germans and Jews after the Holocaust. Members of the third generation face challenges to their self-understanding which are different from the challenges faced by their parents and grandparents. That to the older generations the memory of NS and the Holocaust often is the lens through which they view their lives has prompted particular theological reflection which enabled these generations to respond to their own or their parents' memories of the Holocaust and NS. However, the identity formation of the third generation is no longer confined to the issues which challenged the self-understanding of their parents and grandparents. Having inherited memories of events and experiences they do not share personally, the self-understanding of the third generation is less defined by or dependent on the memory of NS and the Holocaust, while their identities are still influenced by these inherited memories. It would be the responsibility of German Protestants to enable

---

[5] I follow Gavin Langmuir's definition of antisemitism as a combination of prejudices in the form of outside definitions of Jews which deny the right to self-definition, of generalisations of behaviour which is attributed to all Jews and of claims which have no observable reality (such as Christ-killers, desecration of the host, poisoning of wells etc.), (cf. Langmuir 1990, 328ff). Hence I do not argue for a distinction between antisemitism and anti-Judaism common in Christian theology. This distinction is meant to indicate that the theological expression of anti-Jewish sentiments changed mainly in the 19th century with the inclusion of racist elements and the creation of antisemitism which is enacted socially. It is argued that the Bible is free from antisemitism and that its anti-Jewish interpretation in theology can be changed if the texts are understood correctly. Part of the argument for a distinction between anti-Judaism and antisemitism is the understanding that anti-Judaism refers to opposition to the religion and not the people, and that such an opposition is legitimate. What is illegitimate are the social consequences of such attitudes. I do not support such an argument. "Anti-Judaism" draws on images encompassed in the above definition of antisemitism and the distinction between theological statements and their social impact is difficult to ascertain. For the spelling of antisemitism cf. Almog 1989, 1f. Quotations with different spellings have not been changed.

this generation to articulate their relationship to the history and memory they have inherited and make their concerns for the memory of the Holocaust part of theological texts.

The chapters are arranged chronologically. Three chapters follow the development of Protestant theology since the 1980s. These alternate with two chapters concerning the development of narratives of collective memory of NS and the Holocaust in German society and in the third generation in particular. Two contexts of collective memory, FRG society and the third generation of Germans after the Holocaust, inform the evaluation of Protestant representations of the Holocaust and Jews. As such the theological narrative presented in this study becomes increasingly complex through the inclusion of social and generational issues of Holocaust remembrance in Germany.

There are two criteria for choosing the 1980 Rhineland statement *Towards a renewal of the relationship of Christians and Jews*, Friedrich-Wilhelm Marquardt's theology, in particular, *About the misery and affliction of theology* and Britta Jüngst's doctoral dissertation *In the realm of death there is life* from a variety of Christian theological interpretations of Christian-Jewish conversations in Germany:[6] (1) the theological suggestions must explicitly reflect on the Holocaust; they need to be rooted in the context of the FRG and therefore address the history of NS, the war and the Holocaust which preceded the founding of the FRG and the memory of which impacted on post-war society, and (2) the theologies must not only consider a renewed reflection on Jews and Judaism in the context of post-Holocaust Protestant theology, but also intend to transform Christian theology according to insights from the study of the Holocaust and Christian-Jewish encounters. How Protestant theologians have come to articulate their interpretations of the Holocaust and Jews can best be discerned when analysing theological texts that directly address the self-understanding of Christian theology in relation to Jews after the Holocaust. The three theological works I have chosen are each representative of different areas and stages of Christian interpretation of Christian-Jewish conversations. The three examples have been formulated over a period of twenty years and each unites practical experiences of Christian-Jewish conversations with the concerns of academic Protestant theology. All three theological texts originate in the context of the FRG, pre- and post-unification, hence they are rooted in West German discourses.

---

[6] Cf. EKiR (ed.) [2]1985; Marquardt [2]1992 ([1]1988) and Jüngst 1996.

1. The context

The FRG in the 1980s and 1990s suggests itself as a distinct context for reflection on the memory of the Holocaust[7] with regard to the third generation after the war for three reasons. Firstly, the Holocaust originated in NS Germany, Germans being the architects and chief executors of policies and practices that led to the murder of Jews in Europe. Secondly, the reflection on the NS past as a responsibility in the present has been an explicit feature of the self-definition of the FRG since its founding in 1949. As a state that historically succeeded NS, the FRG has acknowledged the history of its predecessor as part of its national heritage. This self-understanding in relation to NS has found expression for example in restitution payments to people persecuted by NS and trials of war criminals in the FRG in the 1960s and 1970s. Thirdly, in the past twenty years in particular a distinct discourse regarding the memory of the Holocaust has developed in the FRG.[8]

Both German states, founded in 1949, succeeded NS and thus had to define their relationship to their political predecessor. This posed the question of how to interpret

---

[7] In this study term Holocaust refers to the implementation of discriminatory policies of the NS state towards the Jews of Europe, beginning in 1933 in NS Germany. In particular it refers to the systematic murder of Jews in mass executions, ghettos and death camps which resulted in the genocide of Jews in Europe. This limitation to a particular group of victims of a particular NS policy does not ignore the fact that NS also persecuted and murdered a large number of other people. However, the persecution of Jews in NS Germany as a state policy sets a precedent in the history of persecution. Therefore, how Germans choose to remember publicly and officially the victims of this policy and how they treat their relatives and supporters reflects the morality and humanity of FRG society and the concern it is prepared to give to all other victims of NS. I prefer "Holocaust" over against other terminology available for three reasons. Firstly, Holocaust has become the most widely known term in the Western world to describe the murder of Jews in Europe during NS. However, for some this term carries sacrificial overtones (Greek/Latin for the Hebrew "*olah*", meaning "whole burnt offering") and that it has been appropriated in other contexts such as "nuclear holocaust", "ecological holocaust" etc. makes its usage problematic. In order to distance myself from the sacrificial context and its appropriation into other contexts I capitalise Holocaust. Secondly, other terminology such as "Auschwitz" is equally widely known, but lacks the scope of Holocaust in the sense that it refers to a particular location of the Holocaust to the exclusion of other places of atrocity and mass murder. Also to Poles Auschwitz is a place of Polish suffering and murder and conflicts regarding the ownership of memory at the site of the Auschwitz camp(s) repeatedly have become the subject of controversy. Thirdly, because I am writing about a German, predominantly non-Jewish, context, the use of terminology which relates Jewish interpretations of the Holocaust in particular (such as for example Shoah and *Hurban*) is not appropriate since it does not capture German relations to this history. Whereas Holocaust has its origin in Jewish texts and is employed by Jewish authors, its use has broadened to include predominantly non-Jewish contexts. For a discussion of different terminologies cf. for example Young 1988, 85ff.; Tal 1989, 218-224 and Petrie 2000.

[8] Cf. for example Loewy (ed.) 1992; Moltmann/Kiesel/Kugelmann/Loewy/Neuhaus (eds.) 1993; Schreier/Heyl (eds.) 1992 and Geyer/Hansen 1994.

NS in the context of German history. The FRG as well as the GDR regarded 1945/49 as a new beginning. In their self-definitions as states they built on a negation of NS and at the same time on the negation of each other.[9] Claudia Koonz points to the initial differences in the confrontation with NS in East and West Germany which were created by a "twofold negation":

> In the West, memory was sealed off in post-traumatic oblivion behind the "Zero Hour" of 1945. In the East the government enshrined courageous Communist anti-Fascists and omitted other victims from its memorials. In both sectors, the camps were put to pragmatic use or razed. Not until the 1960s did war and Nazism return to public consciousness in East and West Germany. When the Third Reich emerged in memory, the political and cultural histories of who remembered what differed significantly.[10]

The GDR understood itself as the state which emerged from the politically left-wing (antifascist) resistance movements to NS. From the start the interpretation of NS was officially limited by the antifascist self-understanding of the GDR and the analysis of political movements in economic terms only. The foundation of the state in the resistance movement led to the claim of a complete break with NS and thereby the denial of any responsibility for NS crimes. NS was not as prominent in the historical consciousness of East Germans and therefore did not become the subject of public discussion as it did in West Germany.[11] In his study *Divided Memory* Jeffrey Herf argues that the immediate post-war developments in both German states did not indicate that the memory of the Holocaust would surface more strongly in the FRG than it did in the GDR.[12] For the GDR he states that

> The East German marginalization of the Jewish question in the Nuremberg interregnum and its suppression during the anticosmopolitan purges of 1950-1956 crushed the public sympathy for the Jews which, though peripheral, had been a dissonant current within German communism before 1945.[13]

After the denazification programme, from 1955 onwards, the official interpretation and remembrance of NS was planned and engineered by the GDR government.[14] Dan Diner observes that this restricted the remembrance of the Holocaust:

> The memory of groups of victims who had been stigmatized and murdered by the Nazis – neither because of political resistance nor for economic exploitation, but merely because of their origin – clashed with the GDR's semiofficial identity and its foundational antifascism.[15]

---

[9] Cf. Koonz 1994b, 111.
[10] Koonz 1994a, 265.
[11] Cf. Lutz 1993, 160.
[12] Cf. Herf 1997, 380f.
[13] Ibid. 382f.
[14] Cf. Koonz 1994a, 265-267.
[15] Diner 1996a, 130.

Since this study restricts itself to the FRG in its immediate pre- and post-unification contexts it can refer to the former GDR only in passing. The discussion of National Socialism took its own form in the GDR, differing inherently from its treatment in the FRG. A simultaneous and comparative analysis of the West and East German contexts pre- and post-unification and in their coming together in the unified Germany is outside the scope of this study.[16]

According to Herf in West Germany the debate on responsibility for NS crimes originated with the founders of the FRG:

> The beliefs of the founding democratic leaders were indispensable for realization of even the minimal program of restitution and public memory which took place in the early years. [...] While Adenauer gave priority to reintegration of compromised elites over vivid reminders and timely justice for past crimes, Heuss and Schumacher inaugurated a tradition of public recollection in which the Holocaust eventually found an enduring place in the dominant West German public narratives of the Nazi era.[17]

In particular since the Eichmann trial in 1961 the debate about German responsibility for the Holocaust surfaced and has never since left the West German political scene.[18] It was significantly reinforced by the student movement of the 1960s and 1970s which generated a challenge to the strategies of coping with the NS past developed by their parents and grandparents.[19] Thus it appears right to conclude that "East and West official histories of Nazism could hardly have been more different when unification occurred."[20] The Cold War on the one hand, and the development of a politically engineered official memory of NS in the GDR and the emergence of a democratic society in the FRG which is able to challenge official versions of the past on the other hand, account to a large extent for the differences in relation to the memory of NS, the war and the Holocaust in East and West Germany.

Since the 1980s a distinct culture of Holocaust remembrance developed in the FRG, beginning with the screening of the American miniseries *Holocaust* in 1979.[21] Public debates on the memory of the Holocaust and other aspects of NS are frequent and highly emotional. Participation is often confined to intellectuals of the first and second generations. Still nearly all participants in public debates have personal memories of the NS period, and if not, the personal link is established via the relationship with one's parents. The "general public" engages in these debates only on a secondary level, in private or in opinion polls and case studies which estimate their

---

[16] For analyses on NS memory in the GDR cf. for example Fulbrook 1999 and Fox 1999.

[17] Herf 1997, 387.

[18] Cf. Koonz 1994a, 268f.

[19] Cf. for example Fulbrook 1999, 171.

[20] Koonz 1994a, 269.

[21] Cf. for example the discussion of the impact of *Holocaust* in Rabinbach/Zipes (eds.) 1986. The issues arising in the debate on *Holocaust* (and *Heimat*) are explored in greater detail in chapter II.

opinions on Holocaust memory and related subjects. Arguably all public debates, such as the discussion surrounding *Holocaust* (1979/80), the Bitburg Controversy (1985), the *Historikerstreit* (1986), the continuing discussion about a Holocaust memorial in Berlin, as well as the Goldhagen Controversy (1996) and the Walser Debate (1998/99) are West German debates. Even after the unification in 1990 East German historians and journalists only reluctantly engage in the public discussions on the memory of the Holocaust and NS.[22] Felix Philipp Lutz argues that whereas in West Germany only the older generations were affected by significant political, social and economic changes in the immediate post-war time, in East Germany all generations since the war had to face up to life-transforming political changes.[23] Lutz concludes therefore that the confrontation with the former GDR takes precedence for East Germans over against the confrontation with NS in constructing a viable identity for the present.[24] When discussing the impact of the Holocaust on German national identity in the context of the post-unification FRG these different traditions in the interpretation of NS and the Holocaust in the history of the two German states have to be considered. However, since the focus of this study is West German East German perspectives on the memory of the Holocaust cannot be discussed.

2. Methodology

The methodology underlying this study and its argument relies on research concerning collective memory. Concepts of history, memory and representation are interrelated and associated with different academic subject areas. Research on collective memory is rooted in a variety of disciplines and therefore the methodologies which analyse the processes and manifestations of memory vary.[25] History, sociology and cultural studies in particular, have developed the concept of collective memory.[26]

---

[22] The only East German response to Goldhagen's *Hitler's Willing Executioners* was Pätzold 1998.

[23] Cf. Lutz 1993, 172.

[24] Cf. ibid. 172.

[25] Jeffrey Olick and Joyce Robbins provide an excellent summary of the development of social memory studies which delineates the different approaches to memory since the late nineteenth century, cf. Olick/Robbins 1998. For the following account of interpretations of collective memory I am guided by their overview.

[26] Cf. the pioneering studies of Halbwachs 1950/1980 and Nora 1996 as well as Lowenthal 1985; for recent appropriations of their work in related areas cf. the collection of interdisciplinary essays in Antze/Lambek (eds.) 1996; for social psychology cf. Middleton/Edwards (eds.) 1990 and for cultural studies cf. Hobsbawm/Ranger (eds.) 1983; Huyssen 1995. Cf. also Burke 1989; Hutton 1993 and Friedlander (ed.) [3]1996. Saul Friedlander is referred to in the literature also as Saul Friedländer. The spelling of his name particular to each publication is left unchanged in references and quotations; in the main text, however, I use Friedlander.

Collective memory refers to a set of selective reconstructions of the past for the present which is subject to social conditions and change. Mary Fulbrook introduces an important aspect in her definition of collective memory as

> "Historical pictures" and collective "discourses" about the past [...] It is in this sense that the notion of patterns of collective memory is being used here. The plural is used intentionally: for there never was one single "collective memory", one generally accepted "conversation about the past." [...] Memory is not simply given, passively present: an effort is required to reconstruct, in what has been termed "memory work".[27]

The plurality of collective memories in any given context is of particular significance when examining conflicts of memory. When different perspectives on a shared historical territory are narrated, depending on the role of the narrators or the communities identified with these, conflicts of memory arise. Such conflicts do not necessarily dispute facts of what happened, but clash over the reconstruction of historical responsibilities and present reconstructions of these. Hence the conflict concerns claims to morality and truthfulness of the individuals and communities identified with particular memories.

Since Maurice Halbwachs' pioneering study *The Collective Memory*[28], the process of defining memory and its social functions first of all took place in distinction from the writing of history. Whereas Halbwachs believed in the objectivity of the writing of history, thus distinguishing it from the socially constructed collective memory, "current studies of the history of historical writing treat it much as Halbwachs treated memory, as the product of social groups such as Roman senators [...] and so on."[29] Hence the understanding that history reconstructs objectively "what actually happened" whereas memory manipulates the past for present aims was challenged. Peter Burke characterises "history as social memory" and argues "that we have access to the past (like the present) only via the categories and schemata (or as Durkheim would say, the "collective representations") of our own culture."[30] Thus Historians have become complicit in legitimising political movements, a process which

> calls into question not only the success of historians in being objective, but the very notion of objectivity itself [...]. Furthermore, postmodernists have challenged the "truthclaim" of professional historiography by questioning the distinction between knowledge and interpretation, and derivatively between history and memory [...]. If "experience," moreover, is always embedded in and occurs through narrative frames, then there is no primal, unmediated experience that can be recovered.[31]

---

[27] Fulbrook 1999, 146.
[28] Halbwachs 1950/1980.
[29] Burke 1989, 98.
[30] Ibid. 99.
[31] Olick/Robbins 1998, 110.

Any historical work, beginning with the choice of subject, sources and method of inquiry, is shaped by the assumptions and preconceptions of the society in which the historian has been educated and works, as well as by the scholar's personal relation to the subject studied. Safeguarding a notion of historical objectivity over against the social construction of memory and its treacherousness and corruption for political and ideological uses appears desirable, in particular when faced with obvious manipulation and denial of historical events for present political aims such as in the recent court case of David Irving. However, while complete objectivity is unattainable, questions concerning the uncertainty of historical knowledge are worth considering in conjunction with notions of collective memory.

A distinction between the writing of history and the construction of memory is as much needed as it is difficult to establish. Jan Assmann distinguishes four forms of memory.[32] Of particular importance in this context are his characterisations of communicative memory and cultural memory, which describe forms of collective memory distinguished by the temporal distance of the speaker to the events recorded. The communicative memory is rooted in language and relates eye-witness recollections of individuals and groups. As such it is bound to a time-span of eighty to one-hundred years and encompasses three to four generations.[33] Cultural memory transcends the boundaries of communicative memory and reflects

> the stock of re-used texts, images and rituals [...], particular to every society, the "cultivation" of which stabilises and mediates its self-understanding, a collectively shared knowledge mainly (but not exclusively) about the past, on which a community bases its consciousness of unity and individuality.[34]

Historical research depends on both communicative and cultural memory in its efforts to find and evaluate evidence, and therefore has to deal with their uncertainty.[35]

Reflecting on the denial of the existence of gas chambers of the French revisionist Robert Faurisson and responding to Hayden White's argument about the emplotment of truth,[36] Omer Bartov addresses the question of "the very nature of truth and its historical reconstruction."[37] The issue at stake is how we gain knowledge about historical events and how we reconstruct them.[38] Arguably this is relevant for both

---

[32] Cf. Assmann 1992: mimetic, material, communicative and cultural memory.

[33] Cf. Assmann 1988, 10f.

[34] Ibid. 15.

[35] Cf. Young 1997 on issues regarding the relationship between the historian and survivor testimony. The use of survivor testimony in the historiography of the Holocaust is contested, because it is considered unreliable. For a discussion of related issues cf. Roseman 1999.

[36] Cf. White [3]1996.

[37] Bartov 1993, 108.

[38] Cf. ibid. 108ff. Bartov discusses Lyotard's argument that "in order for a place to be identified as a gas chamber, the only witness I will accept would be a victim of this gas chamber; now, according

the construction of (collective) memory and the writing of history. Bartov asks "whether [...] [an] event exists independently of our own reconstruction of it and whether any reconstruction of an event is equally legitimate."[39] Caught between the dichotomies of "event and non-event" and "truth and relativity",[40] Bartov struggles to find a way in which the insights regarding the constructed nature of knowledge and truth can be appreciated without conceding historical facts.[41] He characterises the task of the historian as that of a judge who establishes responsibility in a murder case:

> Obviously, there are numerous ways of telling the story of a murder, and those depend on the witnesses as much as on the person reconstructing the event. But a murder has taken place; we did not construct it in our imagination. In that sense it is not relative. Moreover, it is important to adjudicate who was responsible [...][42]

Hence, relativism escapes the choices demanded by "a commitment to truth and morality"[43]. Bartov concludes that historians need to assume their role as "critics of society, as representatives of a moral view, as persons seeking the truth and exposing lies."[44] Hence the issue of how we gain knowledge about historical events and how we reconstruct them, addressed in theories of emplotment and historical relativism, concern the morality and commitment to truthfulness of the historian:

> In this sense, the question of whether the gas chambers existed or not is vital, for if this can be doubted, or if it is a relative issue open to multiple emplotments, then everything is. Hence the question is not one of the limits of representation, but the limits of truth.[45]

Regarding the distinction of memory from history which prompted the above paragraphs, the issue at stake concerns the commitments of individuals and collectives to morality and truthfulness.[46] Whether historical roles, actions and experiences of individuals or collectives are recalled truthfully depends on the morality of the speaker. However, historiography and collective memory exist in

---

to my opponent, there is no victim that is not dead; otherwise this gas chamber would not be what he or she claims it to be. There is, therefore no gas chamber" (Lyotard quoted in Bartov 1993, 109).

[39] Bartov 1993, 110f.

[40] Ibid. 113: "One is the argument that an event cannot be proved to have taken place if no one who had experienced it directly, with his or her own eyes, can testify to it. This is the dichotomy between event and non-event [...] The last is between truth and relativity. The assumption is ultimately that the event took place and yet at the same time it did not. It did, in the sense that it can be emplotted in innumerable ways. It did not, in the sense that no one emplotment is better than another, or rather, that one is no more truthful than another. If the event has no objective reality, then it is free to transform itself into whatever we may like."

[41] Cf. ibid. 113.

[42] Ibid. 113.

[43] Ibid. 114.

[44] Ibid. 115.

[45] Ibid. 114.

[46] Arguably, morality is a contested subject and it cannot be taken for granted that morality means the same thing to everyone (NS can also be understood in "moral terms", cf. Haas 1988).

relation to each other if only because the writing of history takes place in social contexts informed by narratives of collective memory. Arguably the most important distinction between historiography and memory is the relevance of the latter to the identity of communities and individuals. Historical narratives can become part of collective memory, but they do not need to. To that extent historical research concerns "the past that is no longer an important part of our lives"[47], whereas memories narrate what matters of the past for our present identities. However, when historians assume their task as critics of society and are committed to morality and truthfulness, their research on historical events that inform our present identities will challenge narratives of collective memory and expose what these try to obscure. Yet, the memories that inform our identities as individuals and as part of communities also relate the commitments of the individuals and their communities to morality and truthfulness.

Remembering involves decisions about which events and experiences to include in a narrative and which to omit. The notion of remembering necessarily entails the notion of forgetting. The way experiences are formulated and transmitted by individuals and communities indicates how they understand their role in history and how they interpret events they experience. Iwona Irwin-Zarecka identifies the tools that are used to organise experiences and events into narratives that shape identity as "framing devices" or "framing strategies".[48] These strategies are particular to communities and individuals. What is included in the narratives indicates what is relevant to the identity of a community of memory.[49] What is omitted or "forgotten" by the narratives indicates what communities and individuals regard as non-essential to their self-understanding or what is understood as potentially damaging to their identity. Forgetting can be both, "natural" or accidental and deliberate or ideological. Similarly, the genre of a "text", the relationship of its author and the audience to which it is addressed and which receives it, as well as the context of its publication decide about the authority and credibility of its narrative.

Arguably it is the reflection on the memory of trauma that shapes accounts of the Holocaust. The writings of Saul Friedlander, Dominick LaCapra and Alexander and Margarete Mitscherlich, for example, testify to the significance of traumatic memory in Jewish as well as German representations of the Holocaust, NS, and the war.[50]

---

[47] Olick/Robbins 1998, 111 (paraphrasing Halbwachs).

[48] Cf. Irwin-Zarecka 1994, 4ff.

[49] Cf. ibid. 47ff.

[50] Cf. Friedlander (ed.) [3]1996; Friedlander 1994; LaCapra 1998; Langer 1991 and Mitscherlich/ Mitscherlich 1968. Cf. also Freud 1912-1913. In agreement with the literature I use Germans and Jews as terms characterising largely separate communities. To speak about non-Jewish Germans and Jews would identify Germans via a negative and imply that Jewish identities are the reference point for what it means to be German. The non-Jewish character of mainstream German society has to be recognised by a positive identification. This implies that Germans are identified as they

Memory of trauma ruptures the continuities of people's individual and collective lives. Thus traumatic memory conflicts with the notion that memory is built on continuity, while arguably creating new continuities resting on the memory of trauma. This is particularly true for the memory of the Holocaust, NS and the war. The fact that individuals and collectives draw on a shared history which is traumatic in different ways to the communities involved, creates conflicts for the individual and the community as well as between communities and individuals who remember a shared past in antagonistic ways.[51] Here concerns of justice, truth, ethics and right and wrong enter the discourse.[52] Conflicting notions of justice and truth inform Jewish and German memories. The construction of memory of a shared history has placed Germans and Jews, in particular, on opposite sides, namely as the communities of victimisers and victims.[53]

If the past changes according to who is doing the remembering, at what time and in which context, the need to assess its truthfulness and morality arises. According to Irwin-Zarecka, narrating the memory of an unjust past, for which justice in terms of reparation and rehabilitation cannot be achieved, functions as a way of establishing a form of justice:

> When killings, expulsion, oppression go unacknowledged, when these bring rewards rather than punishments, when those responsible are allowed the comforts of forgetting, the wounds remain open. The passing of time does not heal these wounds; the fact that people who had committed the crimes are long dead does not seem to matter. If the historical moral accounts have never been settled, in other words, time collapses.[54]

Conflicts of memory arise, because a past for which justice cannot be achieved is not neutral to the people who care about it.[55] German and Jewish memories of the Holocaust, NS and the war narrate stories which are constructed in a mutually exclusive way.

---

identify themselves, namely as Germans. Although I agree that this distinction of communities who are divided by an antagonistic memory of the Holocaust and NS is largely correct, it prejudices against people who identify as German and Jewish at the same time. This identification, however problematic it remains, is possible and is testified to in Germany every day. However, I will not use terms such as "German Jews" and "Jewish Germans" in relation to Jews who live in contemporary Germany, since these remain definitions still rarely chosen by Jews themselves. Cf. also Brenner 1997 as well as Gilman 1991, 249-278 and Brumlik (ed.) 1998.

[51] To apply the notion of trauma to both victims and perpetrators in connection to NS and the Holocaust is problematic. Being traumatised implies that a person is a victim and to describe perpetrators of crimes as traumatised would compare their situation to that of their victims. However, for want of a better word, I will continue to use trauma.

[52] Irwin-Zarecka 1994, 9.

[53] Cf. for example Diner 1996b, 23.

[54] Irwin-Zarecka 1994, 77.

[55] Cf. ibid. 81.

Across the world, there are people who fled from, or whose parents and grandparents fled from, the Nazi system of terror. Their memories and the impact on their lives and personalities should form part of this story [of German society]; but it is a part which more often contributes to the development now of other cultures, other societies, and has for the most part been excluded from what is deemed to be "German" today.[56]

That reconstructions of NS history are frequently at the centre of controversies on the memory of the Holocaust in Germany demonstrates how difficult it is to formulate narratives of the past which communicate justice to the community of victims as much as to the community of victimisers. Here the conflict of memory also involves the writing of history and the methodologies used to do so.[57] If memories of a past matter to historians researching that past, their scholarly work in particular can become the source of conflict where it involves decisions about which events to report, which sources to access and how to present the research.[58] Whereas the underlying facts are not disputed their historiographical representation is. Hence the role of the historian as critic of society and agent of morality and truthfulness is contested in as much as he or she is also part of a particular community of memory.

Conflicts of memory are inherited by subsequent generations, because the memories that influence communal and individual identities are passed on. Hence the assessment of the moral integrity and commitment to truthfulness of the narrators of collective memory becomes increasingly complex the further their temporal distance to the events they relate. The heirs of memory have not reconstructed the past themselves, they rely on the reconstructions of previous generations. However, if they do not question the memories that are transmitted to them, they become complicit in the lack of morality and commitment to truthfulness of previous generations.

2.1. Communities of memory

Communities of memory bind people together because they share experiences or traumas and then a particular interpretation of their history. They are not homogenous and constantly re-define themselves, being continually in flux in terms of their collective identity as well as their membership.

The framing of collective memories and the drawing of boundaries around communities often employs the creation of an Other against which the self-understanding of one's own community can be established. In particular, memories of

---

[56] Fulbrook 1999, 147.

[57] Cf. for example the *Historikerstreit* and the Goldhagen Controversy, to be discussed in chapter II.

[58] Cf. for example Münz [2]1996, 43ff. regarding the historiography of the Holocaust in Germany.

victimisation create powerful identifications and facilitate the establishment of boundaries.

> If the memory of victimization can so well serve the cause of communal unity, it is not only because of its particular emotional strength. Structurally as well, the self-definition as a victim clearly marks the boundary between "us" and "them" in ways only matched by ties of kinship. To construct a sense of community, one almost inevitably needs the presence of the Other; the oppressor serves this role very well indeed.[59]

Employing the concept of communities of memory allows the identification of different voices and their individual and communal investments in debates on the memory of the Holocaust in German society. The debates are characterised by the interaction of contesting narratives about the same history. Therefore, it is helpful to differentiate between communities of memory, which are associated with different versions of the past according to the relevance of Holocaust remembrance to their communal identities. Thereby the tendency simply to dismiss narratives *a priori* as immoral or wrong and prioritise others can be avoided from the start. This is not to suggest that any version of the past is acceptable.[60] Rather the concept of communities of memory enables the recognition that all participants in the debates have a particular motivation to remember this past and that this motivation can change when the membership of the communities of memory changes. Since in the present the narratives of collective memory of NS and the Holocaust have already been twice transmitted and inherited, they have to be acknowledged with all their distortions and omissions, falsifications and obliterations of history, before they can be challenged, transformed and overcome. Hence the awareness of the different motivations to remember and forget regarding NS and Holocaust history is part of the task of analysing and contributing to collective memory.

In the case of Holocaust memory in Germany historical facts are (mostly) not disputed, whereas their relevance to the identities of Germans and Jews is the source of conflict. Robert Moeller and Bartov suggest that post-war German identity strongly rests on the identification of Germans as victims.[61] However, this self-understanding clashes with Jewish memories of the Holocaust which are constructed as victim narratives against the Other of the German victimisers. As will become clear, in particular in chapter II, in the identification of Germans as victims alongside Jews, Jewish memory of atrocity and suffering hardly entered German narratives.[62] The investment of these competing narratives of victimisation with such communal relevance accounts for the emotive nature of debates on German Holocaust

---

[59] Irwin-Zarecka 1994, 60.
[60] As argued above I am not following White's suggestion of emplotment, cf. White [3]1996. Cf. also Bartov 1993, 110ff. on the limitations of White's theory, as well as Young 1997.
[61] Cf. Moeller 1996 and Bartov 1998 and 2000. Cf. also Marcuse 2001.
[62] Cf. Bartov 1998, 788-790.

remembrance. Allowing Jewish memories to enter German narratives of NS in their own right, challenges German self-understandings as victims of NS alongside Jews as well as it undermines the exclusion of Jews from German narratives.[63]

At present the communities of memory of victims and victimisers – Jews and Germans – increasingly shift their membership from the first generation who has experienced NS and the Holocaust themselves to their descendants of the second and third generation who have learned to negotiate their identities through the communicated memory of the previous generations. However, with the third generation reaching adulthood and the first generation declining, the memory of both communities relies more and more on inherited discourses. The memory productions of Germans and Jews, twice transmitted and inherited, transform into representations of a history that soon will no longer be identifiable in the biographies of people one personally knows. The challenge for both communities is to create narratives of memory which are able to preserve the immediacy of the previous generations' memories so as to ensure their relevance in the construction of Jewish and German identities. Manfred Jurgovsky asks:

> And what is the perspective of the following generations, who do not only have to examine the actions of their parents and grandparents, but also their own position as actors in the present. Remembrance simply because of the fact that one's own relatives were perpetrators, fellow travellers or beneficiaries of National Socialism defines their situation only as something derived and dependent on others, but not as something genuinely owned. But only if it is recognised as genuinely part of oneself can remembrance acquire a function for change, and even that is disputed.[64]

Irwin-Zarecka's book *Frames of Remembrance*[65] provides a set of tools for students of collective memory which enables the recognition of different dynamics in the development of collective memories. The approach she chooses is interdisciplinary and her examples are located in the context of Holocaust remembrance in Polish and Jewish communities. Her analytical tools are not bound to one subject area, and can equally address the representation of the Holocaust in German and Jewish historiography, the transmission of Holocaust memory in families, as well as the construction of collective memory in theology. Thus neither a particular genre of a text nor groups of people who do the remembering need to be privileged. Peter Reichel observes that the democratisation of societies allows access to and participation in the creation of collective memory to an ever larger number of people:

> The former community of memory of scholars and religious specialists for remembrance and transmission has become a field of aesthetic-political action, which includes a large number of

---

[63] Cf. Fulbrook 1999, 147ff.
[64] Jurgovsky 1998, 27.
[65] Irwin-Zarecka 1994.

participants, pluralistically organised and with sophisticated cultural media, strategies of discourse and political functions.[66]

This "democratisation of memory", i.e. that the location as well the actors in the construction of collective memory have broadened to include the variety of cultural texts available in a society underlines Irwin-Zarecka's argument. Her approach allows for the examination of texts relating to the memory of the Holocaust in the different subject areas combined in this study.

---

[66] Reichel 1995, 24f. Cf. also for a brief overview of the development of cultural memory.

I.   The Evangelical Church in the Rhineland – Instituting Christian-Jewish conversations

The 1980 statement of the Rhineland synod *Towards a renewal of the relationship of Christians and Jews*[1] addresses Christian-Jewish relations in the context of post-Holocaust Germany for the first time as an issue which needs to be considered as part of a Christian confession of faith. As such it has been interpreted as a milestone in Protestant reflection on Christian-Jewish relations in Germany which has paved the way for further theological considerations.[2] Yehuda Aschkenasy's comment sums up the positive appreciation the statement received:

> I understand the decision of the synod as a real change, as a first, but decisive, step to an existential renewal of the relationship of the Rhenish church, but also of other churches, to the Jewish people – as a beginning of a significant learning process.[3]

Taking the Rhineland statement as example, this chapter outlines the context in which Holocaust remembrance is conceived in the Protestant community in Germany and develops questions about the location of Protestant Holocaust remembrance in the context of German society. The evaluation of representations of the Holocaust and Jews in the Rhineland statement, helps understand the significance assigned to both in Protestant theological thought concerned with Christian-Jewish relations. The analysis will be guided by the following questions:

(1)   what understanding of the Holocaust is presented in the document and what function does it assign to the events?

(2)   how does the document describe the Christian-Jewish relationship, i.e. are they equal partners or asymmetrical, and if so what asymmetries are assumed to exist? what is the basis for their interpretation, i.e. particular understandings of biblical texts, historical contexts etc.? and what are the aspirations of the theologies regarding the Christian-Jewish relationship?

(3)   how does the Christian understanding of Jews as formulated in the Rhineland statement reflect Jewish identities and what significance is assigned to Jews in Christian theology?

This analysis aims to develop a deeper understanding of the guiding principles structuring institutional Christian-Jewish encounters in the FRG by exploring how the EKiR, in particular, represents Christian-Jewish relations and the Holocaust.

---

[1] EKiR (ed.) [2]1985. An English translation of the statement (excluding the commentary provided by the authors) can be found in Brockway et al. 1988, 92-94.

[2] Cf. for example the discussion of the statement presented in Klappert/Starck (eds.) 1980 and the contributions in Brocke/Seim (eds.) 1986.

[3] Aschkenasy 1980, 4.

However, the wider context of the following analysis of Christian-Jewish relations in Germany are Christian-Jewish encounters on an international level.

1. Approaches of churches to Christian-Jewish relations since 1945

Learning lessons from the Holocaust was a factor in initiating Christian-Jewish encounters after the Second World War, the centre of the conversations being churches of the North Atlantic region, particularly the USA.[4] After 1945 (Western) Christianity felt the need to state their rejection of antisemitism in conjunction with a moral condemnation of the Holocaust. As Rolf Rendtorff points out, "All statements from those years took as their starting point what had happened to the Jews under the Nazis. This was seen as the result of antisemitism."[5] Antisemitism and the Holocaust appear as issues particularly linked with Western societies and thus with Western Christianity, given the self-understanding of the Christian churches as social forces in Europe. Thus church statements concerning Christian culpability for the development of antisemitism and the possibility of the Holocaust were issued by individual Western church institutions and centrally by the Vatican, for the RCC, and by the WCC, for Protestant churches. In particular since the 1970s antisemitism and the Holocaust are explicitly linked in documents of regional churches in the West.[6] The statements clearly reflect a language of acknowledgement of guilt and repentance since they all make a connection between Christian contributions to the development of antisemitism and Christian failure to defend Jews during the Holocaust. No

---

[4] Since the 1930s and in the immediate aftermath of the war scholars such as James Parkes and Bill Simpson made significant contributions to Christian-Jewish relations, the centre of the conversations being the UK. Two Christian-Jewish organisations originated in the UK, CCJ and ICCJ. The founding document of CCJ identifies Nazi policy toward Jews as proof "that antisemitism is part of a general and comprehensive attack on Christianity and Judaism and on the ethical principles common to both religions" (Braybrooke 1991, 14). Then Christian delegates at an ICCJ conference formulated *The Ten Points of Seelisberg* (1947). These constitute the first guidelines for a change in the representation of Jews and Judaism in Christian teaching. They point to Jewish origins of Christian faith, represent post-biblical developments of Judaism in its own right and argue for a limited culpability of Jews for the death of Jesus (cf. Croner [ed.] 1985, 32f.). Whereas the centre of Christian-Jewish conversations has since moved to the USA, Britain's significance for Christian-Jewish relations in Europe cannot be underestimated. Before the founding of the Centre for Jewish-Christian Relations in Cambridge in 1998, institutes for Christian-Jewish learning were established, for example, in Birmingham (Selly Oak), Southampton and Oxford, so that Christian-Jewish relations in this country have achieved recognition as an academic subject in their own right.
[5] Rendtorff in Brockway et al. 1988, 141.
[6] Cf. the collection of documents in Brockway et al. 1988; Croner (ed.) 1985; Fisher 1999 and Secretariat for Ecumenical and Interreligious Affairs/National Conference of Catholic Bishops (eds.) 1998.

difference in formulation and theological approach can be identified between statements originating in Europe and the USA. Antisemitism became the paradigm with which the churches and individual theologians approached the Holocaust. Scholarship evaluated Christian representations of Jews and Judaism as contributions to the development of racial antisemitism.[7] A significant field of study is concerned with the involvement of the churches in NS.[8] And Christian feminist theology, in particular, has begun to debate its own contribution to antisemitism in Christian feminist theology.[9]

Stephen Haynes has developed three paradigms to characterise recent scholarship on the relationship between Christianity and antisemitism.[10] According to Haynes scholars following the "reformist paradigm" understand antisemitism as "essentially foreign to authentic Christianity."[11] Associated with scholars such as James Parkes, Jules Isaac, Edward Flannery and Leon Poliakov, Haynes argues regarding this paradigm that

> Today, Christian theologians and church spokespersons unwittingly operate within this paradigm whenever they regard Antisemitism as a corruption of true Christianity or an aberration from faithful Christian behavior. In fact, the analyses and suggestions of most official post-Holocaust church statements on Jewish-Christian relations are reformist in tenor. It is probably the case that among Christians who are sensitive to this problem the majority view anti-Judaism as a historical accretion to Christian teaching that is fundamentally opposed to the gospel and correctable by a return to biblical Christianity.[12]

Evolving from the "reformist paradigm" Haynes locates the "radical paradigm" which is argued for, in particular, in the works of Rosemary Radford Ruether and Franklin Littell. It presents a continuation of "reformist" arguments, applying them to Christian theology and New Testament[13] texts. According to Haynes

---

[7] Cf. in particular Ruether 1974 as well as Braham (ed.) 1986; Davies (ed.) 1979 and Gager 1983.

[8] Cf. for example Ericksen/Heschel (eds.) 1999; Littell/Locke (eds.) 1974 and Siegele-Wenschkewitz (ed.) 1994.

[9] Cf. for example Kellenbach 1994 and Siegele-Wenschkewitz (ed.) 1988.

[10] Cf. Haynes 1995b as well as Haynes 1996.

[11] Haynes 1995b, 65.

[12] Ibid. 66f.

[13] Since this study examines Christian texts, I acknowledge this context by following traditional Christian terminology using Old and New Testament for the two parts of the Christian Bible. Alternative suggestions have been made, such as Tanach and Hebrew Bible for the Old Testament and Second Testament or Greek Testament for the New Testament in an attempt to acknowledge the Jewish context of interpretation of the Old Testament texts alongside their Christian use. However, these suggestions are not satisfactory, given that the assumption that the Tanach/Hebrew Bible is synonymous with the Old Testament appears flawed. Firstly, the order of the texts in the Tanach/Hebrew Bible is different from the Old Testament and reflects Jewish usage – hence it matters and cannot simply be assumed to be a formality. Secondly, although the number of the books in the Tanach/Hebrew Bible is identical with general Protestant editions of the Old Testament, the Catholic Bible includes the Apocrypha and as such differs from the Tanach/Hebrew

It begins with the acknowledgement that anti-Judaism is woven into the fabric of the Christian story, yet it never relinquishes the belief that vigorous scholarship can extricate authentic Christian faith from the Second Testament *kerygma*. Radical scholars are willing to acknowledge that Christianity is not only historically anti-Jewish but also doctrinally and to some extent textually so. Anti-Judaism can be detected in some of the earliest expressions of Christian theology but is not essential to saving faith in Jesus.[14]

Haynes locates a further evolutionary development in the works of Hyam Maccoby and Gavin Langmuir which he names the "rejectionist paradigm". A difficulty presented with the emergence of this paradigm is the fact that both scholars do not understand themselves as part of the Christian community and as such do not share the commitments of the majority of scholars who advance the "reformist" and "radical" paradigms. However, the insights offered by both Maccoby's and Langmuir's thought "seriously problematize the bases for arriving at the conclusion that Antisemitism is a historical corruption of the Christian gospel."[15] The scholars challenge the existing paradigms in two ways:

that Christian attempts to understand the religious roots of anti-Semitism, no matter how ostensibly critical and objective, must be carefully scrutinized for apologetic concerns; that qualitative distinctions between anti-Judaism and anti-Semitism are only apparent; and that there exists no version of Christian faith, regardless of how "authentic" it is alleged to be, that is rescued easily, if at all, from the taint of anti-Semitism.[16]

Haynes goes on to suggest an approach to research on antisemitism and Christianity which takes seriously the challenges posed by the "rejectionist paradigm". He argues that much of the criticism of the "rejectionists" concerns the prejudices with which "radical" scholars have approached biblical texts. In applying results of historical research directly to the needs of a contemporary theology in the context of Christian-Jewish relations,

the distinction between ancient history and contemporary need becomes quite blurred. Examples range from the specific claim of Paul van Buren – that Paul "could never have said" that Jews rejecting the gospel convict themselves as unworthy of everlasting life – to the

---

Bible in more ways than the order of its contents. Arguably the naming of the holy scriptures of a community should reflect their context of interpretation. Hence Old and New Testament still appear to be appropriate, in a temporal sense of the origin of the scriptures as well as in the importance attached to them in the Christian community where the New guides the reading of the Old (which does not exclude a strengthening of interpretative influences of the Old over the New Testament).

[14] Ibid. 69.

[15] Ibid. 71.

[16] Haynes 1996, 307. In as much as I agree with Langmuir's definition of antisemitism, I also adopt his paradigm to describe Christian attempts to analyse antisemitism. I follow Haynes' suggestion that the moral imperative of Christian theology to rewrite theology in a non-antisemitic fashion needs to be argued for and historically verified in such a way that it is intelligible to non-Christians.

broader and quite dubious contention of Alice L. and A. Roy Eckardt that there was no conflict between Jesus and the Jews of his day.[17]

The moral need to rewrite Christian theology in such a way that it is not antisemitic is in danger of unwittingly establishing a new Christian imperialism regarding how the Bible should be read. Haynes concludes that

> post-Holocaust theologians have failed to articulate or defend a moral imperative for embracing tenuous interpretations of history. [...] The life of the radical paradigm will be prolonged, and its role as a catalyst for post-Holocaust theology preserved, if theologians pay closer attention to the limits of historical inquiry, and if they better explain why Christians are morally obligated to read the New Testament in a pro-Jewish way.[18]

However, both the "reformist" and "radical" paradigms continue to shape Christian theology in the context of Christian-Jewish relations. In particular statements of churches regarding antisemitism and Christian-Jewish relations remain – as Haynes suggests – within the boundaries of the "reformist paradigm". Haynes' analytical categories inform the argument of this study.[19]

In an effort to reform Christian perceptions of Jews, both Protestants and Catholics identify the foundations of the Christian-Jewish relationship as a "common spiritual heritage"[20] derived from what is assumed to be a "Judeo-Christian" tradition shared by Christians and Jews.[21] Both the RCC and Protestant churches issued the majority of statements between 1960 and the early 1980s inspired by recent developments in biblical scholarship.[22] A reinterpretation of Jews as the chosen people whose election by G-d[23] must also be acknowledged alongside or together with the election of the Christian community was developed in so called single and double covenant theologies. Theologies suggesting a single covenant approach for the definition of the Christian-Jewish relationship maintain that both the Jewish people and the church are chosen. They are chosen to be part of the same covenant at different times in history.[24] Double covenant theologies introduce a separate, but equally valid covenant for gentiles which is initiated by Christ. It is argued that, while this was not

---

[17] Ibid. 310.

[18] Ibid. 313.

[19] Cf. also his books Haynes 1991 and Haynes 1995a which are significant both later in this chapter and for the analysis of Friedrich-Wilhelm Marquardt's theology in chapter III.

[20] Flannery (ed.) [9]1992, 741.

[21] Cf. Münz [2]1996, 478f. for a problematisation of this assumption.

[22] The 1970s initiated widespread research into the social, political and religious reality of the first centuries CE, shedding a new light on the development of the early church in its relationship with Jewish communities of the time. As has been indicated, Ruether 1974 can be regarded as a watershed for subsequent scholarship. For an evaluation of this scholarship cf. Haynes 1996.

[23] I use non-gendered language, avoiding male and female pronouns in connection with G-d. Direct quotations and translations, however, reflect the choice of their author.

[24] Cf. for example Buren 1981/1987/1988 and Eckardt/Eckardt [2]1988.

recognisable in direct confrontation with Christ's death and resurrection and thus did not find its way into the New Testament, the recognition of two separate, but equal and related covenants is necessary in retrospect so as to remain respectful to Judaism in its own right.[25]

The RCC officially approached Christian-Jewish relations in the declaration *Nostra Aetate*[26] issued as one of the last documents of Vatican II in 1965 and thereby initiating a new beginning in Catholic thinking about Jews. Followed by the 1974 *Vatican's Guidelines and Suggestions for Implementing the Conciliar Declaration Nostra Aetate 4*[27] and the 1985 *Notes on the Correct Way to Present the Jews and Judaism in Preaching and Catechesis in the Roman Catholic Church*[28] which further elaborate on the basis laid by *Nostra Aetate* the RCC achieved acceptance of the importance of Christian-Jewish relations for Christian self-understanding at the highest level of the institution. A recognition of Catholic responsibility for aspects of Jewish history in Europe which is characterised by antisemitism, found a most recent expression in the document *We Remember*.[29]

The WCC's founding assembly in 1948 in Amsterdam issued the first international Protestant statement which condemns antisemitism and argues for a "special solidarity"[30] of Christians with Jews as basis for the re-evaluation of the Christian-Jewish relationship.[31] The assembly shows awareness of the closeness in time and geography of its meeting-place to the Holocaust.[32] However, the WCC displays an ambiguous attitude towards Jews. On the one hand the assemblies are keen to condemn antisemitism and acknowledge Christian responsibility for the Holocaust.[33] However, antisemitism is never defined in the documents. This is problematic, since on the other hand the WCC cannot find agreement on the subject of a Christian mission to convert Jews.[34] In particular the report of the Committee on the Church and the Jewish People which was accepted by the Commission on Faith and Order and commended to further study displays this ambiguity in the area of mission. Whereas there is no disagreement on an eschatological vision of integrating the Jewish people into the church, it is controversial whether Christians should witness to

---

[25] Cf. for example Parkes 1948 and Ruether 1974. Cf. also the discussion in D'Costa 1990.

[26] Cf. Flannery (ed.) [9]1992, 738-742.

[27] Cf. Fisher/Klenicki (eds.) 1990, 29-37.

[28] Cf. ibid. 38-50.

[29] Cf. Secretariat for Ecumenical and Interreligious Affairs/National Conference of Catholic Bishops (eds.) 1990, 47-56. Cf. also Fisher/Klenicki (eds.) 1996.

[30] Brockway et al. 1988, 5.

[31] Cf. ibid. 5f.

[32] Cf. ibid. 5.

[33] Cf. ibid. 6, 12.

[34] Cf. ibid. 7f., 10f.

Jews with the intent of conversion.[35] However, the Commission shows no awareness that such an ambiguous attitude might display a form of antisemitism and such present an obstacle to a genuine conversation between Christians and Jews as envisaged by the Commission. The report pays attention to difficulties Christians have in terms of the terminology and definitions they use when talking about Jews.[36] While acknowledging historical development and change in the Jewish community and the reality of different forms of Jewish life, not all of which acknowledge a form of religious belief, the report nevertheless speaks of Jews only in religious terms, because only in a salvation historical framework is the existence of Jews relevant to the authors.[37] Jews are relevant to Christian theology only as witnesses to G-d and the covenant.[38] Thus the document tries to reconcile mutually exclusive concerns of Christians regarding Jews: (1) the wish to understand Jewish life in history and today from Jewish perspectives and at the same time presenting a salvation historical interpretation of Jews as continuing witnesses to G-d's intentions for humanity; (2) the wish for dialogue with Jews while the intention of conversion of Jews to Christianity is still part of the Christian agenda. The WCC struggles to reconcile the need to uphold traditional Christian thought about Jews for theological reasons with the no less recognised need for change in the attitude of Christian churches to Jews to counteract and prevent antisemitism.

Both the RCC and the WCC are aware of the particular significance a renewal of Christian-Jewish relations has to Western churches in their social-historical situation after the Holocaust. However, both RCC and WCC are institutions speaking on behalf of a wider Christian community and any statements issued must be acknowledged as significant for the larger Christian community they represent. As long as antisemitism, the Holocaust and Christian-Jewish relations are understood as issues pertaining only to Western Christians statements on these subjects have to be justified regarding their significance to the entire Christian community represented by RCC and WCC.

In the context of the WCC, the awareness of failures of Western churches with regard to NS is meant to serve as a warning sign to non-Western churches without precluding their individual theological approach to Christian-Jewish relations.[39] Thus non-Western Protestant churches have not issued statements on their own on this

---

[35] Cf. Brockway ibid. 22ff. The WCC prohibits proselytism which it defines as an aggressive form of mission (cf. ibid. 24).

[36] Cf. ibid. 13ff.

[37] Cf. ibid. 27: "We should also be aware that many, while affirming that they belong to the Jewish people, do not call themselves believing Jews [...] We should always remain aware that we are dealing with actual, living people in all their variety, and not with an abstract concept of our own."

[38] Cf. ibid. 17ff.

[39] Cf. Croner (ed.)1985, 158, 173.

subject, but only as part of the community of the WCC.[40] The Orthodox churches only very recently issued official documents regarding the relationship of Christianity and Judaism. However, some Orthodox churches share in the formulation of statements by the WCC since they became members in 1961.[41] Also some joint statements of Orthodox Christians and Jews have been published.[42]

The RCC in particular is sensitive to the fact that its non-Western institutions have not been directly involved in the development of antisemitism in Europe that contributed to the possibility of the Holocaust.[43] However, when deciding on Christian teaching the difficulty of having to represent centrally a very diverse Christian community can be as much an obstacle as an advantage. A decision on Christian teaching is issued centrally and therefore binding to all local churches. Thus the understanding of dialogue promoted by the *Guidelines*, which excludes mission with intent of conversion, has made the position of the RCC in conversations with Jews clearer than that of the WCC.[44] Whereas individual Protestant churches have prohibited mission with intent of conversion of Jews, either for historical or theological reasons,[45] there is no authority that could make such a decision on behalf of all the member churches of the WCC.

Haynes placed the rationale of Christian representations of Jews as part of Christian theological thought in an analytical framework. In his discussion of church statements and theological reflections on Christian-Jewish relations he introduced the term "witness-people myth" to characterise the dominant concept used in Christian publications.[46] Haynes offers his own definition of "myth": "As I am employing it, then, 'myth' refers to a specific set of beliefs, assumptions and convictions about Jews that have been expressed consistently by Christians over centuries."[47]

Haynes argues that the assumption of a historical dependency of Christianity on Judaism, and therefore of Christians on Jews, is a recurring feature of Christian theology and can be found in traditional representations of Christian-Jewish relations. According to the German theologian Bertold Klappert, these traditional interpretations of the church's relation to the Jewish people can be categorised into five negative models. They are the Substitution Model, the Integration Model, the

---

[40] Cf. Brockway in Brockway et al. 1988, 181.

[41] Cf. also the reflections of Papademetriou 1990.

[42] Cf. Rendtorff/Henrix (eds.) ²1989, 691ff. and 705ff.

[43] For the RCC cf. Stransky ²1995, 57. He mentions the difficulty in the formulation of the document *Nostra Aetate 4* on antisemitism which should represent universal Catholic theology and could thus not operate on a background limited to European experience.

[44] Cf. Fisher/Klenicki (eds.) 1990, 32f.

[45] Cf. for example Brockway et al. 1988, 97f. and Croner (ed.) 1985, 182f.

[46] Cf. Haynes 1995a, 7.

[47] Ibid. 9.

Typology Model, the Illustration Model and the Subsumption Model.[48] These aim to explain the nature of the Jewish people's relationship to G-d as reported in the Old Testament and the continuing existence of Jewish people alongside the church in a way that is not threatening to Christians. All these models understand the Jewish people as being replaced by the church. The Substitution Model can be understood as the overarching category for the other four models. These differ from the Substitution Model in their definition of the way in which the Jewish people are replaced by the church.

These models understand Jews essentially as "signs" rather than real people. According to the "witness-people myth" Jews effectively assume a role as "signs" or "witnesses". While presenting Jewish life alongside the church in negative terms, the "witness-people myth" also assigned to Jews a necessary role in a Christian interpretation of the world. Jews were understood to witness to a life that is not in accordance with G-d's will. Whereas it can be argued that historically the negative aspects of the "witness-people myth" dominate, Christian interpretations of continuing Jewish life have always retained some ambiguity. Formulation of a collective Christian identity takes place in opposition to and defence against what is perceived as a threat to the truth of Christianity. In particular the definition of collective Christian identity often took place in opposition to Jews. On the one hand, the Jewish community represented an antithesis to the church and as such questioned Christian claims to be the "new Israel" in continuity with the biblical Israel. On the other hand, the Jewish community was understood as a sign of G-d's judgement which needed to be visible to illuminate the truth of Christianity. The church established its collective identity in narratives of continuity as well as discontinuity with Jews. Thus, despite, as much as because of, the negative stereotyping of Jews by the church, the existence of a Jewish community was always needed as a living witness to G-d's intentions for humanity. Ultimately the aim of the church regarding the Jewish community was conversion to Christianity and integration into the church. Murder was not necessarily part of a Christian vision for the fate of the Jewish community. Jews were not favoured in these concepts, but Jewish existence alongside the church was still necessary.

Haynes argues that since the Enlightenment and the development of modern racial antisemitism the image of "the Jew" was transformed into a wholly negative one, in which any religious identity of Jews loses its significance. As a consequence Jews are understood to lose the possibility of redemption through baptism, immediately or as part of an eschatological vision. This development culminates in NS thinking about

---

[48] For the following presentation of these models cf. Klappert 1980a, 14-25. Klappert then goes on to develop three models defining the relationship of Israel and the church in ways that invest Israel's relationship with G-d with a continuing positive meaning. These models pertain to the 20th century but predate the Holocaust (cf. ibid. 26-37). Cf. also Liebster 1980, 55-65.

Jews.[49] According to some theologians the Holocaust challenged the dominant narrative of Christian self-definition in relation to Jews, making the traditional negative, although ambiguous self-understanding of the church in relation to Jews morally indefensible. The aim to murder every Jew also made impossible any Jewish witness in the salvation historical narrative of the church. Therefore, the Holocaust has sometimes been interpreted as an assault on Christianity as much as on Jews, because with the murder of one of G-d's witnesses the witness of the church as successors of the Jewish people was implicitly undermined as well.[50]

Since the 1960s so-called Holocaust theologians[51] have begun to transform the negative image of Jews in the "witness-people myth". Holocaust theology reacts against the negative connotations of the "witness-people myth", as well as against its distortions in modern racial antisemitism and NS.[52] Haynes argues that Holocaust theology represents an inversion of the traditional "witness-people myth" and does not overcome the interpretation of Judaism, Jews and contemporary Jewish life as "signs for the church".[53] He identifies this transformation of the traditional "witness-people myth" in five characteristics common to the work of Holocaust theologians: (1) The "privileging of anti-Judaism as a topos in Christianity is an updated version of the witness-people conviction that Jewish fate is extraordinarily relevant for Christians"[54]; (2) the State of Israel "operates as a sign of God's presence, power and intention in the world, just as in pre-Holocaust Christian theology Jewish existence in exile was assumed to be a sign of the divine plan"[55]; (3) Christian reflection on the State of Israel shows that "they have again placed 'Israel' at the center of Christian reflection"[56]; (4) Holocaust theologians assign great significance to the very survival of Jews, a feature which is part of the "preservationist impulses" of the pre-Holocaust "witness-people myth";[57] (5) the emphasis on the belief that the Jews remain G-d's chosen people and its consequences was part of the "witness-people myth" throughout Christian history,[58] so that

---

[49] Cf. Haynes 1995a, 60f.

[50] Cf. most strongly Marquardt [2]1992; also Eckardt/Eckardt [2]1988 and Littell [2]1988.

[51] For a definition of Holocaust theology cf. Haynes 1991, 6-8.

[52] Cf. for example the discussion in Fleischner (ed.) 1977 and Schüssler Fiorenza/Tracy (eds.) 1984 as well as Jacobs 1993b.

[53] Cf. Haynes 1995a, 7.

[54] Ibid. 124.

[55] Ibid. 130.

[56] Ibid. 132.

[57] Cf. ibid. 132f.

[58] Cf. ibid. 136.

with their convictions that Jewish history is the primary arena for God's interaction with human beings and that Christians and Jews are inextricably linked through covenant and election, the Holocaust theologians implicitly reestablish the witness-people tradition.[59]

Haynes is careful not to judge this renewal of Christian theological thinking. He points out the dangers the "witness-people myth" has historically carried for Jews, while at the same time appreciating the positive changes Holocaust theologians have introduced to the Christian reflection on Jews in an effort to counteract and abolish the negative aspects of the "witness-people myth". However, he appears convinced that "witness-people thinking" is intrinsic to Christian theology. According to Haynes, Christian theology cannot but think about Jews other than in terms of them being somehow "signs for the church",[60] since "For most Holocaust theologians this connection [between Judaism and Christianity] is unique and the church's relationship with Israel is sui generis."[61]

The significance of the post-Holocaust changes in Christian perception of Jews and Judaism can hardly be underestimated. In particular, the speed with which both the RCC and Protestant churches have implemented this reversal in the understanding of Jews and Judaism in their teachings and in the formulation of their self-understanding is remarkable, given that Christian concern for Christian-Jewish relations and a renewal of Christian self-understanding that reflects the impact of the Holocaust remains at the margins of the established churches. However, this change in Christian perception of Jews has also inscribed a Christian perspective on the Holocaust which is in danger of unintentionally ignoring Jewish self-understandings before, during and after the Holocaust. To initiate a new self-understanding of the church and develop a new collective Christian memory concerning Jews and Judaism, Christians have "Christianised" the Holocaust. In post-Holocaust Christian narratives the Holocaust is seen as an event that endangers the future of Christian life as much as it threatened the future of Jewish life. Thus the theological focus moves away from Jews as victims of the Holocaust and of Christian theological antisemitism and centres instead on the implications of the Holocaust for the credibility of Christianity. Christians have developed an understanding of the events of the Holocaust which impacts on them and makes the Holocaust relevant to their self-understanding. To do so churches have (re-)created an interpretation of the victims of the Holocaust using the framework of the "witness-people myth" and have moved Jews into the centre of Christian theology, thus employing these ideas to redefine Christian identity. Post-Holocaust Christian thought relies on the assumption of Jewish peoplehood and accepts particular Jewish religious identities as normative. The legitimacy of such a

---

[59] Ibid. 136.

[60] Cf. ibid. 183.

[61] Ibid. 1995a, 133. Regarding the implications of this claim for post-Holocaust theology cf. the analysis in 3. The statement of the Rhineland synod, as well as chapters III. and V.

move is not yet discussed in the churches, but its consequences are already becoming apparent as the following paragraphs will indicate.

The "witness-people myth" emerges as the organising principle with which the churches approach Christian-Jewish history as well as the Holocaust. As such the "witness-people myth" is the uniting narrative of the churches with regard to the interpretation of Jewish history. In this context the "witness-people myth" can be characterised as the vehicle that carries the collective memory of Christians in their relation to Jews and Judaism. To understand who Christians are in relation to Jews, the church employs the framework of the "witness-people myth" which is able to forge a collective Christian identity in relation to Jews. What has changed after the Holocaust is the meaning the "witness-people myth" carries in the re-evaluation of Christian-Jewish history. It has been turned inside out and the negative connotations have been invested with positive meaning. This aspect of post-Holocaust Christian theology[62] is well summarised by Haynes in his characterisation of church documents on Christian-Jewish relations:

> Two conclusions emerge from this review of ecclesiastical documents which address the church-Israel relationship in the shadow of the Holocaust. First, these statements utilize witness-people terminology and conceptions in a remarkably consistent way. Second, despite continual references to the "turning point" in Christian thinking about Jews and Judaism that is supposedly represented by documents like "Nostra aetate" and the dozens of official pronouncements that have followed it, the theological grid through which Christian theologians view the Jewish people has not been shattered by the Holocaust and the birth of the State of Israel. These documents are distinguished by ubiquitous references to "Israel" in terms of salvation history, covenant, election, uniqueness, divine calling; and they repeatedly affirm the mystery of Jewish suffering, Jewish survival and Jewish restoration.[63]

The implications of this renewed Christian perception of Jews for the development of Holocaust memory in Christian-Jewish relations in Germany will now be explored.

---

[62] Haynes uses "post-Holocaust theology" to describe theologies which translate the insights of Holocaust theology into systematic theological reflection, cf. Haynes 1991, 8.

[63] Haynes 1995a, 174.

2. Approaches of Protestant churches to Christian-Jewish relations in Germany

Scholars agree on the identification of roughly three phases in post-war Protestant efforts to reflect on the relationship of Christians to Jews.[64] The first phase was the immediate post-war years with their expression of shock about the evidence of the Holocaust.[65] The 1960s with the first official encounters of Christians and Jews launched the second phase which came to fruition in the 1970s and 1980s in the formulation of confessional church statements on Christian-Jewish relations. The first two phases took place almost exclusively in the context of institutional churches. Since the 1980s, which marked the beginning of the third phase, academic theology has been actively involved in the reflection on Christian-Jewish relations.[66]

The knowledge of the atrocities of NS and the Holocaust challenged the churches' moral self-understanding. In their reaction to the evidence of atrocities committed in the name of the German people questions about Christian responsibility for NS dominated. The question of how official representatives of the Christian churches, as well as private members of church communities, could have become involved in NS and the atrocities of the Holocaust initiated confessions of Christian guilt and failure during NS. The years 1945-1949 were characterised by statements that recognised Christian responsibility for, and also involvement in, the antisemitic atrocities of NS and the Holocaust.[67] This process of Christian self-examination called into question the traditions which enabled, or which failed to prevent or facilitate resistance against, private and official Christian involvement in NS and the Holocaust. However, it also initiated a "Christianisation" of the Holocaust, because the Holocaust was understood as an initiator of a crisis for (Western) Christianity. Thus the focus of subsequent analyses were Christian traditions, not events of the Holocaust or its dead and surviving victims. The question was and also remains: what does the Holocaust mean to Christians? not, what has it done to Jews? However, the evaluation of Christian understandings of Jews was also from the beginning part of the process of Christian self-examination. While maintaining traditional theological models to speak about Jews, statements from these years emphasise the continuing need to spread the message of salvation in Christ among the Jewish community,

---

[64] Cf. Rendtorff 1989a, 41-55. Eberhard Bethge argues for a differentiation into four phases, a first phase of moral condemnation of the Holocaust, a second phase when Christians gathered information about Jews and studied Christian-Jewish relations by themselves, a third phase of a beginning of actual encounters between Christians and Jews and a fourth phase which saw the formulation of church statements on the Christian-Jewish relationship (cf. Bethge 1980, 95-98).

[65] For a commentary on German statements cf. Rendtorff 1989b.

[66] Cf. for example the initiation of a guest-lectureship in Judaism in Wuppertal as a consequence of the 1980 Rhineland statement. For a further specification of the relations between church-based Christian-Jewish encounters and academic theology cf. Petersen [2]1998, 35ff.

[67] For the following cf. the collection of church documents in Rendtorff/Henrix (eds.) [2]1989.

albeit sometimes with the recognition that this missionary effort might not be appropriate at this particular moment in time and should be suspended for a while.[68] The language of these early statements is theological in the sense that it speaks about Jews first and foremost in terms of salvation history and about particular roles Christian faith needs to assign to Jews. Since the terminology is not clearly defined, terms such as "Jews" and "Israel" are used interchangeably for biblical and post-biblical times, regardless of whether the context is the Holocaust or the State of Israel. The way traditional theology speaks about Jewish people is different from the way it treats other peoples mentioned in the Bible. Greeks and Romans, for example, are not assumed to be identical with Greeks and Romans in the modern world. Here historical developments are taken for granted and it is clear when biblical terminology is used to point to types of behaviour rather than to characterise actual people in the present who are also assumed to represent biblical typologies. Thus if the biblical terms Greeks and Romans are applied to a situation today they refer to groups of people quite different from contemporary Greeks and Romans. However, regarding Jews and Israel the terminology is ever more confused in Christian theology. Haynes argues that defining "Jew", "Judaism" and "Israel"

> requires historical, political and theological judgments which might be debated at great length. [...] while the terms "Jew" and "Judaism" have held generally negative connotations in Christian theology since the second century, "Israel" has found a more ambiguous function in Christian thought.[69]

He goes on to say that

> Although the question "what constitutes Jewishness?" is generally not belabored by serious Christian theology, the relationship between "Israel" as people and "Israel" as state has received a great deal of attention. [...] Most Christian theologians concerned with Jewish-Christian relations agree that whether or not the state of Israel is afforded theological significance, use of the term "Israel" must not be divorced from the present reality of the Jewish people – that is, it must include an affirmation of "the Jews" as the people "Israel," and Judaism as the form of life and worship given these people by God.[70]

This issue has been considered by a number of theologians in responses to the Rhineland statement.[71]

With the EKD synod in Berlin Weißensee 1950 the Holocaust entered the discussion as an event that challenged Christian theology. As a consequence of the atrocities committed in the Holocaust, and the recognition of Christian responsibility for their occurrence, the synod also indicated that relations with Jews in the form of

---

[68] Cf. for example ibid. 530, 537, 539f., 541ff., 544f.
[69] Haynes 1991, 12.
[70] Ibid. 14.
[71] Cf. the discussion in 3.2. The Christian-Jewish relationship.

conversations and encounters would be desirable.[72] Hence initiating relations with Jews in the form of conversations surfaced only in the 1950s, and then in particular with the initiation of the workshop "Jews and Christians" at the biannual German Protestant church congress, *Deutscher Evangelischer Kirchentag*, in 1961. In 1975 the EKD commissioned a group of theologians to research the social relations of Christians and Jews during the history of the church. Historical in its focus the study entitled *Christians and Jews*[73] addresses the development of Christian-Jewish relations through the centuries and examines how Christians formulated and enacted their identity in opposition to the Jewish communities in Europe and in particular in Germany. However, at that point no effort was made to draw conclusions from these historical developments for the formulation of Protestant theology.

The 1980 statement of the Rhineland synod was conceived in this context of Christian thinking about Jews, Jewish history and Judaism. Preceded by two decades of developing Christian-Jewish encounters in Germany, it acknowledges the importance of working with Jews on Christian self-understanding as a major factor in the formulation of this document.

3. The statement of the Rhineland synod *Towards a renewal of the relationship of Christians and Jews* (1980)

When the synod of the EKiR accepted the motion *Towards a renewal of the relationship of Christians and Jews*, it was the first of the member churches of the EKD to declare the relationship of Christians and Jews in the present to be of fundamental importance for the self-understanding and well-being of the Christian church. A pamphlet documenting the resolution together with commentaries on its development and appraisal followed the document.[74] Although not binding as a confession of faith, the document is confessional in its approach. Thereby the synod wanted to invite theologians and lay people alike to engage in a process of considering a renewal of Christian interpretations of Jews and Judaism, which, they argue, affects the basis of Christian confessions of faith.[75]

Since 1965 the synod of the EKiR was active in the pursuit of Christian-Jewish relations when it initiated the Study Commission for the Relation of the Church to

---

[72] Cf. Rendtorff/Henrix (eds.) [2]1989, 549.

[73] Ibid. 558-578. Extracts are printed in translation in Brockway et al. 1988, 74-82.

[74] Cf. EKiR (ed.) [2]1985. The statement of the Rhineland synod has generated discussion and criticism among theologians as well as a number of Jewish responses. For collections of responses cf. Brocke/Seim (eds.) 1986; Klappert/Starck (eds.) 1980 and Klappert/Gollwitzer/Bethge/Lapide (eds.) 1980. The majority of the commentators were instrumental in facilitating and supporting the theological progress of the Study Commission.

[75] Cf. EKiR (ed.) [2]1985, 8.

Judaism in the EKD. Its own study group, "Jews and Christians", was founded a decade later after the publication of the EKD study *Christians and Jews* with the intention of formulating a response to the EKD study and indicating possible practical consequences.[76] According to the then president of the EKiR, Karl Immer, the acceptance of the statement *Towards a renewal of the relationship of Christians and Jews* symbolises a new dimension of theological work:

> If we discover in this plan [G-d's plan for the world] the place of the people Israel who received the first promises, then the objective of all history will become clearer. [...] In this work we do not have to correct statements of the fathers, but we practice the continually new speaking about the father of Jesus Christ who is the God of Abraham, Isaac and Jacob.[77]

This sentence summarises the context, purpose and audience of the statement. All reflections are part of the church and for the church with the intention of discovering G-d's intentions for the world by understanding how "Israel" figures in this plan. The statement intends to define the relationship between Christians and Jews for the purpose of understanding where the Jewish people is situated in relation to a Christian perception of reality. Again, the "people Israel" are important as players in G-d's plan, they appear to be significant primarily as signs. The theological perspective is that of the "reformist" paradigm, which suggests that it is possible to change theological understandings of Jews, because their "pro-Jewish" interpretation is part of Christianity and only has to be discovered.[78] As such the president was able to assure members of the synod who found this new departure of Christian theology difficult that they would not have to discard their traditions, but in addition could discover what should have been part of Christianity in the first place. Eberhard Bethge emphasises precisely this point:

> Here we were concerned with the decision of general principle, that our Christian faith will become purer only if it takes its starting point from a newly to be gained partnership with the Jews.[79]

A close reading of the text and commentary of the Rhineland statement will clarify the understanding of the Holocaust and Jews promoted by the synod.

---

[76] Heinz Kremers traces the history of the Rhineland statement from its beginning in the emerging Christian-Jewish conversation in the EKiR, cf. Kremers 1980. It is significant that Jews were members of the Study Commission and were given an advisory function throughout the process.

[77] EKiR (ed.) [2]1985, 7.

[78] Cf. also Klappert's exposition of the Rhineland statement in Klappert 1980b, 51f.

[79] Bethge 1980, 98. Theologians in particular of the Department of Protestant Theology at the University of Bonn have disputed the legitimacy of this covenantal approach to Christian-Jewish relations and assert that the suggestion of such a close community with Jews denies fundamental tenets of Christian faith which in its universality extends its mission also to Jews (cf. Klappert/Gollwitzer/Bethge/Lapide [eds.] 1980, 14-17).

The authors of the Rhineland statement chose a confessional approach to describe their insights into the Christian-Jewish relationship as developed through recent encounters with Jews. The entire statement is framed in biblical theological terms, beginning with a quotation from Rom 11:18 ("it is not you that support the root, but the root that supports you"), thereby establishing what the synod understands to be the basis of Christian-Jewish relations. In this they follow the understanding suggested in previous documents, but promoted in particular by the EKD study *Christians and Jews*, which is preceded by the same biblical verse.[80] From this basis the synod argues that it is historically necessary to re-think the relationship of the church to the Jewish people for four reasons:

> (1) The recognition of Christian co-responsibility and guilt for the Holocaust – the defamation, persecution and murder of the Jews in the Third Reich. (2) The new biblical insights concerning the continuing significance of the Jewish people within the history of God (e.g. Rom. 9-11), which have been attained in connection with the struggle of the Confessing Church. (3) The insight that the continuing existence of the Jewish people, its return to the Land of Promise, and also the foundation of the state of Israel, are signs of the faithfulness of God towards his people (cf. the study "Christians and Jews" III, 2+3). (4) The readiness of Jews, in spite of the Holocaust, to (engage in) encounter, common study and cooperation.[81]

These four reasons are concretised in confessions of faith ("we confess, we believe").[82] Basic to these confessions is the assumption of a shared "Judeo-Christian" tradition, interpreted positively as the continuing election of the Jewish people and the understanding that the church has been elected into the one covenant of G-d with G-d's people.[83] Six paragraphs of commentary elaborate what the statement confesses, dealing with the Holocaust, the shared Bible, Jesus between Jews and Christians, the one people of G-d, justice and love in Judaism and Christianity and, finally, the question of Christian mission to Jews.[84]

This brief characterisation of the Rhineland statement clearly places it in the context of a re-evaluation of church history with the purpose of revising church teaching to influence the construction of collective memory for the community of the EKiR. The fact that it is confessional in character, but that it is not binding as a confession of faith,[85] demonstrates that it understands itself as the beginning (rather than a

---

[80] Cf. Rendtorff/Henrix (eds.) [2]1989, 558.

[81] Brockway et al. 1988, 92 and EKiR (ed.) [2]1985, 9.

[82] Cf. EKiR (ed.) [2]1985, 10.

[83] Cf. ibid. 10. Cf. also Barkenings 1980 in particular 180: "Bedienen wir uns des 'Ökumene'-Begriffs dabei, erkennen wir im jüdischen Volk den 'Bundesbruder', sehen wir uns mit den Juden als *ein* durch die Geschichte wanderndes Gottesvolk, so bleibt doch die schmerzliche Tatsache, daß wir, so wahr wir *ein* Gottesvolk sind, eben als ein 'gespaltenes' unterwegs sind."

[84] Cf. EKiR (ed.) [2]1985, 12-28.

[85] Cf. ibid. 8f.: "Dieser Synodalbeschluß ist kein Bekenntnis der Kirche, das Kirchengemeinschaft verpflichtend beschreibt und umgrenzt. Er ist aber ein entscheidend wichtiger erster Schritt in einem

completed product) of a process of recreating a theological narrative which expresses a new self-understanding of the church in relation to Jews. However, Paul Connerton argues that

> All beginnings contain an element of recollection. This is particularly so when a social group makes a concerted effort to begin with a wholly new start. There is a measure of complete arbitrariness in the very nature of any such attempted beginning. [...] But the absolutely new is inconceivable. [...] More fundamentally, it is that in all modes of experience we always base our particular experiences on a prior context in order to ensure that they are intelligible at all; that prior to any single experience, our mind is already predisposed with a framework of outlines, of typical shapes of experienced objects. [...] The world of the percipient, defined in terms of temporal experience, is an organised body of expectations based on recollection.[86]

This process of relying on continuities with what went before when developing a new and conflicting collective identity with its own historical narrative is also evident in the formulation of the Rhineland statement. The question of what the existence of the Jewish people in history and the present means to Christians differentiates Christian statements concerning Jews from statements concerning people of other faiths. In history as much as today Jewish existence as such appears to pose a problem to Christian faith – a situation which is singular in interfaith relations. Historically the continuing Jewish life after the death and resurrection of Christ as understood by the church posed a challenge to the credibility of Christianity to which a theological solution had to be found.[87] With the Holocaust this situation appears to be reversed. As explicated in the EKD study *Christians and Jews*, Christian theologians now place emphasis on historical and spiritual developments shared by Christians and Jews and argue that these common elements call for a commitment of Christians to explore Judaism so as to understand their own faith better.[88] The authors conclude that "Christians and Jews are called to enact their responsibility for the world together according to the will of God, rather than in confrontation with or alongside each other."[89]

Even more radically, some Christian theologians have turned traditional understandings of Jews in salvation history upside down. Now it is argued that Christian faith depends on the life – if not the religious life – of the Jewish people.[90]

---

uns allen aufgetragenen Lernprozeß, durch den wir auf theologische Fragen hingewiesen werden, denen wir nicht ausweichen dürfen."

[86] Connerton 1989, 6.

[87] Cf. Münz [2]1996, 470f.

[88] Cf. Rendtorff/Henrix (eds.) [2]1989, 558-564.

[89] Ibid. 564.

[90] Cf. for example most strongly Metz 1984 and Klappert 1980b, 50f.: "Nach Auschwitz und d.h. nach dem Holocaust können wir nicht mehr allein Theologie treiben, sondern nur noch zugleich in der grundsätzlichen Angewiesenheit auf die jüdischen Opfer von Auschwitz und auf das Judentum nach Auschwitz. [...] Die Kirche ist seit dem Holocaust auf das Judentum als den Zeugen der Erinnerung angewiesen, der zum Bekenntnis eigener Schuld anleitet und in die messianische

The Catholic theologian Johann Baptist Metz, one of the most prominent theologians in the field of Christian-Jewish relations, formulates this position as follows:

> Because of Auschwitz the statement "Christians can only form and appropriately understand their identity in the face of the Jews" has been sharpened as follows: "Christians can protect their identity only in front of and together with the history of the beliefs of the Jews."[91]

Metz understands "the Jews" to mean all Jews, past and present.[92] Thus Christian faith becomes dependent on Jewish life. The assumption of a threat to Christian faith inherent in the continuity of Jewish life through the centuries is exchanged for the claim that Jewish life is extremely important to Christian faith.[93] Jewish people living today as contemporaries of Christians assume theological significance to an unprecedented extent. This inversion of the "witness-people myth" which places positive meaning on Jewish life alongside Christians has serious implications for Christian theology and also for Jewish self-understandings. A consequence of this inversion is that the existence of Christianity would be endangered if Jews were to cease to exist. In other words, the church now has the duty to do everything in her power to facilitate the life of Jews as Jews, in particular of religious Jews.[94] Thus Jews and Jewish life have been moved into the centre of Christian theology, becoming its primary concern. Christianity is supposed to find its identity in supporting Jews, safeguarding Jewish security. Jewish life is now interpreted as enabling Christian life and faith, rather than as threatening it, and Christians have to assume responsibility for enabling Jewish life. Thus the hermeneutical principle of the "witness-people myth" assumes central significance as the organising principle of this renewal of a Christian collective memory. In an effort of self-preservation of Christian faith in the face of the crisis of the Holocaust, Christian theology shifts its focus and makes Jews – in particular religious Jews – the central theological subject. Here questions arise concerning the legitimacy of such a Christian definition of Jewish identity, as well as concerning Christian understandings of what it means to be religiously Jewish. In the Rhineland statement these consequences of a permanent dependency of Christians on Jews are implied, but not made explicit.[95]

Hoffnung einweist [...]." Paul van Buren goes much further when he describes the task of the church as "the ADL of the Jewish people" (Buren 1987, 334). ADL stands for "Anti-Defamation League".

[91] Metz 1984, 28. Cf. also Klappert [2]1993.

[92] Cf. Metz 1984, 26.

[93] Another interpretation would be that the key challenge is the potential discontinuity of Jewish life. Hence the threat would be that which was previously considered the goal.

[94] Cf. for example the work of Alice and Roy Eckardt, Bertold Klappert, Franklin Littell, Friedrich-Wilhelm Marquardt and Johann Baptist Metz.

[95] For a more explicit exploration of a dependency of Christian faith on the continuing existence (and well-being) of Jews cf. Marquardt [2]1992.

3.1. The Holocaust[96]

The paragraph entitled "The Holocaust as turning point" is introduced with a prayer ascribed to Rabbi Leo Baeck[97] which is then not reflected on further. The citation of this prayer has received strong criticism from Jewish commentators, primarily because its attribution to Baeck is improbable. Nathan Peter Levinson argues that the prayer

> bears no similarity to the style of Leo *Baeck's* writings, even apart from the fact of its content, which I would reject for myself as well as for most Jews. My teacher *Baeck* would never have written that the abandonment of the victims should be attributed to their hangmen.[98]

The Rhineland statement interprets the Holocaust as one crisis amongst others and offers a definition of the term "Holocaust", derived from Lev 1:3 et al., meaning "complete burnt offering". The Rhineland synod attributes its application to the context of the destruction of Jews in Europe to Elie Wiesel. The synod defines Holocaust as follows: "Six Million people were murdered by heirs to Christianity only because they were Jews."[99] This choice of terminology has received criticism, in particular for its sacrificial overtones and its popularisation with the miniseries *Holocaust*.[100] However, Klappert favours the term "Holocaust", because he interprets it as an attempt to exchange German use of NS terminology such as "Final Solution" (*"Endlösung"*).[101] Günther Bernd Ginzel argues that the sacrificial overtones of the term "Holocaust" are blasphemy. He suggests "Hashoah" as appropriate name for the events in question, because

> Shoah literally means catastrophe, destruction. In connection with the definite article, Hashoah became synonymous with "the catastrophe" in Jewish history. I plead for the use of the Hebrew term "Hashoah" if we use a technical term at all.[102]

However, if adopted by the EKiR, this suggestion, thought of in a Jewish context, would pose serious problems for the perspective assumed by the synod. To speak of *Hashoah*, means to characterise the events of the Holocaust from a Jewish perspective. The destruction of Jews in Europe in the Holocaust signifies the loss of

---

[96] For the following cf. EKiR (ed.) [2]1985, 12-19.

[97] Leo Baeck was an influential rabbi of Reform Judaism in Germany, teaching at the *Hochschule für die Wissenschaft des Judentums* in Berlin. He was deported to Theresienstadt in 1943 and emigrated to London in 1945 where he died in 1956. His writings pre-and post-war reflect his interest in Christian-Jewish relations and exert a strong influence on Christian theologians in Germany. Cf. also Rothschild 1996, 21-108.

[98] Levinson 1980, 234f.

[99] EKiR (ed.) [2]1985, 12.

[100] Cf. EKiR (ed.) 1993, 11.

[101] Cf. Klappert 1980b, 44.

[102] Ginzel [2]1993, 250.

an entire Jewish culture and civilisation which in itself is a catastrophe.[103] However, another implication of the term "catastrophe" is that catastrophes happen, they do not necessarily have to be understood as being comprised of human decisions and actions. Earthquakes, for example, are catastrophes, that are not brought about by human actions. Human responsibility for their casualties can be perceived in the construction of cities in danger-zones as well as in disregarding safety measures in the construction of buildings. Applied to representations of the Holocaust from a non-Jewish German perspective in particular this interpretation, implicit in the term "catastrophe", obliterates the perspective of the victimisers which has been inherited by post-war Germany. This change of perspective, however, appears to be intended in Ginzel's argument, because he goes on to suggest that it is unhelpful to claim a direct culpability of Christians in general for the Holocaust since Christians were also victims of NS.[104] He wishes to make Christian resistance against NS the foundation of Christian-Jewish conversations while bearing in mind Christian antisemitic traditions.[105] In particular, it is important to him that the young generations are not pushed to identify as children of victims and murderers:[106] "The only constructive starting point is the joint shock, the joint mourning of that which is no more and the shared responsibility for a future in which Hashoah is not repeated."[107] That such a sharing of each other's reactions and learned discourses on the Holocaust is hardly part of the reality of Christian-Jewish encounters, and that such a joint perspective of Christians and Jews (in Germany) might not be desirable, is not considered by Ginzel.[108]

The danger of not distinguishing between perspectives of victims and victimisers on the Holocaust is particularly evident when the statement argues that not only Jews, but also Christians in Germany, are affected by the Holocaust, because the Holocaust is understood primarily as a crisis of the civilisation, culture, politics and religion of the people who supported NS. That Jews are affected by the genocide of Jews in Europe is mentioned in conjunction with the fact that it has taken Jews twenty years to be able to address lessons from the Holocaust with the help of survivors. However, in this context, the impact of the Holocaust on Christians in Germany is the main concern who, the statement argues, have been affected no less than Jews by the consequences of the Holocaust. What does it mean to say that Christians in Germany are no less affected by the Holocaust than Jews? The authors do not explore the implications of this statement. The question of a "Christianisation" of the Holocaust arises which derives answers to the crisis perceived in Christian theology from

---

[103] Cf. Tal 1989, 218-224; Young 1988, 85ff. and Bartov 1996, 59f. Regarding Zionist usage of Shoah cf. also Segev 1993, 434.
[104] Cf. Ginzel [2]1993, 251.
[105] Cf. ibid. 252ff.
[106] Cf. ibid. 256.
[107] Ibid. 256.
[108] Cf. in particular the discussion in chapters IV. and V.

Jewish reactions to the Holocaust, thereby failing to engage with Jewish responses in their own right. This "Christianisation" is particularly evident in the understanding of the Holocaust as a turning point.

The statement argues that as a crisis the Holocaust initiates a turning point in the sense of repentance and renewal. A turning point for what is not explicitly stated and can only be concluded from the content of the following paragraphs and commentary by theologians. Klappert argues that the Holocaust is a turning point for the relationship between Christians and Jews.[109] He develops four categories in which the Holocaust is significant to the statement: in a confessional sense which calls for a confession of guilt of the church, in a hermeneutical sense which influences the reading of biblical texts, in a historical-political sense which contemplates Christian theological implications of the founding of the State of Israel, and in a dialogical sense which reflects on the willingness of Jews to partake in Christian-Jewish conversations after the Holocaust.[110] In this context the hermeneutical function of the Holocaust is of particular relevance.

Because New Testament texts can only be accessed with their history of interpretation (*Wirkungsgeschichte*) which is antisemitic, the Holocaust is assigned a hermeneutical function in order to interpret and discover new biblical insights.[111] Klappert argues that

> The hermeneutical function of the Holocaust regarding new biblical insights signifies [...] that only from the recognition of the history of interpretation and in giving up of our anti-Jewish pre-judgement we will be able to understand again the real intention of the biblical text itself.[112]

This interpretation of the hermeneutical function of the Holocaust remains within the framework of the "reformist paradigm". The authors and commentators believe in the possibility of rewriting Christian theology, because the texts of the New Testament are considered to be free of antisemitism. This is manifest in the statement's discussion of the Holocaust in the context of theodicy.

The statement appears to understand the Holocaust as a turning point for theology, in particular for theodicy. In fact, the crisis of religion appears to be the severest in the description of the statement. In the Holocaust

---

[109] Cf. Klappert 1980b, 38.

[110] Cf. ibid. 39.

[111] Cf. ibid. 38f. Cf. as well Bethge 1980, 98ff. and Haacker 1986, 142ff.

[112] Klappert 1980b, 45.

all professions of faith to the God of Abraham, Isaac and Jacob, who has chosen this people [the Jews], have been ridiculed, because to Christians the planned and executed extermination [sic] of God's chosen people is blasphemy [...].[113]

Consistent with the biblical basis of the statement in Rom 11:18 the synod identifies Jews as "G-d's chosen people", thus privileging what the authors understand to be "Jewish religious experience". The fact that the statement uses "the Jews", "Jewish people" and "Israel" interchangeably further emphasises the assumption that Jews are understood as a homogenous group and primarily in religious terms, in particular represented by the understanding of Jews as "the chosen people of G-d".[114]

This first paragraph on the Holocaust closes with an imperative for Christians to remember. The content of this remembrance is not clear at this point. However, the obligation to remember forms the link to the following paragraph, where Holocaust memory in the form of theodicy becomes the theme.

The following four paragraphs explore the question of theodicy in three forms listed by the statement: (1) the general question of "how can G-d allow the suffering?", (2) the concrete question asked when doubting "my G-d, my G-d why have you forsaken me?" and (3) the final culmination "why did G-d no longer guard his chosen people as the apple of his eye?"[115] Thus theodicy is concretised from the universal to the individual, to the particular context of the Jewish people. In this sequence the third point, then, needs to encompass the prior two and set the standard for answering questions of theodicy.

Only a few pages earlier the statement had explicitly mentioned the involvement of Christians in and the responsibility of Christians for the Holocaust as major insights which led to the formulation of the document. However, now this concrete historical context for the statement appears to be no longer part of the reflection. It has receded into the background and functions only as the initiator of the statement and as hermeneutical principle for the evaluation of theological consequences of the Holocaust. The questions now addressed focus on theodicy and thereby on G-d rather than human involvement. By placing the debate on the implications of the Holocaust into a traditional theological framework of thinking about evil and its relation to G-d, the statement employs a second principle of Christian interpretation of history which is part of the framing strategies of Christian collective memory. Thus the attempt to root the new theological narrative in concrete historical events, with which the statement opened in its introductory paragraphs, is now obscured by a return to traditional theological language and reflection. The concreteness of the challenge

---

[113] EKiR (ed.) [2]1985, 13.

[114] Regarding implications of this choice of terminology cf. 3.2. The Christian-Jewish relationship.

[115] Cf. EKiR (ed.) [2]1985, 14f.

which Holocaust memory, according to the statement, poses to Christian life and theology has been evaded.

As an introduction to the exploration of theodicy by the statement itself, the synod now briefly summarises some Jewish and North American Christian reflections on the implications of the Holocaust for Christianity.[116] Except for Wiesel and Emil Fackenheim, all Jewish religious reflections are formulated by contemporaries who have themselves not experienced events of the Holocaust or NS atrocity. According to the statement Richard Rubenstein, Fackenheim and Irving Greenberg emphasise the uniqueness of the Holocaust and the difficulties of relating this event to their inherited religious commitments. Rubenstein can no longer affirm the concept that G-d punishes a disobedient Jewish people with suffering; Fackenheim hears a positive commandment from Auschwitz, that Jews should live as Jews so as not to grant Hitler a posthumous victory; Greenberg emphasises the incomprehensibility of the Holocaust alongside the need for a confrontation with the events to enable a religious renewal in the present; Abraham Heschel understands the State of Israel as the possibility to enable Jewish life with G-d after the Holocaust; and Wiesel interprets Jewish life after the Holocaust as continuing to tell the story of G-d with G-d's people even though faith in this story has been destroyed by experiences in the Holocaust.[117] The Christian responses of Roy Eckardt and Franklin Sherman address the North American context of Christian-Jewish relations after the Holocaust. Eckardt understands the State of Israel as an answer to the Holocaust, demonstrating G-d's positive involvement in history which manifests a form of repentance for the sin G-d committed in allowing the Holocaust to happen.[118] Sherman emphasises the cross of Christ as the symbol of G-d's participation in the suffering of humans and calls for humans to share in the suffering of G-d.[119] However, the statement does not reflect on the cultural, social and political contexts in which these religious responses to the Holocaust have been formulated. The authors understand that Jews and Christians are in different situations after the Holocaust, but they do not explore the implications of these differences. Instead they appear to ignore the challenge they claim has been posed to Christian theology by the Holocaust and Jewish responses to it. A reason for this evasion of questions raised by Jewish responses to the Holocaust is indicated by Edna Brocke's commentary on the statement. She argues that it is difficult from a Jewish point of view to understand the Holocaust as a turning point, because Jewish responses confirm as much as dispute such an understanding and as such disagree among themselves whether it was a turning point.[120] Faced with such diversity, it

---

[116] Anthologies in German of Jewish responses to the Holocaust as known in English speaking contexts are rare. However, cf. for example Brocke/Jochum (eds.) 1982. For Christian responses cf. for example Jacobs 1993b.

[117] Cf. EKiR (ed.) [2]1985, 15f.

[118] Cf. ibid. 15.

[119] Cf. ibid. 16.

[120] Cf. Brocke 1980, 108.

seems that Christian theology has to choose which Jewish responses it includes in its own theological reflection and which it bypasses. Such a choice has implications for Christian representations of the Holocaust and Jews and thus for Christian-Jewish conversations.[121] It is noticeable that the statement excludes any traditional orthodox Jewish responses to the Holocaust.[122] In view of the emphasis the Rhineland synod places on Jewish religious life this lack of traditional responses is quite ironic.

The aim of the statement in exploring theodicy is twofold and represents a dialectical tension: responses to theodicy are supposed to maintain the divinity of G-d (in the traditional sense of being omnipotent and omniscient) and at the same time incorporate the reality of the experience of the forsakenness of the murdered.[123] Thus according to the statement the Holocaust has only reinforced the question of theodicy, but not radically altered its focus. The traditional concept of understanding G-d as the "lord of history" has not been questioned and thus traditional forms of Christian belief in G-d appear not to have been challenged by the Holocaust. What has been challenged appears to be only their expression in the present, not their defensibility in general. It can be concluded that the statement's efforts to renew the collective memory of the church remain within the traditional framework of Christian theology. The authors refuse to think through the arguments put forward by people such as Rubenstein and Wiesel to their logical conclusion. The question of what would happen if one could not be certain that G-d was in charge of history (Rubenstein) – or if G-d's ruling of history became morally indefensible (Wiesel) – is successfully evaded by the authors. In his commentary on the Rhineland statement Friedrich-Wilhelm Marquardt recognises these questions as the all important ones.[124] He concludes that the synod enables itself to confront these questions by assuring itself of the "nevertheless" of Ps 73 while at the same time acknowledging silence as the only appropriate response.[125] Brocke comments that such an evasion of the questions asked by Jewish thinkers may be necessary for Christian theology if it wants to remain Christian theology. She is satisfied with Christian acknowledgement of the contributions Christian representations of Jews have made to the possibility of the Holocaust and recognises the Rhineland statement as a first practical consequence of

---

[121] For a different suggestion of how to address the diversity of Jewish responses to the Holocaust cf. Wollaston 1995.
[122] Cf. for example Berkovits 1973; Schindler 1973, 88-104 and more recently Rosenberg (ed.) 1992.
[123] Cf. EKiR (ed.) [2]1985, 18.
[124] Cf. Marquardt [2]1992, 420: "Theologie steht mit dem Gottsein Gottes. Und darum fällt sie auch damit. Ihre letzte Frage könnte darum lauten: ob sie gefallen ist, nicht wieder aufsteht, weil sie zerschmettert wird von einer Frage, die sie weder stellen kann (ohne sich selbst damit aufzuheben): ob Gott Gott sei – noch beantworten kann: daß er es nicht (mehr) sei oder daß er es 'dennoch' sei (die rheinische Erklärung versieht sich des Geschenks des 'dennoch' im 73. Psalm)."
[125] Cf. ibid. 420.

this acknowledgement.[126] However, such a refusal of Christian theologians to address the questions of Jewish thinkers ultimately implies a refusal to take these seriously. Whereas Christian reluctance to engage with Jewish responses to the Holocaust in all their diversity may be understandable with regard to these pioneers in post-war German Protestant theological reflection on Christian-Jewish relations, this reluctance may no longer be acceptable for younger theologians.

In the fourth paragraph, considering the implications of the Holocaust for the future of Christian faith, historical experience once again enters the debate. The statement recognises that the enormity of the Holocaust and the impossibility of providing an adequate explanation forces people to fall silent. However, silence is understood as too weak a response since it appears implicitly to confirm the aims of the Holocaust by refusing to remember what happened and as such paves the way to oblivion. At this point the statement refers again to the fact that Jewish thinkers have begun to respond to the Holocaust and that their responses provide help to find a Christian answer.[127]

The fifth paragraph concludes with a list of theological concerns which correspond to the four areas in crisis – civilisation, culture, politics and religion. The first three concerns are general, and seem only to be re-emphasised by the Holocaust. The fourth, regarding religion, sets the agenda for the next paragraphs of the statement and for Christian-Jewish conversations in general which consider the Bible, Jesus, the one people of G-d, justice and love, and mission to Jews.

This chapter of the statement closes with the wish for a prayer of Ps 73 which can be shared by Christians and Jews. However, the implications of this hope for a joint prayer are not explored. How would such a prayer reflect Jewish experiences of the Holocaust? Can the theoretical (theological?) possibility of such a shared prayer be taken for granted, the implication being that Christians and Jews "only" have to concentrate on creating the right circumstances for this exercise?

The statement's narrative of the Holocaust for the purpose of the future collective memory of the church tries to take seriously the historical situation in which the statement is conceived and the historical reality which it addresses. However, it organises these experiences according to the principles of traditional theology, i.e. theodicy and the "witness-people myth" and thereby circumvents its own questions. The statement reaffirms Christian faith by suggesting that answers to the (traditional) question of theodicy can be found which are as satisfactory as the traditional answers to theodicy have been.

---

[126] Cf. Brocke 1980, 108f.

[127] Cf. EKiR (ed.) [2]1985, 18f.

However, the interpretation of the Christian-Jewish relationship itself has undergone changes. Whereas a dependency of Christians on Jews was traditionally understood as a hindrance and a relationship the church would rather relinquish, but could not, Christian dependency on Jews is now elevated to a virtue and is understood to be of primary significance to Christian faith. Christians need the survival of Jews and the ability of Jews to respond to the Holocaust. To be dependent on Jews not only historically, but permanently, is understood as an honour and Jews are invited to be the teachers of Christians. In fact, the desperate situation in which Christians in Germany find themselves after the Holocaust can be turned into a gain: by learning from Jews, much of Jewish religious heritage can be incorporated into Christian theology.

The dangers in this approach to the creation of a new collective memory of the church regarding Jews and the Holocaust are all too clear. Too little attention is paid to differences between Christian and Jewish situations and realities of life prior to, but particularly also after, the Holocaust. Thus the statement's approach to Jewish responses to the Holocaust is in danger of a misappropriation of Jewish traditions and religious responses to the Holocaust. Arguably Christian theology appears to be oblivious to the danger of syncretism, which is recognised in interfaith relations, when relations with Jews are concerned. The reasons for using Jewish traditions to redevelop Christian theology and the legitimacy of appropriating Jewish thought to Christian use would need to be explored by the authors.[128] Although the statement's narrative of the Holocaust does not exclude Jewish perspectives on the events, nevertheless, the focus remains on the crisis for Christianity which is addressed with the help of Jewish responses to the Holocaust. In a sense the church – unintentionally – assumes the role of the suffering and appears to ask very much like Henryk Broder in his sarcastic comment on the recent debate about the Holocaust memorial in Berlin: "What have we brought upon us by murdering the Jews".[129]

3.2. The Christian-Jewish relationship[130]

The following five chapters of the Rhineland statement address the areas in which the church sees a need to change its teaching with regard to Jews and Judaism. The emphasis throughout these five chapters is on what the statement understands to be the common heritage of Christians and Jews. Where the differences between Christian and Jewish teachings have been traditionally emphasised and portrayed as antagonistic and mutually exclusive, the Rhineland synod focuses on aspects of Christian and Jewish teaching which demonstrate what the authors consider to be the shared concerns and expectations of both traditions.

---

[128] Cf. also Brocke 1998, 124.

[129] Broder quoted in Reemtsma 1999 (emphasis mine).

[130] For the following cf. EKiR (ed.) ²1985, 20-28.

The synod argues that both Christians and Jews read the scriptures they share as a testimony to G-d's actions and intentions towards humanity, that the G-d witnessed to in the New Testament is identical with the G-d of the Hebrew Bible, and that both the Hebrew Bible and the New Testament witness to the two modes of G-d's concern for humanity which Luther signified as law and gospel.[131] The synod goes as far as to claim that "Jews can say that the God of Abraham, Isaac and Jacob has made himself known to the nations through the Christian witness."[132] However, how this generalisation can be justified by the synod is unclear, given that it has no authority to claim what Jews may or may not acknowledge as part of their self-understanding as Jews. Even if this statement is possible for some Jews, there is no reason for the synod to believe this to be the case for all Jews. Jürgen Seim understands this statement mainly in the tradition of the *Haskalah* and the German reform movement and names the medieval mystic Yehuda Halevi, the philosopher Hermann Cohen, Baeck and Franz Rosenzweig as protagonists of this idea.[133]

The synod recognises the different presuppositions with which Christians and Jews read the texts of the "Hebrew Bible" when considering the Christian interpretation of the scriptures as a witness to Christ and to the second coming of Christ.[134] That the shared body of biblical scriptures has been read in antagonistic frames of reference, i.e. that they have been part of collective memories of two distinct and often opposing communities, is understood as an unfortunate historical development. The synod argues that the differences in approach to the shared texts are not to be eliminated, but that the implicit and explicit antagonism which separates Christian interpretations from Jewish understandings of biblical texts should be counteracted. Thus the synod suggests that

> In view of this difference in the understanding of the "scriptures" Christians and Jews are challenged to read the "scriptures" together. Since the "scriptures" have their roots in the history of the Jewish people, in their faith, thought and actions, Christians have to learn anew to listen to the Jewish voice in the interpretation of scripture. This would be for their benefit also regarding a deeper understanding of the New Testament.[135]

However, that Christians have to listen to Jews in order to interpret biblical texts is neither logical nor self-evident. The synod bases the assumption that Christians and Jews should read biblical texts together and that Christians need to pay attention to Jewish readings of biblical texts on what it understands to be the *sui generis* nature of the Christian-Jewish relationship. As such it is presented as a statement of faith. However, Haynes points out that such a faith commitment needs to be argued for

---

[131] Cf. ibid. 18-21.
[132] Ibid. 21.
[133] Cf. Seim 1980, 122.
[134] Cf. EKiR (ed.) [2]1985, 21f., 22-24.
[135] Ibid. 22.

rather than just stated and assumed to be *sui generis*.[136] To assert that a situation is *sui generis* renders it inaccessible to any debate. It has to be believed or denied, but cannot be accessed by reason and argument. Hence the description of a situation as *sui generis* is defensive since it avoids argument by hiding behind a statement of faith.

The aim of the synod is to show the continuing salvation-historical significance of the Jewish people. To do so the statement emphasises what it perceives as common ground between the two faiths and stresses beliefs shared by Jews and Christians. Seim argues that the statement of the synod that Jews and Christians have biblical scriptures in common "formulates a fundamental commonality which Jews and Christians are allowed to and need to refer to."[137] Arguably this statement constitutes a contradiction. Either one is allowed to do something, describing an option and excluding necessity, or one needs to do something, in which case there is no option. According to Seim, the fact that Jews and Christians refer to this body of scriptures with different terminologies demonstrates the history of their separation and that although problematic,[138] the adoption of the name Hebrew Bible by Christians

> has the advantage that it clearly indicates the limitation of the canon common to the synagogue and the Protestant church. This reference to the language [of the texts in their name] indicates at the same time the basic hermeneutical claim that the thorough reading of a book must be done with all possible attention to its historical location and its intrinsic intellectuality.[139]

However, the problematic nature of this suggestion becomes clear when the synod goes on to argue that Christians and Jews share the same body of scriptures but read them from different points of view. While the texts of the Hebrew Bible/Old Testament are shared by Christians and Jews, the different names of the books in which they are compiled for use by the communities indeed begs the question whether they can be understood as shared. The different order of the texts and their distinct histories of interpretation witness to Christians and Jews reading two different books which contain the same texts. References to a "Judeo-Christian" tradition and seeming similarities tend to obscure the separation of the two communities of interpretation.[140] While I do not wish to dispute that Jews and Christians can learn from each other in reading the texts interpreted by both communities, their distinct contexts of interpretation should be part of the reflection rather than hidden behind the assumption of commonality. An example of this different usage and history of interpretation is given by Zvi Werblowski in his address to the synod. Werblowski comments that the significance of the Torah to

---

[136] Cf. Haynes 1996, 313.
[137] Seim 1980, 111.
[138] Cf. ibid. 113.
[139] Ibid. 114.
[140] Cf. for example ibid. 123.

Jews can be compared to the significance of Christ for Christians.[141] Thus the Torah reading in synagogue would not be comparable to the Old Testament reading in church, but rather to the reading of the Gospel portion. Hence already the contexts in which a text is read in Jewish and Christian liturgical life are distinct from each other. By extension, learning Torah is a different activity from studying the Old Testament, and the language in which the text is read in liturgical and other settings contributes to the fashioning of the context of interpretation; the list of differences could go on. Again, the aim of this criticism of the statement is not to suggest that Christians and Jews should not read biblical texts together. Rather it is intended as safeguarding the integrity of both communities as well as preventing the usurpation of Jewish interpretations into Christian theological frameworks. All too frequently Jewish understandings of biblical texts are quoted out of context to prove a Christian theological point. Whereas the assumption of a moral imperative for Christians to facilitate "pro-Jewish" readings of biblical texts is honourable, it should not be taken as an excuse for Christian imperialism of Jewish tradition.[142]

However, the aim of the statement is to facilitate a reading of these scriptures which can be shared by Christians and Jews. Christians in particular should learn from Jewish interpretations of the Hebrew Bible. Thus, the writers claim, Christians can discover that they share their eschatological vision of the kingdom of G-d with Jews, that Christians are elected to partake in the already existing and never revoked covenant of G-d with the Jewish people.[143] As a consequence Christians can understand Jews as equal witnesses to G-d and abandon Christian efforts to convert Jews.[144]

The statement identifies Jews only in religious terms, excluding however Jewish debates on Jewish identity and religious expression. Because of the confessional approach of the statement this understanding of Jewish identity becomes a Christian presupposition for Christian approaches to Jews and Judaism. The statement does not address issues arising from the terminology which refers to Jews as a homogenous group ("the Jews") and no attempt is made to explore Jewish identities in history and today. Commentators, however, address the question of terminology used by the statement. Helmut Starck's summary of the negotiations of the Study Commission "Christians and Jews" on the Rhineland statement notes that the members of the Commission were aware of the multiple meanings of the terms "Israel" and "Jewish people":

---

[141] Cf. EKiR (ed.) [2]1985, 39.

[142] An interesting suggestion for theologians to consider is put forward by Michael Hilton who analyses Christian influences in the shaping of Jewish traditions, suggesting a mutual borrowing from each other's cultural expressions (cf. Hilton 1994).

[143] Cf. EKiR (ed.) [2]1985, 25f.

[144] Cf. ibid. 28. Cf. also the development of single and double covenant theories to accommodate the need of Christian theologians to affirm the Jewish witness to G-d positively.

Actually the theological, social and historical aspects as well as aspects of international law inherent in this term can be distinguished from each other if necessary, but they cannot be separated.[145]

Hans-Joachim Barkenings argues in a similar fashion and opts for the use of the term "people Israel", because this would express best the continuity of biblical with post-biblical "Israel" as well as the permanence of "Israel's" election.[146] This emphasis on continuity of biblical and post-biblical Jews is confirmed in the commentary on the suggested change of the constitution of the EKiR. It asserts that Christians have no right to interfere in Jewish self-definition while generalising aspects of Jewish identity as follows:

Jewish self-understanding has thereby [in traditional Christian understandings of Jews] been completely overlooked. Contemporary Jewry understands itself in uninterrupted continuity with biblical history. Jewish women and men in the land of Israel and in the Diaspora understand themselves as belonging to one large unity; centre of Jewish life in the Diaspora has long been the land of Israel, even before the founding of the state.[147]

The understanding of Jews as a people has been problematised by Jews since the 19th century as well as the development of Jewish identities other than religious and the pluralism of Jewish life in different religious and cultural expressions.[148] The social anthropologist Jonathan Webber argues that such a perspective of continuity cannot simply be taken for granted.

Whether the Jews of today, then, are the "same" people as that described in the ancient texts of the Bible is a question that permits no single answer. Jewish identity seen historically reveals both continuity and discontinuity; where the emphasis is to be placed depends on a person's point of view.[149]

In particular when it comes to defining who is a Jew, Jewry is divided and it is often difficult to perceive the divisions as divisions within one people. Webber summarises as follows:

There are many competing definitions that are known from the contemporary European experience, including the classical rabbinic definition (descent from a Jewish mother, or via conversion from an Orthodox court of rabbis), modern Progressive rabbinic definitions (descent from a Jewish mother or father, or conversion from a Progressive court of rabbis), Nazi definitions (a given number of Jewish grandparents, regardless of the individual's personal religious or communal affiliations or identity), and modern personal *ad hoc*

---

[145] Starck 1980, 21.
[146] Cf. Barkenings 1986, 152: "Die jüdische Pluralität ist zu berücksichtigen. Gemeint ist mit dem Neuanfang im Verhältnis von Christen und Juden immer das real existierende jüdische Volk, und zwar sowohl im neuerstandenen Staat Israel wie in der weiterhin vorhandenen Diaspora, also auch bei uns."
[147] EKiR (ed.) 1993, 21.
[148] Cf. for example Goldberg/Krausz (eds.) 1993 and Webber (ed.) 1994.
[149] Webber 1994, 3.

definitions (self-identification with the Jewish people, for whatever reason, such as being married or related to a Jew, or being labelled by others as Jewish).[150]

In any case, there is no authority acknowledged by all who understand themselves as Jewish which would be able centrally to determine Jewishness (comparable to the universal recognition of baptism among the churches which are part of the ecumenical movement). This is not to say that Jews cannot be understood as a people, but to indicate that Jewish peoplehood should not be taken for granted as an unproblematic concept. As a consequence, the concept of Jews as "the chosen people" which can be incorporated into salvation history is in conflict with Jewish reality and self-understanding.[151]

Christian interpretations of Jewish relations to the "land of Israel" and the founding of the State of Israel, as manifest in the Rhineland statement and commentaries on it in particular, have implications for Jewish self-understandings which are not reflected on by their authors. The statement argues "that the continuing existence of the Jewish people, its return to the Land of Promise, and also the foundation of the state of Israel, are signs of the faithfulness of God towards his people."[152] In his explication of the synod's intentions with this statement Klappert concludes as follows:

> [...] this model of a symbolic correspondence initiates a Christological-theological reflection and contemplation on the actual immigration to Israel and the founding of the State of Israel which are understood from the perspective of the confirmation of the covenant of God with Israel in Jesus Christ. These have to be interpreted and respected as signs of the faithfulness of Yahweh [sic] to his people, as signs of the validity of God's promises to the people Israel and also as signs of the still to be expected promises that correspond to the covenant which has been fulfilled in the messiah of Israel.[153]

---

[150] Ibid. 16.

[151] In the context of Christian representations of Jews, Herbert Jochum develops the notion of an exchange of paradigms, moving from the traditional notion of the "evil" to the "pious" Jew in Christian theology since 1945. He suggests that "der 'fromme Jude' der christlichen Literatur nicht aus Gründen jüdischer Selbstbezeichnung übernommen worden sein kann, sondern daß es sich vielmehr um eine verliehene Fremdbezeichnung durch Christen handelt. [In Anlehnung an christliche Frömmigkeitsformen], [...] wird daraus der aus innerer Überzeugung praktizierende 'Synagogen-Jude'" (Jochum 1986, 40). He argues that "Christen müssen sich auf die Wirklichkeit des Judentums einlassen. In all den kirchlichen Dokumenten der Gegenwart ist auf diese Notwendigkeit hingewiesen, auf Konstruktionen und Bilder zu verzichten. Dieser Verzicht erfordert eine selbstkritische Wahrnehmung der Ursachen und Grundlagen der Konstruktionen auf der einen Seite wie auch eine größere Sachkenntnis angesichts der Andersartigkeit und Vielgestaltigkeit des Judentums auf der anderen Seite" (ibid. 43). Regarding the Rhineland statement, however, he concludes that it successfully avoids a limited definition of Jews and as such is not discriminating against Jewish identities, an achievement he attributes to the fact that Jews were consulted as advisors for the formulation of the statement (cf. ibid. 46).

[152] Brockway et al. 1988, 92 and EKiR (ed.) [2]1985, 9.

[153] Klappert 1980c, 86f.

Inscribing such a perspective on Jewish social, political and religious realities appears to be problematic in the context of Christian-Jewish conversations. Such Christian statements of faith without doubt have to be respected and honoured, if not necessarily for their content, then surely for their moral and ethical intentions. However, they also present a "Christianisation" of Jews, in the sense that interpretations of Jewish reality are incorporated into Christian theological frameworks for the confirmation of Christian confessions of faith.[154] The implicit exclusion of conflicting Jewish self-understandings and interpretations of these Jewish social and political realities – ranging in extremes, for example from the rejection of the State of Israel by large parts of the *haredi* community to Reconstructionist dissociation from covenantal thinking – can hardly be taken seriously by this kind of Christian theological reflection, because it would undermine its foundation in a particular interpretation of the covenant and its promises.

The implications of defining a community one is not part of are not addressed by the statement. However, in the context of analysing constructions of collective memory in the Protestant church in Germany, questions about the ownership of traditions and definitions will be part of the following chapters.

Implications of such intrusion upon (or ignorance of or lack of interest in) definitions of Jewish identity have become more significant since 1996 when the synod ratified a change in its constitution and now confesses that the Jewish people are G-d's people and affirms an eschatological vision it understands to be shared by Jews and Christians:

> She (the Evangelical Church in the Rhineland) confesses God's faithfulness, who holds fast to the election of his people Israel. Together with Israel she hopes for a new heaven and a new earth.[155]

This change in the constitution of the Church of the Rhineland has now moved the debate on Christian understandings of Jews and Judaism for Christianity onto a different level. When a particular understanding of who Jews are in a Christian framework of interpretation of reality is inscribed in a confession of faith and the constitution of a church, members of this church are bound to this understanding.[156] Therefore the possibilities of Christians to include non-religious and conflicting understandings of what it means to be Jewish are limited. That the statement assumes a Christian religious perspective is implicit in the fact that it is a church document

---

[154] Krister Stendahl makes a similar point (cf. Stendahl 1986, 14f.).

[155] EKiR (ed.) 1993, 16 (the motion was accepted in 1996). For a detailed discussion of the developments resulting in the acceptance of the motion cf. Kriener/Schmidt (eds.) 1998.

[156] The fact that the formulation of the change in the constitution intrudes upon Jewish self-understandings and is not representative has been criticised during the decision-making process (cf. Seebass 1998, 176f.; Honecker 1998, 199).

addressing a Christian community regarding a Christian confession of faith. Problems with this perspective arise when the intentions of the statement (and the subsequent change of the constitution of the EKiR) are examined. Since the statement (and the addition to the constitution) understands itself as a document which wants to facilitate conversation and make Christian antisemitism impossible, it has to allow for the partners in the encounter, i.e. Jews, to define their own identities, rather than prejudge this question in a confession of faith. When the EKiR intrudes upon Jewish debates on Jewish identity and tries to determine – implicitly or explicitly – what is authentically Jewish, it undermines the efforts and intentions of dialogue. Only in a limited way does it now appear possible for the EKiR to say: "we no longer define what, according to our opinion, Jews should be, but we ask them about their self-understanding."[157]

The document acknowledges Christian complicity in the persecution of Jews which is grounded in Christian theological teaching. With the statement the church intends to rectify this involvement and lay the ground for a Christian theology that does not abuse Jews. However, the method of Christian renewal of the Christian-Jewish relationship is based on a reinterpretation of the significance of Jews for salvation history. Haynes points out, it is based on the understanding that Jews are witnesses to the presence of G-d. Therefore the statement still instrumentalises Jews and does not explore alternatives of looking at Jewish identities apart from what the authors understand as religiously Jewish. The statement suggests that a closer communion of Christians and Jews is desirable, since it believes Jews and Christians to be joined together in one covenant with G-d. In particular the hope for a common future is expressed.

Thus the statement introduces a theological asymmetry into Christian-Jewish relations: Christians believe things about Jews that Jews themselves may reject. The EKiR reflects only on Jewish religious identities which can be recognised by Christians and ignores that the underlying assumption of the statement of the existence of a "Judeo-Christian" tradition is not shared by all Jews. Even if the EKiR chooses to ignore these Jewish realities and can support its decision with Christian theological reasons, the question remains whether the existence of Jewish plurality does not implicitly undermine the intentions of the statement. The statement is in danger of creating new stereotypes about Jews and Judaism, because certain Jewish

---

[157] Barkenings 1986, 156f. Jürgen Seim, in contrast, argues that any explicit recognition of Jewish diversity through terminology used in the statement or constitution, namely the substitution of "Israel" as all-encompassing term with various historically, socially and religiously defined expressions, would suggest Christian interference with Jewish self-definition. He bases this argument on the assumption that Jewish self-understandings do not recognise a separation between biblical and post-biblical times comparable to Christian understandings of history (cf. Seim 1998, 290f.).

identities (even religious identities) are by definition excluded from consideration in this Christian reflection on Jews and Judaism.

A further consequence of the statement's understanding of Jews is related to the suggestion that Jews are at the centre of salvation history and that Christians need Jews to understand their own Christian identity. In these confessions of faith or interpretations of (Jewish) reality, even if addressed to Christians only, the EKiR interferes in Jewish definitions of identity. To some extent this implies that Jews are no longer free to differ with Christian definitions of Jewish identity, since Christian faith depends on them. As a consequence, the statement implies that Jews carry responsibility for the future possibility of Christian faith and life. Whether such an intervention with Jewish definitions of identity is legitimate is not addressed by the synod.

4. Conclusion

The statement of the Rhineland synod has to be welcomed as the first theological statement that reflects on the Holocaust and defines itself as a contextual approach to Christian-Jewish relations in Germany. It presents a great theological achievement to include reflections about the well-being of members of another community into considerations regarding what it means to be Christian. Whether or not the statement introduces a radical change in Christian understandings of and approaches to Jews and Judaism, the statement initially opened the floor for a discussion. An important consequence of the statement of the Rhineland synod is that statements of other member churches of the EKD followed the lines of thought opened by the Rhineland synod.[158]

The statement has an overall emphasis on education. It intends to introduce lectures in Jewish theology in church-run colleges, support teaching on Judaism in parishes and facilitate Christian-Jewish encounters.[159] These efforts have to be welcomed since opportunities for Christians to meet Jews in Germany on a regular basis in everyday life are rare. However, for the same reason education as suggested by the statement is also a problematic proposition, because what is supposed to be taught about Jews are particular kinds of religious Jewish identities and a Christian interpretation of these. Thus the danger of stereotyping Jews, albeit in a well-meaning, positive way, arises.

Furthermore, the context of Christian-Jewish encounters in Germany is governed by a number of asymmetries in Christian-Jewish relations which are not necessarily part of

---

[158] Cf. Rendtorff/Henrix (eds.) [2]1989, 609ff.

[159] Cf. EKiR (ed.) [2]1985, 11.

conversations between Christians and Jews in the USA or Britain. Birte Petersen summarises the asymmetries in Christian-Jewish relations particular to Germany as follows: (1) Jews in Germany are a small minority in a Christian dominated society; (2) Jews who partake in encounters with Christians are either themselves victims of the Holocaust or their descendants, whereas Christians are part of the tradition of victimisers of Jews (in the Holocaust); (3) the theological assumption that Judaism is the "root" of Christianity has as a consequence an understanding of Christianity as the "daughter-religion" of Judaism which needs reflection on its roots as part of its self-understanding; (4) the location of the conversation between Christians and Jews is largely isolated from the reality of contemporary Christian and Jewish life.[160]

What are the implications of these asymmetries and the apparent Christian agenda for Christian-Jewish encounters in Germany? When the conversations of Christians and Jews are dominated by the Christian side – which after all is the initiator – and moved directly onto the level of discussing interpretations of shared scriptures and the use of theological concepts, the danger arises that contemporary identities and social-historical contexts of both sets of participants in the encounters recede into the background of the conversation. Because the agenda of the conversation is set by the Christian side, Jews often function as sources of information rather than as partners. Many of the prominent Jewish participants in the conversations, in particular in advisory functions at church councils and synods, come from a German-Jewish background. Their education was largely German speaking and much of their religious-theological training included famous German-Jewish thinkers such as Martin Buber, Rosenzweig and Baeck, all of whom worked on Christian-Jewish relations in pre-World War II Germany. Their hopes for a togetherness of Christians and Jews in German society which would complement and strengthen the symbiosis of Germans and Jews envisioned by Jews in Germany are very much part of their cultural heritage.[161] To keep alive one's heritage was a concern of first generation emigrants from NS Germany and part of the search for their roots for their children.[162]

The issues that have arisen in this chapter help to set the agenda for the following chapters. In particular the debates in German society on the memory of the Holocaust will clarify implications of the issues which could only be indicated in this chapter. A feature of social and cultural debates on the memory of the Holocaust in Germany is a generational shift in the population away from eye-witnesses to second and third generation Germans whose relationship to the memory of the Holocaust is shaped by their historical distance to NS. Third generation Christians and Jews are still emotionally related to the history of the Holocaust – NS and the Holocaust are still

---

[160] Cf. Petersen [2]1998, 31f.
[161] Cf. Rendtorff 1991, 126.
[162] Cf. for example Friedlander 1990.

part of their communicative memory, i.e. the memory which embraces three to four generations and can thus be directly transmitted.[163] Thus far the traditional theological focus has neglected the inclusion of contemporary experiences with the memory of the Holocaust in Christian and Jewish communities. The biblical foundation of Christian-Jewish relations has created a mutual meeting ground which has thus far not been analysed critically.

This would suggest a refocusing of the conversation on contemporary Christian and Jewish identities and their relation to the memory of the Holocaust. Thereby the Christian religious foundation of Christian-Jewish relations may have to be rethought by concentrating on questions such as: has the confession of a common ground and future of Christians and Jews really helped to eliminate antisemitism from Christian thinking or has it substituted one model of thinking about Jews with another, which again does not take seriously Jewish self-expression? are Jews considered as people in their own right or only as symbols in Christian understandings of salvation history? does Christianity have to focus on the covenant to find a credible theological basis for a Christian-Jewish encounter or are there possibilities which do not patronise Jews by assigning them salvation historical functions and would thus establish equality in a conversation?[164] If Christian-Jewish encounters in Germany can be informed by the memories articulated by third generation Germans and Jews, the need to assert differences in perception and identification with this shared history would call for an acknowledgement of the separation of the communities and a recognition that the memory of this history is not shared.[165] The Christian use of Jewish tradition would have to be evaluated anew – could its function be selfish and be an attempt to disinherit Jews or a sign of syncretism? The process of naming injustices has to be owned anew by each generation of Christians and Jews. For an honest conversation to take place, injustices of the past have to be named; only then can it be asked how Christians and Jews can now distance themselves from traditional theologies/identities and negotiate a new self-understanding.

The following chapters will broaden the perspective indicated here and reflect on the complex field of Holocaust remembrance in the FRG in an effort to gain insights into the socio-cultural background of the specific context of Christian representations of the Holocaust and Jews. Outlining strands of public forms of Holocaust remembrance in the cultural fabric of the FRG provides the background to the analysis of Marquardt's theology in the third chapter. Marquardt's theology explicitly takes as its

---

[163] Cf. Assmann 1988, 10f.

[164] Cf. Münz [2]1996, 478f. regarding imperialistic tendencies in Christian appropriation of Jewish tradition.

[165] A similar set of questions that might be important for the developing Christian-Jewish conversation in Germany was already formulated by Stendahl in the 1980s, but responses have not been forthcoming, cf. Stendahl 1986, 11-15.

starting point the impact of the Holocaust on German society and Christian theology. The fact that the theologians engaged in Christian-Jewish conversations in the FRG are part of the tradition of the victimisers of Jews in the Holocaust (and in church history) becomes a discerning element in his contextual dogmatic theology.

II. From *Holocaust* to Goldhagen – Exemplary debates on the memory of the Holocaust in the last two decades

Public representations of the Holocaust allow the identification of patterns of publicly articulated forms of Holocaust remembrance. The Holocaust is represented in a variety of ways in public debates, films, books, and behaviour. Choice of language – which does not always have to be conscious – indicates particular relations to this part of German history and can thus also be interpreted as enactment of memory. In other words, the complex structure of society frames representations of the Holocaust. These representations of the Holocaust intensify in a number of public debates regarding the place of the Holocaust in German collective memory. I will explore the representation of the Holocaust and Jews in the following five exemplary events of the last twenty years in the FRG: the debates surrounding the films *Holocaust* (1979/80) and *Heimat* (1984), the Bitburg Controversy (1985), the *Historikerstreit* (1986) and the Goldhagen Controversy (1996). All these debates are firmly rooted in the cultural context of West Germany.

Commentators have repeatedly pointed out that the debates surrounding the first screening of the American miniseries *Holocaust* in 1979 were a turning point in the enactment of Holocaust remembrance in Germany.[1] Arguably *Heimat* represented a version of NS history in an effort to reclaim German history from its representation in *Holocaust* where the Jewish victims of NS had been the focus of the narrative.[2] In the mid-1980s the controversy surrounding Chancellor Kohl's and President Reagan's visit to the German war cemetery near Bitburg and the *Historikerstreit* illustrated conflicting political and moral perspectives inherent in the representation of NS history in public ceremonies and historical scholarship.[3] Ten years after this cluster of debates, the publication of Daniel Jonah Goldhagen's book *Hitler's Willing Executioners*[4] caused a public controversy about the representation of the Holocaust, German perpetrators and Jewish victims.[5] The controversy testified to particular structures of German public debates on the memory of the Holocaust while also indicating a generational shift in the participants in the discussion. As such *Holocaust* and the Goldhagen Controversy indicate a beginning and a recent example of German public debates of the past two decades. An analysis of public debates will demonstrate how relations to the Holocaust and Jews are publicly enacted in Germany.[6]

---

[1] Cf. for example the discussion of *Holocaust* in Rabinbach/Zipes (eds.) 1986.

[2] Cf. for example the discussion in Murray/Wickham (eds.) 1992 and Kaes 1989.

[3] Cf. for example Levkov (ed.) 1987; Hartman (ed.) 1986 and Augstein et al. ³1987.

[4] Goldhagen 1996a.

[5] Cf. Heil/Erb (eds.) 1998; Schoeps (ed.) 1997 and Shandley (ed.) 1998.

[6] The years between the *Historikerstreit* and the Goldhagen Controversy and since witnessed a number of events concerning the representation and remembrance of the Holocaust, such as the

The contested field of Holocaust remembrance can be understood as a series of debates concerning the ownership of memory where different groups focus upon what is relevant from the past for their contemporary self-understanding. All debates on the memory of the Holocaust in Germany concern the meaning of the past for the present. Any representation of the Holocaust in Germany reflects on German self-understanding and thus relates constructions of national identity. Since the end of the Second World War the crucial question in Germany has been: How should Germans relate to their NS past? This question generates a string of subsequent questions concerning what should be remembered of 1933-1945 and what place the memory of the Holocaust should assume, indeed what should be remembered of the Holocaust and how other memories of this time are to be interpreted in relation to the memory of the Holocaust. When examining cultural texts it is important to bear in mind that the terms NS, war and Holocaust are not interchangeable but represent differences in content as well as in the function assigned to their memory. Confusion arises when each term is understood to include the others' content. NS, the war and the Holocaust are arguably the most frequently discussed subjects in German political, historical and cultural debates. Numerous books are published each year on the subject and the number of conferences, exhibitions and monuments relating to NS is ever increasing.[7] However, commentators on Germany frequently speak of a culture of collective amnesia, arguing that German society refuses to confront its past and evades the memory of the Holocaust.[8] This raises the question of what Germans think they remember and what commentators understand them to forget or refuse to confront.

Remembrance of the Holocaust and the NS past in Germany is often described in terms such as "working through the past", "mourning the past", "coming to terms with the past", "normalising the past" and "drawing a line under the Nazi past", terms which reflect different relations to NS history. Commentators on the debate accuse Germans of "collective amnesia", "collective silence" and "wilful forgetfulness", thereby criticising German representations of NS history and formulations of identity in relation to that history. The descriptions used in public debates on the

---

debate on the museums of German history in Bonn and Berlin (cf. Maier [6]1994), the creation of a Jewish museum in Berlin (cf. for example Libeskind 1999; Young 2000 and the discussion in Wiedmer 1999), the refurbishment of the *Neue Wache* in Berlin as a memorial to the dead of all wars, the planned construction of a Holocaust memorial in Berlin (cf. for example Cullen [ed.] 1999 and Brumlik/Funke/Rensmann 2000), the introduction of 9 November and 27 January as memorial days (cf. for example Brumlik/Kunik [eds.] [2]1988; Bodemann 1996b and Domansky 1992), the box office success of *Schindler's List* (1994) (cf. for example Loshitzky [ed.] 1997 in particular 171-192 on the impact of the film in Germany), the controversy surrounding the exhibition *Crimes of the Wehrmacht* (cf. for example Thiele [ed.] 1997 and Hamburger Institut für Sozialforschung [ed.] 1998), the Walser-Bubis exchange (cf. for example Brumlik/Funke/Rensmann 2000 and Stiftung für die Rechte zukünftiger Generationen [ed.] 1999) as well as numerous local events.

[7] Cf. Kaes 1992, 310 and Buruma 1994, 8; for an overview of aspects of the development of a distinct culture of memory in the FRG in the past twenty years cf. Geyer 1996.

[8] Cf. for example Traverso 1995; Bartov 1992 and Nolan 1988.

remembrance of the Holocaust reflect the variety of functions that are assigned to its memory. Common to all of them is the recognition that in Germany the Holocaust cannot be remembered without the memory of NS. The memory of both is part of the historiography of the German nation state(s). The interpretation of NS affects the understanding of the Holocaust and vice versa. And the memory of both and the perception of their relationship to each other impacts on German national self-understanding in the present. Eric Santner observes that "Germans are faced with the paradoxical task of having to constitute their 'Germanness' in the awareness of the horrors generated by a previous production of national and cultural identity."[9]

Debates on the memory of NS, the war and the Holocaust are, then, debates on the definition of German identity. Two questions arise in this context: first, how can a society remember national failure without losing a sense of a positive national identity? Second, how can this be achieved while doing justice to the memory of the victims of NS and the Holocaust at the same time? Michael Geyer argues that

> If the Germans wish to be a nation, then they can in no case refer to a normality of others (such as the French or the Americans), but must take an interest in their own history and their own dead, the victims as well as the culprits, and their equally divided and interrelated histories. Not too long ago that was a matter of assigning guilt. But now it will increasingly become a question of protecting the civility of succeeding generations in light of a passing era.[10]

How these questions have been negotiated in the representation of the Holocaust and Jews in the five debates on the remembrance of the Holocaust outlined above is the subject of this chapter.

1. *Holocaust* and *Heimat* – Staging the opposition of Jewish and German memories

1.1. *Holocaust*

With *Holocaust*, the German public was confronted with a version of recent German history which had hitherto gone largely unnoticed. While it is wrong to say that the Holocaust was not remembered in the German media,[11] the American miniseries for the first time directly confronted the perspective of the perpetrators of the Holocaust with its victims. Through the fates of two fictitious families, one Jewish (Weiss), one German (Dorff), the series narrated a history of the Holocaust.[12] Focusing on the Weiss family the series follows its members who suffer a variety of NS atrocities,

---

[9] Santner [3]1996, 145.

[10] Geyer 1997, 20f.

[11] Cf. Geisler 1992, 223.

[12] Regarding the more general (mainly American) discussion of Holocaust cf. American Jewish Committee 1978; Wiesel 1978; Doneson 1987 and Shandler 1999, in particular 159-178.

ranging from the November pogroms 1938, the T4 programme, the expulsion to Poland, the establishment of the Warsaw ghetto, the ghetto uprising and deportation to Auschwitz, Babi Yar, fighting with a Jewish Partisan group, Theresienstadt, and finally liberation and emigration to Palestine. The main protagonist of the Dorff family ascends through the ranks of the SS, is present at Hadamar, Babi Yar, the Wannsee Conference as well as being involved in the development of gas chambers. While being itself a very graphic representation of atrocity and mass killing, the narrative is also intersected with documentary footage.[13] Thus the series manages to provide the audience with a chronology as well as introduce them to major events, names and places of the Holocaust. The portrayal of the Holocaust through the fate of two families contributed to its accessibility which invited the identification of the audience with its characters. Siegfried Zielinski comments:

> "Holocaust" wants to denounce and condemn anti-Semitism, to show the suffering of its victims and render them comprehensible to the audience, to touch the emotions of the guilty, the uninvolved, the successive generations, and to arouse identification with the victims.[14]

Holocaust generated a public debate of an unprecedented scale.[15] Screened in the USA in 1978, sold to Israel and most European countries, the series had attracted such an amount of publicity that Germany could not refuse to televise *Holocaust* if it wanted to be taken seriously in its efforts to commemorate the Holocaust.[16] However, the national television stations were less than enthusiastic about putting *Holocaust* in the schedules and the decision was made to show it on the regional third television channels – reserved for educational and "serious" cultural programmes.

Criticism of the miniseries objected to its commercial roots in the American television industry, which were deemed unsuitable for the representation of such a sensitive subject as the Holocaust, and argued that *Holocaust* trivialised the subject it depicts and therefore did not live up to the standard of high culture (*Kultur*).[17] However, Geyer rightly points out that

> The separation of intellectual and popular culture is highly artificial, in any case. Both sides shared in the same public space, and there was much more overlap between the two than the distinction between "high" and "low" culture would allow. [...] it was only through film and television that a memorializing culture finally took hold.[18]

---

[13] Cf. for example the scene in which Dorff shows films and slides of the killings by the *Einsatzgruppen* to Heydrich in order to inform him of the "progress" of the programme of murder. The films and slides are documentary evidence produced by members of the NS killing squads.
[14] Zielinski 1986, 234.
[15] Cf. ibid. 259. For a collection of material on *Holocaust* cf. Kampen (ed.) 1978.
[16] Cf. Zielinski 1986, 265. *Holocaust* was not shown in the GDR, but viewers with access to West German television channels were watching the miniseries (cf. Buruma 1994, 88).
[17] Cf. Herf 1986, 214f.
[18] Geyer 1996, 183.

When considering how German filmmakers had thus far represented the Holocaust, the argument that *Holocaust* did not qualify as an expression of *Kultur* can be read as an evasion of the issues presented by the miniseries. NS, the war and in particular Hitler himself were subjects addressed by German filmmakers, the Holocaust, however, had not been chosen as a subject.[19] To defend this lack of cultural interest in the murder of Jews in Europe, critics were willing to undermine their own genre by saying that it is unsuitable for the representation of the Holocaust, as well as accuse their American colleagues of trivialising the issues *Holocaust* represents.[20] Political needs were hidden behind an aesthetic agenda, as Dieter Zimmer, one of the editors of the weekly paper *Die Zeit* argues:

> The wish not to remember these events, especially when the impulse to do so comes from abroad, hides behind a high-minded disapproval of form. The need to repress the past couldn't find a better alibi.[21]

Der Spiegel also feared that the series could arouse anti-German feelings.[22] Issues concerning the representation of atrocity and mass murder were mixed with concerns of political correctness and the international image of the FRG.[23] According to Jeffrey Herf, "the sanctimoniousness and hostility to 'Holocaust' emanating from West German conservatives was fully consistent with the highly practical purposes of amnesia"[24], thereby supporting the argument of Adorno, who in his essay "What Does Coming to Terms with the Past Mean?" had concluded that

> The forgetting of National Socialism should be understood far more in terms of a general social situation than in terms of psychopathology. Even the psychological mechanisms that defend against painful and unpleasant memories serve highly realistic ends. This is revealed when those who are defensive point out, freely and in a practical mood, that too vivid and lasting remembrance of those events could harm Germany's reputation abroad. [...] The effacement of memory is more the achievement of an all-too-wakeful consciousness than it is the result of its weakness in the face of the superiority of unconscious processes.[25]

Holocaust was shown in January 1979 at a time of particular political tension. The *Bundestag* debated the statute of limitation for murder (*Verjährungsdebatte*) which would, if it was not abolished, make war crimes trials in Germany impossible once thirty years had elapsed since the crime had been committed. Herf comments that "'Holocaust' was telecast in a climate of growing West German public criticism of the post-war failure to live up to basic liberal principles of justice."[26]

---

[19] Cf. Geisler 1992, 224-233.

[20] Cf. Herf 1986, 213-218.

[21] Quoted in ibid. 215f.

[22] Cf. Zielinski 1986, 264.

[23] Cf. Herf 1986, 208-233.

[24] Ibid. 219.

[25] Adorno 1959/1986, 117.

[26] Herf 1986, 213.

Zielinski, one of the main commentators in the *Holocaust* debate, argues that the miniseries functioned in a number of ways as a watershed for Holocaust memory in Germany. He argues that during the week in which *Holocaust* was shown on four consecutive evenings, the miniseries was the main topic of conversation in the media, the workplace, schools and universities, at home and in other places of social life.[27] Immediately after the programme a panel of experts was available to answer questions of the television audience and debate issues raised by the programme.[28] Many viewers wrote to the broadcasting company WDR and expressed their opinions on the programme.[29] In particular, for younger viewers *Holocaust* appeared to be a source of information about – and confrontation with – a history which had so far been taboo in public debates.[30]

> This visceral reaction is symptomatic of the gaping hole that must have existed in the minds and emotions of the viewers. "Holocaust's" impact sheds by no means a favourable light on the Federal Republic. On the contrary, it demonstrates the thirty-year-old failure of the mighty culture industry to transmit the experience of fascism and its capital crimes to the mass of the inhabitants of this country – moreover, to transmit them as complex, in a way that does not relegate the problems to an affair of intellectuals and does not bypass the emotions.[31]

Responses to *Holocaust* by the audiences indicated that the watershed was interpreted to mean different things. On the one hand, it signalled the breaking of a silence around a subject that so far could hardly be addressed in public. Education appeared to be the main concern of critics who viewed the series in a favourable light.[32] On the other hand, it also appeared to legitimise wartime experiences. Repeating the pattern of the 1950s' and 1960s' confrontation with NS

> it became rather socially decorous to have "been around then" and to publish your sincere or just recently concocted struggles with your conscience. It was not the resistance fighters nor the victims who were now put forward as an example but instead, the pitiable fellow travelers.[33]

Again the focus of the discussion did not shift to the (Jewish) victims, but remained mainly on the victimisers and their traditions. However, in the aftermath of *Holocaust* there followed a greater recognition of other minorities persecuted by NS who had so far and still have not been heard strongly enough.[34] In addition a renewed process of discovering history began with *Holocaust* and was continued with *Heimat*. The

---

[27] Cf. Zielinski 1986, 267.

[28] For numbers of recorded calls cf. Markovits/Hayden 1986, 240.

[29] For statistics on the audience of *Holocaust* cf. Magnus 1979, 221-224.

[30] Cf. Zielinski 1986, 249.

[31] Ibid. 269.

[32] Cf. Markovits/Hayden 1986, 238f. Cf. also the material distributed to educators by the Landeszentrale für politische Bildung, Northrhine Westphalia (Kampen 1978).

[33] Zielinski 1986, 271.

[34] In particular Sinti and Roma gained recognition as victims of NS, as well as homosexuals, and also prisoners of conscience such as Jehovah's witnesses began to be named publicly more often.

personalisation of historical events in *Holocaust* led to numerous local history projects, occupied with unearthing the biographies of Jewish communities.[35]

1.2. *Heimat*

Criticism, however, did not only concern the aesthetic qualities of *Holocaust* and the question of whether it is possible to represent the Holocaust. When Edgar Reitz's *Heimat* was televised in 1984 the debate concerned the nature and ownership of memory. The question of who had the right to represent German history was at the heart of Reitz's inquiry.[36]

> Germany, it seemed, had to import the images of its own past from Hollywood. German history – made in Hollywood: that was the real scandal someone like Edgar Reitz tried to counter with his film *Heimat*, which was originally entitled "Made in Germany".[37]

Thus, Reitz' *Heimat* was produced as an antithesis to *Holocaust*. By narrating almost a century in the history of one family in an imaginary village in the Hunsrück (Schabbach) he wanted to reclaim German history, arguing that history can only be owned by the people who remember it. Memory, according to Reitz, is a personal concept which cannot transcend national boundaries.

> As such it [*Heimat*] is one of the most intriguing interpretations of German history in recent years, a bold attempt to set the rules as to who is permitted to talk about German history and what is permitted to be said.[38]

According to Reitz, Americans, by definition, cannot represent German history, because they cannot remember it.[39] For him remembrance is tied to direct experience or to generational transmission of experience in a continuous cultural context, thus excluding non-Germans from the representation of German history.[40]

> *Heimat* originated as a project of national identity, seeking, like every national identity, to claim an authentic national voice that differentiated what Germans "know" about themselves from what others "know" about them.[41]

Commentators have criticised the film mainly for its omission of representations of the Holocaust, because such an omission can facilitate an uncritical construction of German identity.[42] However, Alon Confino disputes this conclusion, arguing that the

---

[35] Cf. ibid. 276f. Cf. also Geisler 1992, 240f. and Geyer 1996, 180f.

[36] For Reitz's own contribution to the subject cf. Elsaesser 1992; Kaes 1989 as well as Reitz 1984.

[37] Kaes 1992, 313. For Kaes' influential analysis of the film cf. Kaes 1989, 161-192.

[38] Confino 1998, 185.

[39] Cf. ibid. 200. The conflict about the right to represent German history arises again in the Goldhagen Controversy.

[40] Cf. ibid. 200.

[41] Ibid. 199.

[42] Cf. for example Kaes 1992; Kaes 1989 and Santner 1992.

symbolic manual of the Heimat-idea[43] does not by definition exclude representations of the Holocaust.[44] According to Confino the concept of Heimat as developed since the end of the 19th century is a key to the interpretation of the film and of the demands it places on the interpretation of the relationship between the writing of history and memory. He argues that *Heimat* demonstrates the ambiguity of memory and the treacherousness of its uses. Confino links the success of *Heimat* in the wake of *Holocaust* to the flourishing of the concept of Heimat in Germany, arguing that with the founding of the German nation state in 1871 Heimat became

> a key concept in German culture and a central word in German discourse. The logic of Heimat was that it represented a community, real or imagined, tangible or symbolic, of people who shared a transcended common denominator.[45]

However, this common denominator changed depending on the way in which the concept of Heimat was used. Whereas until the 1940s "Germans understood the word Heimat to mean both local and national territory"[46], Germans today will associate Heimat only with "local territory that is immediate and tangible – a hometown, a village, or home itself."[47] Confino argues that

> The meaning of Heimat in the past two hundred years thus appears to have made full circle defining local territory in the first half of the nineteenth century when a German nation-state did not exist, local and national territory in the period of the nation-state, and local territory again after 1945 following the bankruptcy of German nationalism and the dismemberment of the nation-state.[48]

However, the link between the local and the national has not been completely obliterated in post-1945 usage of Heimat. According to Confino, *Heimat* was successful "because it appropriated this culturally familiar symbolic manual"[49] which understood Heimat "not simply [as] a mediator between national and local identity, but [...] [as] an actual representation of the nation."[50] While Reitz "sets out to tell the story of some ordinary Germans, but not others",[51] Confino argues that this constitutes a problem only when such a representation is not augmented by other

---

[43] I use Heimat as a concept without indicating the German origin of the word by italicising. When *Heimat* is italicised it refers to the film.

[44] Cf. Confino 1997, 185-208.

[45] Ibid. 126.

[46] Ibid. 126.

[47] Ibid. 126.

[48] Ibid. 127.

[49] Confino 1998, 193.

[50] Ibid. 191. For Reitz Heimat signifies harmony and represents an antithesis to nation which stands for conflict. However, given the fact that *Heimat* "sets out against the concept of national history, the underlying assumption of *Heimat* is that Schabbach is a metonymy of German history" (ibid. 190).

[51] Ibid. 201.

stories. Given Reitz's limitation of the interpretation of German history to Germans who have communicative memory of the events narrated, Confino concludes that

> In a past which is determined by experience, everyday life, and personal recollections, there is no reason why Reitz cannot film *Ordinary Men*, with Christopher Browning as historical adviser, about the experience of a group of lower-middle-class folks from Hamburg who, as members of Police Battalion 101 in Poland in the Second World War, shot to death 38,000 Jews and helped deport to Treblinka an additional 45,200. The symbolic manual of the Heimat idea, in itself, does not prohibit the inclusion of Auschwitz into *Heimat*; [...] Auschwitz, too, was a German world of everyday life, not only Schabbach. But in a past which is determined by personal memory, the chances that Germans would prefer to remember Auschwitz are slim, while the chances that they would prefer to repress it are infinitely greater.[52]

In contrast, I would argue that Auschwitz cannot be understood as "a German world of everyday life" which corresponds to the Heimat idea. Heimat refers to an identity rooted in everyday life owned by a community which is defined by the exclusion of non-Germans. Confino demonstrates this in his analysis of Heimat museums:

> Every community in Germany had, as everybody knew, a long history and Heimat museums therefore proliferated rapidly, legitimizing local history and identity. [...] The very existence of a local Heimat museum symbolized the worthiness of one's local past [...].[53]

Heimat only relates traumatic or disturbing memory as part of narratives pertaining to the community of Heimat with the aim of establishing its solidarity, but not traumatic memories of victims of the Heimat community which would undermine its self-understanding. Instead as the Heimat museum did, narratives of Heimat represent

> the identity of a community of people who shared a past and a present. The community in question [...] [is] not only the local community, but also an intangible community that extended to larger territories and inclusive identities.[54]

Heimat is a concept of solidarity, extending to the members of a specific community. I would contend – incidentally in agreement with Confino – that in the framework of the relationship between local and national identity represented by the Heimat idea, the members of a Heimat community are defined by exclusion.[55] German Heimat narratives will, for example, not include French or English experiences in their own right, and more importantly in this context, they will not relate Jewish memories. Auschwitz does not represent a community which could be understood as Heimat. It was not a world of everyday life that could forge identity by connecting to a past and

---

[52] Ibid. 201.

[53] Confino 1997, 140.

[54] Ibid. 145.

[55] Cf. Confino 1998, 200. However "basing his understanding of the past on memory, Reitz excludes non-Germans from evaluating German history [...]" (ibid. 200), a limitation which – in agreement with Confino – I would reject, since it limits historical inquiry and renders the writing of history beyond the life of two generations impossible.

a present. Inasmuch as Auschwitz was by definition the exact opposite of what Heimat is supposed to signify, it cannot be included in any German narrative about Heimat. Auschwitz in its conception as "a page of glory in our history which has never been written and shall never be written"[56] excludes its representation as part of the Heimat idea. NS was aware that with Auschwitz it was creating an antithesis to Heimat and any narratives that can represent this idea. The museum of an extinct culture where NS intended to represent Jewish life was not planned as a Heimat museum where one is asked to identify. Rather it is the opposition to such a museum, which is meant to discourage from deriving any positive experiences from an encounter with Jewish culture. Confino concludes that "Reitz's masterpiece is a historical film based on a moral decision to conceal parts of history and to highlight others so that they will not be 'too much for our mind.'"[57]

But, by definition, Heimat is never "too much for our mind". The moral decision to exclude experiences of people considered as Other is part of the existing symbolism of the Heimat idea. Heimat symbolises the refuge from everything that might be challenging, gruesome and hard to confront and endure.[58] Auschwitz does not have to be concealed, it simply can never be part of a Heimat narrative which defines communities of Germans by exclusion. However, Michael Geisler argues that *Holocaust* served to undermine this concept of narratives of German history, because "The taboo *Holocaust* broke in Germany [...] was precisely the embedding of the terror in the matrix of everyday reality"[59]. By juxtaposing two narratives of human experience, *Holocaust* and *Heimat* demonstrate different approaches to everyday history and as such criticise what thus far could be included in the Heimat symbolic.

This Heimat narrative has also subtly been undermined by local history projects. In Michael Verhoeven's film *The Nasty Girl* (1990), which is based on the real-life experiences of Anna Rosmus, the protagonist Sonja Wegmus[60] began to unearth the NS past of her hometown and thereby shook the foundations of what the local population was prepared to accept as their Heimat history. Ian Buruma observes that

> Her subject was also Heimat history, but she had always been at home. She had never rejected her local identity; it was her opponents who tried to take the Heimat away from her, by

---

[56] Heinrich Himmler in a speech to a group of SS leaders in Posen, 4 October 1943.

[57] Confino 1998, 202.

[58] Cf. Ibid. 197f.: "Heimat history has never been about getting the facts of German history right, such as establishing some sort of a causality between Schabbach's residents and Nazism. On the contrary, it is about getting the story crooked, about inventing a causality in Heimat museums between the Germanic tribes and the Second Empire, or obscuring a causality in Heimat films between the crimes of the Third Reich and West Germany."

[59] Geisler 1992, 235.

[60] The choice of names is interesting as well. Wegmus appears to be related to "wegmüssen", having to leave. The "real" Sonja, Anna Rosmus, emigrated to the USA.

making her feel she didn't belong, that she was a "Jewish whore," to cite one of the more common phrases in her hate mail.[61]

What makes Heimat for Sonja is the inclusion of destructive aspects of local history in her narrative. It is important that all memories she includes are local. She does not try to include "Auschwitz" or "the war", but rather works within the tight framework of her community.[62] This does not stop her from identifying, but makes Heimat a more honest place to live in. Hence for Sonja the idea of Heimat includes challenges as long as identification with the place and the community is not abandoned. However, it ceases to be part of the Heimat museum approach to Heimat. Because Reitz refused to question the narratives underlying the Heimat idea he implicitly rejected any changes to the perception of what Heimat can mean to people and how to negotiate its memories. To him Heimat is immutable and either exists in its classical idyllic form, or it becomes impossible and disintegrates as the ending of the film shows.[63] Omer Bartov argues that

> Edgar Reitz's film *Heimat* (1984), [...] is a film about authentic (yet imagined) memories, not about authentic (and largely documented) reality. This type of authenticity enabled *Heimat* to avoid precisely those inconvenient issues that the protagonist of Michael Verhoeven's cabaret-like production *The Nasty Girl* (*Das schreckliche Mädchen*, 1990) persistently raised to the consternation of her own community, whose "authentic" memories had very little to do with the reality of the past.[64]

By not allowing the single Jew in the nearest town a voice of his own, Reitz silences his history and his memory in the narrative of *Heimat*.[65] Jews do not belong in a narrative of Heimat, a message of Reitz's film as much as of Sonja's opponents who call her "Jewish whore" to demonstrate that they exclude her from the local

---

[61] Buruma 1994, 266.

[62] In her recent study of Holocaust remembrance in Germany, Caroline Wiedmer includes a discussion of *Nasty Girl*. She argues that the film contributes to what Adorno characterised as conscious forgetting of NS, because it does not directly address the Holocaust, nor does it explore how Sonja's family had been complicit in NS (cf. Wiedmer 1999, 101-103). While I agree with these observations I would not draw the same conclusion as Wiedmer. She appears to imply that any representation of NS necessarily needs to explore the Holocaust. I would argue that the Holocaust is not the subject of *Nasty Girl*. Rather the film's subject is the ways in which representatives of Sonja's hometown deny that they are in continuity with NS and how they would like to omit this part of their town's history from memory. As in *Heimat*, the focus of the narrative is local but, unlike *Heimat*, *Nasty Girl* does not accept the exclusion of conflicting memories from the narrative of her hometown. Thereby Sonja hinders the process of forgetting, but at the same time she does not claim to have explored all there is to explore. The film ends with Sonja rejecting the bust of herself that representatives of her town present to her for her achievements in writing Heimat history. She interprets the bust as a bribe to keep her quiet.

[63] Cf. Kaes 1989, 167. Cf. also Confino 1998, 198.

[64] Bartov 1996, 164.

[65] Cf. Kaes 1989, 188.

community.[66] If Reitz's *Heimat* signifies what Germans can say about themselves and thus claim as their own history, the consequence would be a complete separation of Jewish memory and history from German memory and history. This assumption would not only confirm NS ideology regarding the opposition between Jews and Germans, but also place the Holocaust totally outside of German history as a series of events which cannot be remembered by Germans, because they have no ability to relate to its victims in any way. As a consequence the imperative to remember the Holocaust would become utterly meaningless, because to remember the Holocaust Germans need to have some access to victim memory. However Geisler, writing on *Holocaust*, argues that

> In a sense a miniseries, especially one with such a tremendous resonance in mainstream discourse as *Holocaust*, actually becomes part of the personal life experience and memory of the viewer.[67]

If memory can be acquired through knowledge and empathy, then experiences we do not share can still become part of our memory and can thus be owned by people who lack first hand experience or who do not share in the history of a community in the first place. *Holocaust* began to facilitate such a bridging of German and Jewish memories for Germans:

> The audiences' memories were in this sense part of a specular imagination; in the image of the other (the Jewish family as the victims of Germans) the audience discovered a part of itself that had been lost – and that, indeed, had been betrayed by them. Betrayal and lies surface as tangible accusations. They were the small change of dictatorship and they were the things people remembered. They saw it all on television and many people in the audience saw themselves for the first time in the double of the fictional image.[68]

Germans "know" about the Holocaust, but do not remember it as part of the narratives of their collective memory. In other words, the knowledge of the genocide of Jews in Europe is relevant to their self-understandings, whereas memories of persecution and murder are not. In other words, historical knowledge of NS and the Holocaust has not become part of the memory relevant to the identities of Germans. When such memory is acquired, Germans constantly have to perform a balancing act between the empathic identification with the victims of NS and the historically

---

[66] Regarding post-Holocaust Jewish association with Germany cf. also Borneman/Peck 1995; Feinberg 1997, 161-181 and Gilman 1991, 249-278.

[67] Geisler 1992, 236. Michael Geyer and Miriam Hansen are critical of imagery of the Holocaust conveyed by the media, because "the market-driven interplay between representation and receptive audience led to confessional memories that were the exact opposite of *Erinnerungen* or internalizations. They were *external memories*, expressive acts of a 'spectacular' imagination combining with technology to organize everyday experience" (Geyer/Hansen, 1994, 187). While I would acknowledge the dangers inherent in a confusion of "external memories" with *Erinnerungen*, such "borrowed" memories may nevertheless point into the direction of the creation of a memory of the victims of the Holocaust and their representation as part of German history.

[68] Geyer 1996, 184.

necessary identification with the perspective of the victimisers. For reasons of historical accuracy non-Jewish Germans cannot identify directly with the victims of NS without denying part of the victimiser legacy of Germany. However, identification with the victims and with their memories and historical perspective remains a precondition if knowledge is to become relevant memory. One way to enable an identification that does not bypass the traditions of the victimisers is the inclusion of Jews in the community of Germans, so that the history of Jews in Germany is written as part of German history. As Geyer and Hansen argue

> the most hopeful indication of a German working-through of the past is the possibility of keeping alive the memory of the victims. [...] The ability to sustain – rather than usurp – the memory of Jewish victims depends on a concept of the subject as a divided subjectivity, one that could bear a recognition of the violence of the past. [...] Such memory-work, therefore, recovers not a single history but several histories; not the negating of death through the rhetorical assertion of continuity, but the remembrance of absence.[69]

German-Jewish conflicts of memory of the Holocaust are at the centre of debates on the representation of NS in Germany. This history has generated the formulation of identities which perceive Germans and Jews as separate and antagonistically defined communities.[70] Santner expresses this notion with reference to psychoanalytic concepts of self and Other:

> the tasks facing post-Holocaust societies in general, that is, societies willing to work through the traumatic impact of Nazism and the "Final Solution," include that of a radical rethinking and reformulation of the very notions of boundaries and borderlines, of that "protective shield" regulating exchange between the inside and the outside of individuals and groups.[71]

That Germans and Jews (necessarily) remember differently is already indicated by the conflicting terminologies employed by these two broadly defined communities of memory. James Young argues that names associated with NS, the Holocaust and the war are telling a story about the memories the people who use them connect with the events these names describe: "As one of the first hermeneutical moves regarding an event, its naming frames and remembers events, even as it determines particular knowledge of events."[72]

In Jewish discourses the language relating to the events of the Holocaust is differentiated. To speak, for example, of Holocaust, Shoah, *Hurban* or *l'univers concentrationnaire* signals political, social and religious allegiances.[73] The

---

[69] Geyer/Hansen 1994, 190. By extension this process would also facilitate the inclusion of memories of other victims of NS.

[70] What Saul Friedlander points out regarding the first generation, i.e. "what was traumatic for the one group was obviously not traumatic to the other", has been transmitted to their descendants (cf. Friedlander 1994, 257).

[71] Santner ³1996, 152f.

[72] Young 1988, 87.

[73] Cf. ibid. 85ff.

relationship of survivors and their families as well as many Jews to the victims of the Holocaust is often one of identification.[74] Questions arising in the discourse of Jewish Holocaust remembrance concern, for example, authenticity: who is qualified to speak authentically on experiences in the Holocaust? What language is appropriate in this context? What forms of remembrance should be chosen? Answers concern understandings of victims and survivors, interpretations of Holocaust testimony and attempts to find appropriate places, days and rituals to communicate Holocaust memory to subsequent generations.[75]

In German the name "Auschwitz" has come to signify the murder of six million Jews, locating the murder of Jews outside of Germany in a single place.[76] Another term used to describe the Holocaust in Germany is "Final Solution" which adopts Nazi terminology and aggressively asserts the perspective of the victimisers. Conflicts in Jewish discourses on the Holocaust as testified to, for example, in literature, film and liturgy are hardly found in Germany. Other memories relating to the NS time are prevalent. Terms such as Nazi regime, Hitler regime and *KZ-Zeit* are used to describe German relations to the time in question. By using the term "regime", the notion of an imposed "foreign" form of government is invoked which clouds over the widespread public support of NS. The reference to Hitler can allude to an exclusive allocation of blame for this period of history to Hitler which distracts from the more complicated question of the population's responsibility for and involvement with the actions of the NS state. "*KZ-Zeit*" arguably belies the experience of the majority of the population of the Third Reich who never came near a camp. Everyday language also testifies to a connection between the language of violence inherited from NS and discourses on national identity.[77] Questions concerning German memory relate to the war: was it lost or was Germany liberated?[78] How should German soldiers who were killed in action be remembered? In addition, there are questions concerning recurrent claims to territories which belonged to Germany in 1937 and concerning liability and guilt for NS crimes.[79]

The local history projects of the 1980s present a first attempt to include narratives of the Jewish community in the memory production of German towns and cities.[80] However for the 1980s, Adorno's verdict in his perceptive 1959 essay "What Does

---

[74] Concerning Israel in particular cf. also Segev 1993.

[75] For an overview of Jewish responses to the Holocaust in a variety of genres cf. for example Roth/Berenbaum (eds.) 1989 and Jacobs (ed.) 1993a.

[76] Holocaust is also a popular term and Shoah is increasingly preferred in Christian theological contexts.

[77] Cf. Steiner 1959/1985 as well as Linke 1995, 55ff.

[78] Cf. for example Domansky 1997.

[79] Cf. for example Dregger in Levkov (ed.) 1987, 113.

[80] For literature on such research projects cf. for example Galinski/Herbert/Lachauer (eds.) 1982; Brenner 1983 and Rüter/Westhoff 1985. Regarding methodology of oral history cf. Niethammer (ed.) [2]1985.

Coming to Terms with the Past Mean?"[81] still rings true. He argued that the structures of German society which facilitated NS and the Holocaust are continuing in the FRG. The inability to mourn, diagnosed by the Mitscherlichs at the end of the 1960s,[82] testifies to this as well as the debates surrounding *Holocaust* and the construction of *Heimat* as its opposition. Further examples of the exclusion of Jewish memory from German memory as manifest in German political and historical debates on the memory of the Holocaust are the Bitburg Controversy and the *Historikerstreit*.

2. The Bitburg Controversy and the *Historikerstreit* – Usable pasts

2.1. The Bitburg Controversy

President Reagan's highly symbolic visit to the military cemetery of Bitburg in May 1985, for example, was carefully staged as a public spectacle for television; setting, framing, camera, acting, and sound were planned in detail. The elaborate production triggered a major controversy, resulting in an embarrassment for all involved because the intentions behind this attempt to reshape public memory via television were a shade too obvious.[83]

The Bitburg Controversy was explicitly concerned with German national self-representation and took place against the background of international politics. When Chancellor Kohl and President Reagan embarked on their visit to the site of Bergen-Belsen concentration camp and Kolmeshöhe, a German military cemetery near the border-town of Bitburg, the debate surrounding the motivations and appropriateness of their endeavours reached its peak.[84] The Chancellor had envisaged 5 May 1985, shortly before the D-Day commemorations of the Western Allies in France on 8 May, as a ceremony of reconciliation between the USA and West Germany.[85] In time for the fortieth anniversary of the end of the Second World War, this act of reconciliation

---

[81] Adorno 1959/1986, 114-129.

[82] Cf. Mitscherlich/Mitscherlich 1968.

[83] Kaes 1992, 310.

[84] Bitburg war cemetery at Kolmeshöhe had been chosen for the visit of Reagan because Bitburg was also the location of a US Air Base. Kolmeshöhe contains forty-nine graves of German soldiers of the *Wehrmacht*, the SS and the *Waffen-SS*. This combination of graves of soldiers of different organisations of the armed forces of Germany who died during the Second World War is the same in almost every war cemetery in Germany, cf. Kohl in Levkov (ed.) 1987, 107. To avoid the possibility of pilgrimage-like veneration of graves of SS men by veterans of these organisations and their post-war admirers, the Allied administration of Germany decided not to allow the creation of separate cemeteries for sub-groups of the German armed forces. These are facts of which the FRG government, President Reagan and his advisors were seemingly unaware. Furthermore, when Kolmeshöhe was inspected in the winter of 1984, snow had apparently concealed the existence of the graves of members of the SS (cf. Kennedy in ibid. 52).

[85] As Chancellor Kohl stated at Kolmeshöhe: "Bitburg can be regarded as a symbol of reconciliation and of German-American friendship" (Kohl in ibid. 167).

was supposed to have evolved similarly to the ritual which Kohl and the French President Mitterand enacted in September 1984 on the battlefield of Verdun. There the two heads of state laid wreaths and held hands in silence to remember the soldiers of the French and German armies who fell in World War I (as well as the preceding centuries of German-French conflict), thus intending symbolically to show their mutual respect and readiness to forgive past wrongs. Had Bitburg had the same effect as created in Verdun – namely that of an internationally acknowledged act of remembrance and forgiveness – Kohl would have regarded this as the fulfilment of his ambition to draw a line under Germany's NS past and to establish West Germany as a fully recognised and trusted member of the Western Alliance, and thus of the community of free, stable democracies. But the ceremony at Bitburg created the opposite effect to that intended by the Chancellor. The historian Charles Maier, analysing the Bitburg Affair writes: "Bitburg, in short, became a sacrament of resentment, not of reconciliation."[86]

5 May 1985, its pre-history and aftermath, emerge as a conflict caused by differing interpretations of the same historical and political events. Maier invented the term "Bitburg history" to express what he called a "multiple muddying of moral categories and historical agents."[87] By this he means the uniting of perpetrators and victims of Nazi crimes in one act of remembrance and the avoidance of identifying any real German responsibility.[88] Demonstrating their agreement on the importance of a ceremony of remembrance (and reconciliation), Kohl and Reagan had gone to great lengths in defending their visit to Bitburg after the presence of graves of members of the Waffen-SS became apparent. Whereas Kohl could be sure of enough support from the German public so as not to be publicly embarrassed, Reagan headed for one of the worst public relations disasters of his career.[89]

The West German government led by Kohl agreed with Reagan and his government on a notion of forgiveness and reconciliation which displays exactly what Maier calls "Bitburg history". Kohl said in a speech justifying his visit to Bitburg in the German Parliament (*Bundestag*) on 15 April 1985:

> At the cemetery in Bitburg we intend to commemorate those who died in the war, those who had to die in the war started by Hitler in Europe and overseas, those Germans who were forced into the war by Hitler and perished in it. Reconciliation will be achieved between erstwhile adversaries if we are capable of mourning people irrespective of the nationality of those who were murdered, who fell or died. This we demonstrated at Douaumont in Verdun, and we intend to do so in Bitburg. Commemoration of the victims always keeps alive an

---

[86] Maier [6]1994, 12.
[87] Ibid. 13.
[88] Cf. ibid. 14.
[89] Cf. Reichel 1995, 283ff.

awareness of the guilt of the perpetrators. War graves are always a reminder of those who assisted and committed the crimes of the war and the tyranny.[90]

As in the speech Kohl later gave in Bitburg, he here already communicated his interpretation of reconciliation: "mourning people irrespective of their nationality" just because they happened to die at the same time. He was able to affirm this understanding because he divided Germans neatly into victims and perpetrators which then lead him to ascribe guilt only to Hitler and some unnamed perpetrators. The others, then, were the victims who equally remain faceless and nameless. Kohl intended to commemorate the victims of World War II in Bitburg.[91] Implicitly all soldiers are victims of Hitler, forced into the war and, as such, not to be held responsible for injustices in any meaningful way.

Reagan had expressed a similar opinion in an interview on 18 April 1985, explaining his intentions in visiting Bitburg:

> I think there's nothing wrong with visiting that cemetery where those young men are victims of Nazism also, even though they were fighting in the German uniform, drafted into service to carry out the hateful wishes of the Nazis. They were victims, just as surely as the victims in the concentration camps. And I feel that there is much to be gained from this, and, in strengthening our relationship with the German people, who, believe me, live in constant penance, all these who have come along in these later years for what their predecessors did, and for which they're very ashamed.[92]

Both politicians consciously avoid reference to concrete events or the identities of the soldiers buried in Bitburg. This amounts to a universalisation of the term "victims" which evades any question of agency and responsibility. Thus an ambiguous understanding of victim emerges: on the one hand, it does not deny the status of victims to Jews, on the other hand, it prevents further inquiries into history to understand the conflicts in the present relationship between Germans and Jews.[93] Thereby Jews are victimised a second time, because it is implied that an analysis of the reasons for being a victim of NS is of minor importance. In this case international political aims determined the representation of NS history and thus the purpose and function assigned to its memory. To achieve greater international recognition, the German government was willing to ignore the criminal character of the NS regime and treat its dead soldiers in the same fashion as the US government regarded its fallen soldiers. Hence the agreement in the speeches of the two heads of state, that soldiers are victims in conflicts generated by their governments and that they therefore should be seen as equal in death when the conflict between their countries is ended. However, the question of how to remember soldiers dying in defence of

---

[90] Kohl in Levkov (ed.) 1987, 109.

[91] Cf. Young 1986, 104.

[92] Reagan in Levkov (ed.) 1987, 39.

[93] A further confusion in the use of terminology arises with the ambiguity of meaning of the German word *Opfer*, which can mean both victim and sacrifice (cf. also Czaplicka 1995, 179).

criminal regimes – regimes which have been recognised as criminal by their political successors – was not addressed. Omitting a commemoration of victims of the Holocaust from the original itinerary of Reagan served the purpose of highlighting the perceived commonalities of dead soldiers, not their actual duties during the war. The fact that a visit to Bergen-Belsen was hastily inserted into Reagan's schedule in an attempt to appease Jewish protesters at the proposed ceremony in Bitburg, served to highlight the contradictions in this enterprise of remembrance rather than alleviate any tensions. Frank Stern comments that

> Jews in Germany can still be denounced as persons who wish to "disrupt" the comfortable status quo in mentality and attitude – disturbers of this particular moral, political and spiritual peace. [...] They are supposed either to keep their silence and avoid voicing any critique – or to serve as an assuagement for a bad public conscience and provide society at large with a "clean bill of historical health."[94]

German church leaders who participated in the ceremonies in Bergen-Belsen and Bitburg were criticised for their involvement. Dietrich Goldschmidt, a member of the workshop "Jews and Christians" of the German Protestant church congress, feels that the achievements of recent Christian-Jewish encounters are challenged by the political climate epitomised in the visit of Kohl and Reagan to Bitburg.

> To want to honor the murdered in the same breath as those who covered Europe with war and annihilation [sic] denies their sacrifice [sic] any worth. [...] We are ashamed that the church leadership and the synods let the Jews who demonstrated against this development go it alone; the Jews who were carried away by police from the doors of former concentration camps. Representatives of the Protestant and Catholic church did not show solidarity with them, rather they took part – in contrast to the Jewish representatives – in the ceremony at Bergen-Belsen. [...] In the view of the silence of the church organs and the behavior of the church representatives, we ask ourselves whether the Synodal Declarations on a new, positive relationship to the Jews [...] were formed to remain paper documents instead of to lead to acts of solidarity with Jews in daily life.[95]

However, Richard von Weizsäcker, then President of the FRG, delivered a speech on 8 May 1985 in the *Bundestag* to commemorate the end of the Second World War which stands in stark contrast to the events in Bitburg only three days earlier.[96] While Weizsäcker's speech was initially not well received in the German political sphere, it was warmly applauded in the USA and Israel.[97] He never mentioned forgiveness or reconciliation in the speech, but attempted honestly to recall the suffering and hardship experienced by different groups of people without ignoring who were its perpetrators. In doing so Weizsäcker intended to remember the end of the war in a nuanced way, paying attention to the different perceptions of 8 May 1945 in the

---

[94] Stern 1992, 420f. Regarding the antisemitic reactions in the German media cf. Bergmann 1995, 423ff.
[95] Goldschmidt in Levkov (ed.) 1987, 496.
[96] Reprinted in Hartman 1986, 262-273.
[97] Cf. Benz 1995, 60.

German public, such as defeat and liberation. At the same time he emphasised the importance of remembering accurately as the responsibility of the young generations in Germany. By taking responsibility for the consequences of NS history they should contribute to the process of learning from history.[98] The favourable international reception of Weizsäcker's speech showed that the image Weizsäcker gave of post-war Germany was more conducive for endeavours of reconciliation than Kohl's. Without diminishing the post-war achievements of West Germany in establishing a stable democracy firmly bound to the Western Alliance, Weizsäcker was able to confront cruel historical reality without losing the ability positively to identify as German.[99] Peter Reichel comments on this speech, pointing out its achievement but also questioning its format as an "address to the nation"[100]. He criticises Weizsäcker for not refering to antisemitism being rooted in the population at large, for not mentioning the period of prosperity of large parts of the population before the terror of the regime affected a majority, and for smoothing over the fact that many were implicated in the enactment of the Holocaust on all levels of society rather than only a handful of perpetrators.[101] Reichel concludes that

> It was therefore a political speech, but a speech that did not provoke. On the occasion of the farewell ceremony for the President, Gunter Hofmann, in his friendly ironical manner, characterised this very well as the political style of the President. Weizsäcker's speeches would pad and wrap up politics. As the highest representative of the republic, he embodied something which was not integral to its constitution: "a kind of president of the state (...) seemingly faultless, the wounds well hidden." This way he was able to "ease the moral and aesthetic situation of the republic" (H.M. Enzensberger).[102]

This "padding and wrapping up" of politics proved to be helpful in the international context where Weizsäcker smoothed over Kohl's efforts "to bolster German national consciousness and create a new sense of pride in German identity".[103] However, regarding home politics his style of non-provocation was unable to counteract the "enthusiasm for *Schlußstrich*, a conclusion of the memory debate"[104] advocated by Kohl and desired by the majority of the population.[105]

Ending the debate on the memory of NS and the Holocaust is a subject also in the *Historikerstreit*. There the conflict concerned the construction of German national

---

[98] Cf. also Mary Fulbrook's assessment of the speech in Fulbrook 1999, 99.

[99] Weizsäcker's personal background of having defended his father at the Nuremberg trials and having to work through the implications of his father's conviction at Nuremberg added credibility to his words, but at the same time demonstrated that these are not representative for German society (for Weizsäcker's personal relation to NS cf. for example Buruma 1994, 142f.).

[100] Reichel 1995, 295.

[101] Cf. ibid. 295.

[102] Ibid. 296.

[103] Geyer 1996, 189.

[104] Ibid. 189.

[105] Michal Bodemann as well is critical of this effect of Weizsäcker's speeches (cf. Bodemann 1996a, 42).

identity via the representation of the Holocaust and as such the use of historiography. Arguably, the *Historikerstreit* beginning in the summer of 1986, while focusing on the uniqueness of the Holocaust, implicitly debated the function of history in contemporary politics.[106]

2.2. The *Historikerstreit*

In the summer of 1986 a number of historians debated the uniqueness of the Holocaust and its implications for German national identity in a series of articles published largely in the conservative daily FAZ and the liberal weekly *Die Zeit*.[107] The historians Ernst Nolte and Andreas Hillgruber were the main contestants on one side of the controversy,[108] their opponents being the philosopher Jürgen Habermas and the historians Hans-Ulrich Wehler as well as Hans Mommsen and Martin Broszat.[109] The broader historiographical context was the debate on boundaries of legitimate interpretations of history, exemplified in a discussion about the ethics of interpretations of the Holocaust and NS for present national political ends.[110] Christopher Browning observes that the intensity of this discussion derived from the political implications of the arguments rather than from the originality of the research.[111] It is significant that an academic debate was carried out in the newspapers, rather than the universities, thereby demonstrating that the interpretation of the Holocaust concerns the identity of all Germans.[112]

> Historians must believe in national communities persisting through time. They feel the burden of the Third Reich as their own and seek to come to terms with it. From their confrontation derives much of the compelling fascination of the recent debate.[113]

Hence to some extent the academics participating in the debate reflect the preoccupations and assumptions of the national community of memory. Maier's statement about the *Historikerstreit* in 1986 appears to apply to the debate on the interpretation of NS and the Holocaust not only among historians but with regard to Germany since the end of World War II. The *Historikerstreit* condensed issues which make the interpretation of the Holocaust in German history troublesome and controversial. These issues concerned

---

[106] Cf. Benz 1995, 58f.

[107] For a collection of contributions cf. Augstein et al. [3]1987 and the English version of some of the contributions in Knowlton/Cates (eds.) 1993. For an overview of the development of the debate cf. Wehler 1988.

[108] Cf. also Michael Stürmer, Joachim Fest, Klaus Hildebrand and Hagen Schulze.

[109] Cf. also Jürgen Kocka, Eberhard Jäckel and Wolfgang Mommsen.

[110] Cf. Torpey 1988, 6.

[111] Cf. Browning [3]1996, 27.

[112] Regarding the Holocaust in German historical scholarship cf. Evans 1989. For an overview of different schools in Holocaust and NS research cf. Dawidowicz [6]1993 and Marrus 1987.

[113] Maier [6]1994, 5.

(a) the place of NS in German history (continuity or discontinuity);
(b) the uniqueness or singularity of the Holocaust;
(c) "the distinction between 'victims and executioners,' between *'schlußstrich* and remembrance.'"[114]

All three questions impact on the understanding of German national identity in the present which make answers relevant for contemporary politics. In particular, the issue of responsibility for the Holocaust dominates discussions on the interpretation of NS. The ethical and moral implications suggested in different approaches to this question account for difficulties in assessing the level of remembrance or forgetting of the Holocaust in Germany. According to Enzo Traverso

> The "quarrel of the historians" might, therefore, appear as a symbolic event indicating a simple *transformation of forgetting*, final stage in the flight from a past too dire to contemplate and the beginning of a new form of repression, based on the "normalization" of a past, which now becomes nonproblematical. The banalization of the crime in the national consciousness provides the indispensable passage from one forgetting to another. The Shoah is no longer hidden away; Auschwitz is no longer a nonevent. Quite simply, they will not become a locus for memory: Germany will be able to do without them. This can open the way as much to an absolutory presentation of the past as to new forms of collective amnesia.[115]

Arguably, to many commentators, the *Historikerstreit* became the key example of the amnesiac nature of West German society.[116] Maier, one of the most important commentators on the *Historikerstreit*, summarises the issues at stake:

> If Auschwitz is admittedly dreadful, but dreadful as only one specimen of genocide – as the so-called revisionists have implied – then Germany can still aspire to reclaim a national acceptance that no one denies to perpetrators of other massacres, such as Soviet Russia. But if the Final Solution remains non-comparable – as the opposing historians have insisted – the past may never be "worked through," the future never normalized, and German nationhood may remain forever tainted, like some well forever poisoned.[117]

On 6 June 1986, Nolte published an article in the FAZ, entitled "The Past That Will Not Pass".[118] When Habermas formulated a reply on 11 July 1986, "A Kind of Settlement of Damages"[119], the controversy began. Nolte had compared the NS death camps with Stalin's gulags and concluded that since the gulags historically predated the death camps, NS could have been imitating the gulags by establishing death camps, because they "considered themselves to be potential victims of an 'Asiatic'

---

[114] Rabinbach 1988, 183.
[115] Traverso 1995, 154f.
[116] Major commentaries on the *Historikerstreit* can be found in Baldwin (ed.) 1987; the special issue on the *Historikerstreit* of the *New German Critique* 44 (1988) as well as Evans 1989; Henningsen 1988; Joffe 1987; Kampe 1987; Maier [6]1994 and Miller 1990. For a psychoanalytical reading of the controversy cf. LaCapra 1998, 43-72.
[117] Maier [6]1994, 1.
[118] Nolte 1993b.
[119] Habermas 1993.

deed [gulag]."[120] With this comparison Nolte hoped to prove that the Holocaust was not unique since it could be understood as a reaction to a prior atrocity. In an article published in 1980 Nolte had explained the intention behind this kind of historical comparison: he wanted to show that with the Holocaust Germany had not committed a crime out of the ordinary and that therefore its history should be treated as being as "normal" as the history of any other nation which includes atrocities of some form or other.[121] He thereby employed the writing of history to legitimise Germany's past and its present evasion of the Holocaust morally – effectively saying "we are not worse than others". This defensive approach to German national identity avoids the representation of the Holocaust as a subject that assumes particular relevance to German national self-understanding in the present, with the argument that its atrocities deserve no more attention by German historians than atrocities committed by other modern states. Thereby Nolte hoped to facilitate a positive national identity which can be affirmed as moral and which at the same time has no need to attach any particular moral and political relevance to the Holocaust in this new national narrative.

Hillgruber argued for a similar kind of "normalisation" of history. In the collection of essays *Two Sorts of Demise*[122] Hillgruber analyses the German army's fight against the Russian army on the Eastern front in 1944-45. The defeat of Germany, described in one chapter, is paralleled with another chapter on the murder of Jews in the Holocaust. Hillgruber thus suggests that the Jews of Europe can be regarded as a historical-political community as much as the German state and that their fate can thus be compared. His portrayal of history is suggestive on two accounts. Firstly, he describes the sufferings of the *Wehrmacht* soldiers and the local German population in detail, asking his readers to identify with their fate, whereas the essay on the Holocaust does not dwell on Jewish suffering.[123] The discrepancy in style between the two chapters is such that Maier concludes that "If indeed these two experiences are two sorts of destruction, one is presented, so to speak, in technicolor, the other in black, gray, and white."[124] Secondly, Hillgruber's call for identification with the perspective of the soldiers opens the way to apologetics, because it goes beyond outlining and attempting to understand the choices with which the soldiers were faced. Hillgruber asks the reader to take sides with the German soldiers and implicitly devalues any other perspective on the situation.[125] Similarly, presenting German soldiers as victims comparable to Jewish victims of the Holocaust suggests that NS did not produce any victims other than casualties of war. Here the historical

---

[120] Nolte 1993b, 22.
[121] Cf. Nolte 1993a.
[122] Hillgruber 1986.
[123] Cf. also the commentary by Santner 1992, 265f.
[124] Maier [6]1994, 23.
[125] Cf. ibid. 22f. Cf. also Bartov 1996, 71-88.

distinctions between the social groups of victimisers and victims in NS are blurred beyond recognition.

Both Nolte's and Hillgruber's efforts to historicise NS are part of conservative efforts to "normalise" German history. By arguing

> that the Nazi regime, although reprehensible, had been far from unique when seen in the broader perspective of the twentieth century [...] it no longer remained as an insurmountable barrier to the past, distorting national self-identity, and preventing West Germans from appreciating the positive aspects of the Federal Republic's Weimar and Imperial antecedents.[126]

In dismantling the assumption of decisive continuities in German history running from Imperial Germany via Weimar and NS to the FRG, these historians shift the focus of the inquiry away from Germany. As such they dispute any form of uniqueness of the Holocaust, even if understood as carrying particular significance for the political self-understanding of the FRG. By representing both Jews and Germans as victims of war, remembrance of victimiser history in the FRG is rendered unimportant.

Rejecting such universal claims to the status of victimhood and a marginalisation of the Holocaust for notions of German identity in the present, the opponents of these interpretations of history

> argued that such integration and relativization represented an unvarnished nationalist attempt to gloss over the horrors of the Nazi period and to glorify the Imperial tradition whose peculiarities and weaknesses, as inherited by Weimar, had played a crucial role in allowing Hitler to power.[127]

Habermas in particular

> cannot accept a version of the Nazi past that transforms comparisons into a balancing of accounts. Such an interpretation eradicates the historical legacy of the suffering inflicted by German soldiers that is also part of the contemporary cultural inheritance.[128]

His contributions to the *Historikerstreit* are related to Broszat's understanding of "historicisation"[129]. Habermas agrees with Broszat's interpretation of the possibility for a historicisation of NS and argues that only an analysis of the cultural heritage of the FRG and its rootedness in traditions of NS and before will safeguard the prevention of another Holocaust.[130] This means that Germans continue to bear a responsibility for the Holocaust, a responsibility which cannot cease, because

---

[126] Baldwin 1990, 10.
[127] Ibid. 11.
[128] Torpey 1988, 12.
[129] Cf. Broszat 1990.
[130] Cf. Habermas 1993, 41ff.

Germans of the FRG are bound to Germans of the Third Reich and before through a succession of national communities.[131] Maier explains that according to Habermas

> This responsibility entailed in the first instance an obligation to remember, and not with the head alone, the dead murdered at the hands of the Germans. These dead had a claim on a solidarity that those born afterward could provide only by a renewal of memory.[132]

The debate on "historicising" German history in the sense of interpreting NS and the Holocaust as part of the continuum of German history predates the *Historikerstreit*. Developing functionalist arguments regarding research on NS, Broszat and Mommsen argue for a vertical perspective on NS, namely for the understanding of the Third Reich in the continuity of German history before and after the Second World War.[133] They want to gain a better perspective on the developments in German history and society which led to the Holocaust. For Broszat the inquiry into the daily reality of Germans during NS, which did not focus only on the Holocaust, meant a contribution to a more differentiated understanding of this period of history than that achieved by the approaches so far.[134] Nicolas Berg summarises Broszat's approach positively: "*normalisation*, meaning *Alltagsgeschichte*, close-up, vividness, recovery of authenticity and understanding."[135] Understanding, for Broszat, did not mean condoning the experiences and decisions of Germans in the Third Reich. Rather he wanted to gain a more comprehensive understanding of all aspects of life during NS. Broszat's approach to the historicisation of NS in particular has been criticised by Saul Friedlander who interpreted it to be in danger of diverting attention from the Holocaust.[136] Friedlander argues that the Holocaust is the overarching category which should dominate analyses of NS history. Allowing non-victims to write history from their point of view and on matters which were not concerned with the Holocaust could lead to a relativisation of the Holocaust.[137] Berg shows that Friedlander does not interpret the Holocaust as part of a historical continuity which can be analysed in retrospect:

> When Broszat speaks of "comprehension", Friedländer doubts already "understanding"; when the former demands "explanation", the latter can only just trust "documentation", where the one speaks of "continuity", the other only sees a radical "rupture".[138]

Friedlander fears that the narratives relevant to Germans in the writing of their everyday history (*Alltagsgeschichte*) will omit representations of the Holocaust and Jews. He objects to a writing of history based on the memory assembled in German

---

[131] Cf. Maier [6]1994, 58f.

[132] Ibid. 58.

[133] Cf. also Nolan 1988, 51-80 regarding the concept of *Alltagsgeschichte*.

[134] Cf. Broszat 1990.

[135] Berg 1996, 39.

[136] Cf. Broszat/Friedländer 1990.

[137] Cf. Friedlander 1993.

[138] Berg 1996, 40.

oral history projects without a critical commentary, because the speakers will only report what is relevant to their identities.[139] The project of historicisation suggested by Brozsat implies to Friedlander the loss of the unique quality of the Holocaust which refuses its integration into any historical narrative. For Friedlander this would mean giving in to a representation of the Holocaust which is alien to his memory and follows a moral political agenda which is not his. Bartov comments perceptively that

> the debate is in fact not at all on more or less memory, but on the politics of memory. And once one is in the realm of politics, arguably anyone's politics is as good as anyone else's: some people want to remember Jews and concentration camps, others want to remember German soldiers and their defense of the West against Bolshevism; some study memory through personal accounts, others distribute questionnaires, others still conduct studies of oral history; some speak of collective memory, some of national memory, some of personal memory. Thus the manner in which we speak of memory betrays our political beliefs, just as our political beliefs are molded to a large extent by our memories.[140]

The participants in the *Historikerstreit* were all born before 1945 and thus the fact that the questions debated were of particular personal concern to them added to the intensity of the discussion.[141] However, Habermas' understanding of responsibility and solidarity between generations points to the continuing relevance of these issues for subsequent generations. He demands that Germans accept that the remembrance of German responsibility for the Holocaust is constitutive for post-war German identities.[142] However, the acceptance of such a responsibility of remembrance in solidarity with the dead implies an end to the exclusion of Jewish history and memory from German history.

Both the debate over Bitburg and the *Historikerstreit* avoid representing the Holocaust and, in particular, representing Jews. German historical scholarship has focused on different subjects in the field of NS and, until recently, had hardly worked on the Holocaust itself.[143] Without necessarily acknowledging the heritage of the victimisers, German politicians and historians thus far often express their identity defensively. Thus they follow a strategy of exclusion of Jewish memory from German narratives of the past while at the same time promoting a "politics of memory" which wants to educate about the Holocaust so as to prevent its

---

[139] Cf. for example Friedlander 1994, 258.

[140] Bartov 1996, 122. Geyer employs the term "politics of memory" in a slightly different way, associating it with German academics and intellectuals of the political left who assume "that public knowledge about the Third Reich and the transparency of a reckoning with the past will have a cathartic effect; and that remembering the Holocaust will prevent the recurrence of National Socialism and of the attending evils of racism and anti-Semitism" (Geyer 1996, 169). This politics (and subsequent transformation into a "culture of memory") is counteracted by the conservative government's politics epitomised in Bitburg and the *Historikerstreit* (cf. ibid. 189).

[141] Cf. Bartov 1996, 120f.

[142] Cf. Maier [6]1994, 166.

[143] For an overview of German historiography on NS cf. Herbert 1993 and Münz [2]1996, 37-110.

repetition.[144] Again Jews are relevant only in their absence, not in their present lives with their memories of the Holocaust. Bartov argues that

> if the Nazis strove to ensure the health and prosperity of the nation by eliminating the Jews, postwar Germany strove to neutralize the memory of the Jews' destruction so as to ensure its own physical and psychological restoration. [...] it must be stressed that Nazi criminality itself was persistently associated with the suffering of the *Germans*. Both the murder of the Jews and the victimization of the Germans were described as acts perpetrated by a third party; however, while Germans believed they had little in common with the Jews, they naturally felt their own suffering very keenly. Thus the Holocaust was an event carried out by one group of "others" on another such group, whereas the destruction of Germany was perpetrated by (possibly even the same) "them" directly on "us," the Germans. In this manner, the perpetrators of genocide were associated with the destroyers of Germany, while the Jewish victims were associated with German victims, without, however, creating the same kind of empathy.[145]

German debates on the memory of NS, the Holocaust and the war have created a specific discourse of *Vergangenheitsbewältigung* (generally translated as "coming to terms with the past" or "mastering the past").[146] Horst-Eberhard Richter writes:

> According to Grimm's dictionary *"Bewältigen"* comes from, *"Bewaltigen"*, also *"Begewaltigen"*, which once meant as much as to overcome or to defeat, in particular also, *"frowen bewaltigen und schwechen"*, namely rape in the narrowest sense. It seems as if already the term *"Vergangenheitsbewältigung"* by mistake betrays the image of fighting down and defeating memory like an opponent or an obstacle.[147]

This begs the question whether the connotations of violence connected with rape are only "by mistake" part of the dominant discourse on the memory of NS, the war and the Holocaust in Germany. If it is correct to say that memory builds on continuity, then discontinuities originating in NS, the war and the Holocaust have to be counteracted, if necessary by force. Commentators on German enactments of memory relating to the years 1933-45 have suggested that the work done is often one of repression, rather than remembrance, in the sense that what hinders the formulation of a positive national identity in the present is actively (violently?) prevented from becoming part of national memory.[148] The FRG inherits the history of the victimisers of NS, the Holocaust and the war, and at the same time seeks to acknowledge experiences of victims in its national narrative.[149] However, the Holocaust was perpetrated in a cultural environment of a longstanding antisemitic tradition which suggested the exclusion of Jews from German society. Jewish life in

---

[144] Cf. Geyer 1996, 169-200.

[145] Bartov 1998, 788-790. That the quotation runs over three pages is due to long footnotes and illustrations on 788f.

[146] For an overview of the development and use of the concept in different disciplines cf. Kohlstruck 1997, 13-38.

[147] Richter 1992, 228.

[148] Cf. for example Traverso 1995, 135 and Adorno 1959/1986.

[149] Cf. Geyer 1996, 181.

post-war Germany remains insecure and continues to be regarded with suspicion where it differs from mainstream culture which makes it difficult to acknowledge perspectives of the community of victims in narratives of the community of victimisers.[150]

A good example that serves to illustrate further this separation (suppression?) of Jewish from German memory are the dates chosen for the commemoration of the Holocaust. These are different for Germans and Jews, expressing a dominant relationship of the respective communities to the history of the Holocaust. Germans chose 9th November and recently also 27th January to commemorate the victims of the Holocaust. Michal Bodemann shows that 9th November, the anniversary of *Kristallnacht* 1938, has been developed as a remembrance day that establishes a chronology of 9th Novembers in German history and serves as a reminder of historical lessons to the German population.[151] 27th January 1945 marks the liberation of the Auschwitz camps by the Red Army. As such it also marks the advance of the Russian army from the east and reminds Germans of their expulsion from the eastern territories. Connecting the liberation of the death camp and the expulsion from the east creates a powerful (causal?) connection, which contributes to the "never again" message of rituals of remembrance.

Relating to Israeli constructions of Jewish identity, Jews chose dates according to the Jewish calendar: the 27 *Nisan* as *Yom Ha'Shoah*, symbolising the beginning of the Warsaw ghetto uprising during *Pesach* 1943.[152] This corresponds to the commemoration of Israel Independence Day on 5 *Iyar* a week later, thus interpreting the Warsaw ghetto uprising as the beginning of the armed struggle for Jewish independence,[153] an interpretation of the Holocaust which does not fit with the dominant image of Jews in German culture which perceives Jews as passive victims.[154]

---

[150] Regarding constructions of Jewish identity in the FRG cf. for example Rapaport 1997 and Stern (ed.) 1995. Cf. also Fulbrook 1999, 147ff.

[151] Cf. Bodemann 1996b, 84ff. However, he is critical about the motivation to construct this memorial date: "Ich möchte deshalb behaupten, daß die gesamte Gedenkkultur um die Kristallnacht sehr wenig mit dem real existierenden Judentum zu tun hat, daß dieses Gedenken vielmehr als wichtiges Element in der neuen deutschen Identitätspolitik fungiert. [...] Darüber hinaus hat dieses Gedenken zu tun mit Phantasien über Juden, mit Verlust und Schuld. Hierfür werden jüdische Dramen und jüdische Schauspieler benötigt – keine Hauptdarsteller freilich, sonder eher Statisten" (ibid. 99). Regarding the creation of a united German unity through the suppression of Jewish memory cf. also Domansky 1992, 64ff.

[152] For the function of *Yom Ha'Shoah* in Israeli public discourse cf. Young 1996.

[153] Cf. Kugelmann ²1988.

[154] Cf. Bodemann 1996b, 112ff. Bodemann also highlights the history of pogroms connected with *Martinstag* (10th November) which deepens the archetypal image of Jews as victims.

In agreement with Bartov, Robert Moeller argues that in the immediate post-war period remembrance of NS centred on the victimisation of Germans, i.e. non-Jewish Germans:

> in the first postwar decade the stories of expellees from eastern Germany and Eastern Europe and German prisoners of war imprisoned in the Soviet Union were crafted into rhetorics of victimization in the arena of public policy and in the writing of "contemporary history" (*Zeitgeschichte*). West Germans collectively mourned the suffering of these groups, and their experiences became central to one important version of the legacy of the war: their private memories structured public memory, making stories of Communist brutality and the loss of the "German East" crucial parts of the history of the Federal Republic.[155]

According to Moeller, although narratives of Jewish suffering were not excluded from public memory, these did not assume the same importance as did stories of German victimisation, because they did not easily lend themselves to construct a "usable past".[156]

However, it is also important to remember that the Jewish community in post-war Germany is not in continuity with pre-war German Jewry. Rather it is a community which in the majority grew from "displaced persons" who, for a variety of reasons, did not emigrate. Later Jewish emigrants from NS Germany returned in small numbers.[157] Moreover, German Jews who survived the Holocaust remain reluctant to identify as German.[158] But even in the present with the Jewish community ever more established as a part of German public and social life, its representatives can be, for example, publicly called upon to explain actions of "their government", whenever there is a crisis in Israel.[159] Another peculiarity in the German language is the reference to "*jüdische Mitbürger*" ("Jewish co-citizens") – "co-citizens" being a term usually reserved for people without a German passport who belong to a distinct cultural community (for example *türkische Mitbürger*) – a term not applied to German citizens who happen to belong to distinct cultural or religious communities as for example *Rheinländer, Schwaben, Friesen, Katholiken, Protestanten*, the list is endless and cultural and religious identities overlap (just as they do for Jews living in Germany).[160] This testifies to the continuity of the common perception that Jews cannot be German and points to another reason why Germans have difficulty in recognising Jews as Germans.[161]

---

[155] Moeller 1996, 1013.

[156] Cf. ibid. 1032f.

[157] Cf. for example Bodemann (ed.) 1996; Brenner 1997; Burgauer 1993; Richarz 1986, 23ff. and Schoeps 1990, 97ff.

[158] Cf. Rapaport 1997, 18f.

[159] Cf. Ignatz Bubis in Thierfelder/Wölfing (eds.) 1996, 59f. and on a local level cf. Grözinger 1995, 123f.

[160] Cf. Ginsburg 1986, 108f.

[161] Cf. also the problems of defining German citizenship via descent (Senders 1996; Fulbrook 1999, 180ff. and Huyssen 1995, 78-80).

However, Geyer observes that the discovery of Jewish history in German local history projects initiated a crisis:

> But this discovery [of victim memory] proved to be a strange gift, for it created a manifest tension between German "memory work" and the history and memory of "others". It remains unresolved how this past can be brought back into German history without taking away from the fullness of past life on the one hand and its *shoah*, its utter destruction, on the other.[162]

Jewish memory disturbs and challenges German memory. If allowed space in debates it may counteract the definition of Jews as Other and thereby react against the placing of Jewish memory outside of German memory as an effective way of silencing competing versions of the past. Regarding the past two decades with its conflicts concerning the interpretation of the Holocaust in Germany, it is apparent that an effort is made at keeping the memory of the victims of the Holocaust alive. At the same time the largely critical commentators of this scene of remembrance have to be taken seriously. Their suspicion directed at the "memory movement" of the 1980s and 1990s has to do with the fact that many initiatives serve the educational purpose of increasing knowledge about the past, but at the same time fail to assist its remembrance.[163] The danger inherent in the emergence of such a "memorialising culture" is the effacement of memory where representations of the Holocaust and NS are deposited, so that the process of working through can end. Whereas that process naturally ends with the death of eye-witnesses and their children, the deposits of memory are transmitted to subsequent generations who have to be enabled to transform these carriers of memory into relevant memory.[164]

The Goldhagen Controversy enters into this new climate of debate on the representation of the Holocaust in the 1990s.

3. The Goldhagen Controversy – Owning the past

The controversy beginning in the spring of 1996 surrounding the German publication of Goldhagen's *Hitler's Willing Executioners*[165] initiated a public debate on the Holocaust in Germany. It can be compared in its intensity and length to the discussions following the screening of the American miniseries *Holocaust* in 1979, the *Historikerstreit* on the uniqueness of the Holocaust in 1986, as well as the box office success of *Schindler's List* in 1994. In fact, it seems fair to say that the

---

[162] Geyer 1996, 181.
[163] Cf. ibid. 191 on the effect of *Schindler's List*.
[164] Cf. for example ibid., in particular, 190ff.
[165] Goldhagen 1996a.

publication of a single book on the Holocaust had never before sparked a debate that engaged scholars, the media and the public in Germany alike.[166]

Commentators have approached what has come to be known as the Goldhagen debate, controversy or syndrome from different perspectives.[167] Some comment on the arguments presented in the book itself, others focus on the different readings and criticisms the book has received in and outside of Germany, whereas others still suggest psychoanalytical readings of the book and the debate in Germany.[168] With reference to Robert Shandley, I suggest a structuring of the German debate into three stages, stage one being the publication of book reviews and criticisms in German newspapers in the spring of 1996, before the German translation of *Hitler's Willing Executioners* was available. The second stage begins with the German publication *Hitlers willige Vollstrecker*[169] in August 1996 and ends with the subsequent visit of the author to Germany. Finally the third phase discussed the debates of the first and second stages.[170] Whereas the first phase was characterised by an almost unanimous dismissal of the book, the second phase structured itself into a more differentiated scholarly reception of the work after its German translation was available and a positive acceptance of book and author by the general public.

My reading of the debate engages with the reception of Goldhagen's book, the level of comment on the discussion. I therefore do not engage in a critique of the book's content or methodology. What matters to my analysis is the way arguments are articulated and perceived in the course of the debate. Thus starting point is the question how do participants in the debate articulate their <u>investment</u> in the construction of German collective memory through their representation of the Holocaust?, in other words, how do the contestants articulate the <u>relevance</u> of the memory of the Holocaust to their self-understanding in the context of German collective history and memory?

The Goldhagen Controversy

> is the first major historical debate of the postwar era in which none of the primary participants (apart from Augstein, who served in the war) have their personal histories to defend. Thus the

---

[166] For a critical evaluation of the role of the media in creating the "Goldhagen phenomenon" cf. Schneider 1997.

[167] Cf. Shandley 1998, 2.

[168] Cf. for collections of responses cf. for example Heil/Erb (eds.) 1998; Schneider 1997; Schoeps (ed.) 1997 as well as the translation of many articles reprinted in Schoeps' volume in Shandley (ed.) 1998 and the articles in *Psyche* 51:6 (1997) for psychoanalytical readings of book and debate.

[169] Goldhagen 1996b.

[170] Cf. also for the following remarks Shandley 1998, 2ff. Mitchell G. Ash suggests a division of the debate into two phases, ending with the visit of Goldhagen to Germany (cf. Ash 1997, 401).

memory of the events being discussed is only an acquired "collective memory". It reflects how Germans have come to terms with a history they did not live.[171]

Thus the generational aspect for the first time is part of the debate from the start and significantly shapes its course. Frequently the author as well as his critics appear to be talking at cross purposes, almost entirely missing the other person's line of reasoning. This was particularly visible in the public discussions of scholars from Germany with Goldhagen.[172] However, rather than understanding this as detrimental to the debate on the memory of the Holocaust, it appears to be an integral part of the structure of the discussion. It seems that the discrepancy between the way arguments are advanced and perceived by the participants is an expression of their identification with different memories regarding the Holocaust. Regarding the field of Holocaust scholarship Steven Aschheim suggests that

> The plurality of these continuously changing and revised perspectives are, willy-nilly, the lubricants of historiography: the more we can articulate the tensions, the more vital the history. In our own charged field, then, the fact that divergent needs and interests are at play is not only inevitable but helps to shape and enliven our understanding.[173]

Each argument expressed an aspect of Holocaust memory that has become relevant to the self-understanding of the speaker, sometimes to the extent that any other perspective is understood as threatening one's own integrity. Santner argues that

> The transferential relations of a non-Jewish German historian to Nazism and the Final Solution will differ enormously from those of an Israeli historian to the same events. And certainly not only the national and cultural background but also the age of the historian, his or her temporal distance to the events in question, will play a significant role in the definition of the subject position.[174]

Goldhagen argues that the vicious cruelty with which the persecution and murder of Jews was carried out can be explained by reference to the unique character of German racial antisemitism. According to the author, German antisemitism differed from antisemitism in other Western European countries, because it became the centre of German culture and advocated the genocide of the Jews.[175] Belief in this form of antisemitism was shared by the majority of the population. Therefore Goldhagen claims that he can conclude that the majority of Germans, if put in the situation, could have been tempted to carry out the cruel murder of Jews in the same way as suggested by the evidence gathered in the three case studies – police battalions behind the Eastern front, labour camps and death marches – without voicing any moral objections. Goldhagen argues that he has enough evidence to suggest that the majority of Germans agreed with the Holocaust and the methods with which the

---

[171] Shandley 1998, 19.

[172] Cf. ibid. 25.

[173] Aschheim 1997, 247.

[174] Santner [3]1996, 145.

[175] Cf. Goldhagen 1996a, 72ff.

murders were carried out.[176] He uses the generalising expression "the Germans", because he argues that the belief in this form of antisemitism was characteristic of the majority of the population of Germany at the time.[177]

The ensuing controversy in Germany about the arguments advanced in the book was dominated by non-Jewish contributions and involved some of the key-players of the *Historikerstreit*, such as Eberhard Jäckel, Michael Stürmer, Mommsen and Habermas. In terms of the "contestants" who voiced their opinions in print and at panel discussions open to the public, the older part of the audience experienced a sense of *déjà vu*. However, younger historians also participated and thus new perspectives entered the debate.[178] Whereas the panels dominated by non-Jewish participants were often very confrontational, the dynamic changed where the panellists were in the majority Jewish.[179] There, while the participants disagreed no less with the author, the positions were not expressed in confrontation, but rather in a way of stating obvious differences in their approaches and agreeing to disagree. Identical statements in the discussion were articulated in a different way and thus appeared to take on a different meaning depending on who makes them. Whereas the non-Jewish German participants in the discussions appeared to feel threatened and reacted emotionally, the Jewish participants seemed to have less need to express their disagreement with Goldhagen in emotionally charged statements.

The Goldhagen Controversy developed according to principles different from previous debates. Disagreement with Goldhagen did not indicate that the critics were acting immorally with regard to the historiography of the Holocaust. Arguably, on one level, the debate concerned the explanation of undisputed actions of perpetrators of the Holocaust, the methodology used to do so, and the style of representation. Much of the initial criticism the book received centred on Goldhagen's methodology and definition of antisemitism. Historians whose field of research is NS and the Holocaust dismissed the viability of Goldhagen's thesis, because they reject a monocausal explanation of the Holocaust as a result of antisemitic beliefs of the German population.[180] Goldhagen's response to his critics, which was published a few days before the German publication of the book, focuses to a large extent on the clarification of his argument against the background of criticisms which he refutes

---

[176] Cf. ibid. 20ff.

[177] In a footnote Goldhagen explains that "This usage does not mean that all Germans are included when the term 'Germans' is employed (just as the term 'Americans' does not implicate every single American), because some Germans opposed and resisted the Nazis as well as the persecution of the Jews" (ibid. 476, note 5).

[178] However, the discussions lacked East German perspectives and female scholars were largely absent as well. It remains to be seen if the debate on the memory of the Holocaust changes visibly towards a representation of such so far marginalised positions.

[179] Cf. Ullrich 1998, 199f.

[180] Cf. for example the contributions of Omer Bartov, Christopher Browning, Norbert Frei, Hans-Ulrich Wehler, Moshe Zimmermann and Jäckel in Schoeps (ed.) 1997.

point by point as unsubstantiated by the text.[181] A.D. Moses argues that as a political scientist Goldhagen relies on a different methodological manual than historians, but concedes that "It is all the more curious, therefore, that his most important methodological assumptions are not highlighted and explicitly justified."[182] Moses supplies the methodological justifications missing in the book, arguing that "Goldhagen relies on a blend of three sources: rational choice theory, behavioralism, and cultural anthropology."[183]

> Rational choice reinvests the individual with the agency and autonomy that the concern with bureaucratic structures and social psychology plays down. With behavioralism and cultural anthropology, by contrast, he is able to link the individual to the collective by grounding individual preferences in the national culture that conditions the individual.[184]

Arguably, scholars agreed that different lines of inquiry were not only possible, but also necessary – the most prominent, though non-German, example being Browning who worked on the same material as did Goldhagen, but reached different conclusions about the perpetrators' motivations for their actions.[185] Regarding the academic critics of Goldhagen, Shandley comments:

> Given the obvious fact that this most sensitive of German historical topics was again being dominated by someone outside their sphere of influence, it is not surprising that initial reactions to *Hitler's Willing Executioners* ranged from incredulity to rage. Unfortunately, these early critics and their anxious attitude in this case add little to the cause of learning more about the Holocaust. Their comments are, however, quite revealing of the current state of the cultural battle around a unified Germany's "collective memory."[186]

The arguments concerning *Hitler's Willing Executioners* were personalised from the beginning. The identification of the book with its author and vice versa is evident in many commentaries. By defining his investment in the debate as an academic who happens to work on the Holocaust, Goldhagen aims to place himself outside of inquiries into his personal connections with the events his book examines. He states:

> On the subject of my identity and alleged motives: They are irrelevant to the evaluation of the book. Many of the same critics who fail to acknowledge, let alone discuss, the many issues of method and interpretation that I put forward in the book, who fail to address the central questions of the period, let alone provide coherent explanations where mine are deemed wanting, pointedly mention my Jewish background and that my father is a survivor, the obvious effect of which is to delegitimize me as a scholar by saying explicitly or implying that a Jew is too afflicted to write in a scholarly manner about the Holocaust.[187]

---

[181] Cf. Goldhagen 1998a. Originally published in *Die Zeit*.

[182] Moses 1998, 210.

[183] Ibid. 210.

[184] Ibid. 210.

[185] Cf. Browning 1992.

[186] Shandley 1998, 10.

[187] Goldhagen 1998a, 143.

This response follows the conventional rules of scholarly argument. The author is clearly not interested in doing anything else. His method of engaging in the debate is rooted in his profession as an academic. Therefore he reacts to what he sees as unscholarly criticisms in an academic fashion. Thus Goldhagen himself made a point of refraining from identifying with any community of memory. Indeed he denied that his book can be understood as displaying personal investments in the historiography of the Holocaust, and he did not actively enter in the debate where it concerned communal and personal investments of the participants. However, this position fails to acknowledge Goldhagen's own involvement in the issues debated. He is not willing to recognise that his person is perceived as connected with the subject debated and that he acts as a representative of a particular culture to Germans and thereby poses a threat. That does not imply that he has to give in to the way he is perceived by participants in the debate, but he needs to show an awareness that he is constructed in a particular way. How he is represented in the media and by contestants in the debate and how he chooses to represent himself have to do with the topic and its significance.

The responses to the book demonstrate that Goldhagen's identity and biography mattered a great deal in the debate. Whether this was expressed in explicit antisemitic comments,[188] or more subtly between the lines, it was often the critic's perception of the author that gave his arguments credibility and authority or not. This places aspects of the debate on Goldhagen's book thoroughly in the context of discussions on Holocaust remembrance in Germany. The public discussion of *Hitler's Willing Executioners* dealt not so much with the arguments advanced in the book. Rather, it concerned the questions asked by the author and the style in which these arguments were presented. The debate discussed not so much arguments concerning explanations of the Holocaust, as it focussed on the people who make them. The contributions of the speakers suggest particular investments in the history they are talking about. The understanding of what is "right" and "wrong" concerning the representation of this period of history also depends on the identification with a particular perspective on this history. This would indicate that the participants in the debate were not so much engaged as scholars whose research concerns aspects of NS, the war and the Holocaust, or as commentators who take a particular interest in the publication of research in these areas. Rather they were engaging in a mixture of academic and personal concerns. Shandley observes that "The obvious defensiveness of many of the critics is surprising, given that they have dedicated their lives' work to serious study of the Holocaust."[189] Aschheim has captured the issues at stake very well, describing them as a battle over the ownership of history:

> Goldhagen [...] is offering an inverse of the apologetic and simplified *Historikerstreit* histories of the 1980s, which relativized Auschwitz into the regular annals of human

---

[188] Cf. the analysis of such personalised responses to Goldhagen (Markovits 1998).
[189] Shandley 1998, 7.

murderousness. He, so to speak, returns the Shoah to the Jews, in much the same way as some German scholars sought to rehabilitate German identity by "normalizing" it in the context of other twentieth-century genocides.[190]

By explicitly or implicitly identifying Goldhagen as Jewish, American, (comparatively) young, and as the son of a Holocaust survivor, commentators such as Rudolf Augstein, Jost Nolte, Peter Glotz and Wehler address the community and generation they understand the author to be rooted in.[191] This, then, influences the way in which they are prepared to read his book. In the area of traditional academic scholarship the quality of an argument is assessed according to the methodology and sources employed. It is acknowledged that personal connections can contribute to the topic one chooses to work on and the perspective one adopts. However, it is generally not deemed acceptable to refer to the personal involvement of a scholar with the research topic to explain the conclusions reached.

Wehler's critique of *Hitler's Willing Executioners*, true to the style of argument with which he had gained his reputation, is structured into two parts, each of which divides into six points. The first six points illustrate why Goldhagen's book is worthwhile reading, the second set argues why the book is flawed. It is generally well argued and depends on academic methods to assess the quality of an argument. However, when he reaches the fifth point against Goldhagen's thesis, Wehler slips into polemics, implicitly referring to Goldhagen's cultural identity:

> Take, for example, the Turkish massacres of millions of Armenians: Instead of trying to provide an explanation in terms of a cluster of very varied causes and motives, should we simply give up and hand the job over to a young Armenian historian, so that he can trace everything back to the centuries-old tradition of "Ottoman butchery"?[192]

By analogy the personal connection of Goldhagen with the Holocaust is interpreted as incapacitating him as a scholar of the Holocaust, because his heritage is assumed to predetermine the conclusions he can draw from source material.[193]

Augstein's interview with Goldhagen illustrates well the personalisation of the debate as well as the generational theme, here enforced by a cross-cultural distance between the German and the American.[194] Throughout the interview Goldhagen makes no reference to his cultural or national background to substantiate his argument. In contrast, Augstein relates personal anecdotes and emphasises his biographical connection with NS in order to undermine Goldhagen's theses. Augstein refers to the

---

[190] Aschheim 1997, 245.

[191] Cf. Augstein's, Wehler's and Nolte's contributions in Shandley (ed.) 1998 and Glotz 1997.

[192] Wehler 1998, 100.

[193] Cf. also Shandley 1998, 7: "Wehler's diatribe was remarkable in that it clearly went beyond his reading of the book. It is also remarkable in that he did not adhere to the careful argumentative style that had made him so famous."

[194] Cf. Interview with Daniel Jonah Goldhagen by Rudolf Augstein 1998.

distance of Goldhagen's personal experiences to the Holocaust by virtue of growing up in the USA with the intention of challenging his ability to interpret life in a dictatorship and exculpating German behaviour towards Jews during NS:

> As a young American who grew up in a democracy, you cannot imagine what conformist pressure – in its worst form, moral cowardice – could be like, certainly not during the Hitler dictatorship. Later we had the terror of the dictatorship *and* the terror of the war.[195]

Underlining different perceptions of NS, Augstein argues regarding the Nuremberg Laws and the pogroms of November 1938 that

> many Jews, absurdly enough, reacted to the shameful Nuremberg Racial Laws like this: "Now we finally know where we stand; earlier and elsewhere, too, we've been in dire straits." At that time we advised our Jewish acquaintances: "Get out of here, what's keeping you here?" [...] By their own account they also misevaluated the Reich pogrom night [...] It had only one single advantage: It convinced a great many Jews that they had to get away after all.[196]

Augstein suggests that solidarity with Jews implies the separation of Jewish and non-Jewish Germans – quite in agreement with NS.[197] The "advantage" of the pogroms underlined by Augstein bears a relation to their intention, namely that Jews were (are?) not welcome in Germany. However, in doing so he inadvertently confirms Goldhagen's point concerning the importance of inquiring about the motivations of the murderers. If the desire to separate Jewish and non-Jewish Germans is so strong even in the post-war recollections of someone who claims to be a friend of the Jews (stretching to the extent of giving a positive meaning to the November pogroms), a question arises about the prevalence and intensity of this desire of the German population during NS.[198] Jan Philipp Reemtsma argues that the outrage caused among German scholars was connected to the questions Goldhagen asked:

> Only a few weeks ago I heard a well-known historian speak publicly about Goldhagen's thesis that German anti-Semitism is genetically conditioned, revealing by that statement how foreign to him was the very idea that had actually been Goldhagen's chief concern: not to present human beings as acting with no will of their own but to insist that human beings are also responsible for what they believe to be right. [...] Goldhagen demonstrated that the genre of "historical explanation" is not the only way in which to present historical material and, indeed, is perhaps not even especially useful for some purposes.[199]

Often, Goldhagen's intentions in writing *Hitler's Willing Executioners* were understood as a personal battle conducted against Germans. This perception of author

---

[195] Ibid. 153.

[196] Ibid. 152.

[197] Cf. also Augstein's comment ibid. 154: "Today it's no longer so easy to appreciate that the majority of the population back then was on his [Hitler's] side, and one didn't worry about the Jews."

[198] For an overview of antisemitic attitudes of the population of the FRG cf. for example Jodice 1991.

[199] Reemtsma 1998, 256f.

and book appear linked to Goldhagen's refusal to identify his own investment in the debate. This refusal is ironic as well, given that he himself contributed to the personalisation of the debate by referring "to *Hitler's Willing Executioners* as 'my book' and to see himself as being on a personal mission to change the ways in which the Holocaust was discussed."[200] The style of *Hitler's Willing Executioners* is assertive and its intensity can be read as an indication of the involvement of the author with the subject. He is clearly addressing moral issues with regard to the behaviour of the perpetrators of the Holocaust and the conclusions he draws from that about the character of German society during NS. However, during the debate Goldhagen did not acknowledge that the questions he is asking about the German past affect Germans in the present.[201] Some of Goldhagen's critics understood themselves to be emotionally and communally identified with the community of the victimisers. Therefore for them more than academic arguments were at stake in the controversy. Although they did not have to defend their personal actions during NS, their immediate memories of the time put them in a position in which they felt morally challenged. Shandley characterises this as

> the tension between older historians (or, in the case of Augstein, journalists) who also lived in the period under investigation and younger historians who do not risk being asked for an explanation of their own actions.[202]

The way they defended themselves against this challenge was intense emotional reaction with the aim of placing Goldhagen outside of what they identify as their community of memory. This would suggest that the debate moved for these critics from the consideration of a thesis to the issue of identification, an aspect highlighted by the psychoanalyst Rolf Vogt who writes about his own struggles in reading *Hitler's Willing Executioners*. He is perceptive about his own emotional entanglement with this history, while at the same time advancing a positive academic criticism of the book. In the essay he and his wife wrote together Vogt illustrates his <u>emotional</u> reaction to author and book very well.

> He leaves us Germans with nothing positive. He knows how many great cultural gifts Germany has presented to humanity! Antisemitism and the Third Reich are not everything! He pushes us again and again head-first into the nasty antisemitic mud. That is his revenge for the atrocities the Germans committed against his father and the other Jews. As the LORD sent his prophet Jonah to the corrupt city of Niniveh to preach God's wrath, repentance and self-examination, his father sent him, Daniel Jonah, to Germany to do the same to us Germans. The avenger in the form of a young scholar who gives us a piece of his mind.[203]

---

[200] Shandley 1998, 9.

[201] Goldhagen acknowledged later that he had misread this point in the debate (cf. Goldhagen 1998b, 283f.).

[202] Shandley 1998, 13

[203] Vogt/Vogt 1997, 513.

Vogt has personal memories of the NS period, but is too young to carry any direct responsibility for crimes of the regime. Nevertheless he identifies with the Germans Goldhagen's book is addressing. He also identifies Goldhagen with the book. At the same time Vogt understands the author to be an academic. But the academic engagement of Goldhagen with the Holocaust has merged with the perception of Goldhagen's background, so that the two cannot be separated. This portrayal of the author, written as an account of Vogt's emotions while reading the book, stands in stark contrast to Goldhagen's self-understanding in the debate. Goldhagen is not prepared to speak on any level other than that of academic argument. Author and critics are thus often not communicating. The clash between these different levels of engagement was particularly obvious in the public debates where the atmosphere created by the participants, the author and the audience often proved to be detrimental to the German scholars.

Volker Ullrich illustrates this miscommunication with the description of two very different panel discussions. In Berlin Goldhagen was faced by Mommsen and Jürgen Kocka amongst others. The audience's sympathy was with Goldhagen. Mommsen's evaluation of the book and his own contribution to the study of the Holocaust were lost to the debate, because

> the harder Goldhagen is attacked by German historians, the more forcefully the public takes his side. With his insistence on the perpetrators' individual responsibility, Goldhagen addresses people's feelings better than do Mommsen and Kocka, who ask about complex structures and systemic requirements, and he uses a language that, as it were, focuses on the victims once again.[204]

In Frankfurt the evening took a very different turn. The debate involved no less controversy among the contestants amongst whom were Micha Brumlik, Dan Diner and Norbert Frei. However, the differences were articulated in monologues, the audience applauded and the evening ended without a heated discussion.[205] Shandley argues that this difference in style in which arguments were articulated by participants in the debate as well as their perception by the audience had to do with the biographies of the contestants:

> The role played in the debate by those born during the mid-1940s to mid-1950s [...] was critical. Although they did not represent a uniform opinion, their contribution is remarkable in that for the most part they did not resort to the same identity politics as had the preceding generation.[206]

The reaction of the audience also split along generational lines. Whereas "older Germans attacked Goldhagen for using collective nouns like 'the Germans' to

---

[204] Ullrich 1998, 199.
[205] Cf. Ibid. 200.
[206] Shandley 1998, 23.

describe the killers of the Shoah, [...] younger ones seemed largely immune to such language."[207]

The success of Goldhagen's book in particular with young Germans arguably can be read as a challenge to the inherited cultural discourse on the Holocaust. Aschheim suggests that

> a generational distance [...] enables the young to question the conventional distinction between "bad" Nazis and "ordinary" Germans and to upbraid their elders for fleeing from the concrete murderous acts of the *their* parents by depicting the Holocaust as a kind of historical abstraction, a matter of impersonal industrial and bureaucratic processes, a mass killing operation shorn of flesh-and-blood killers.[208]

However, the Frankfurt panel discussion can also be read from the perspective of Jewish-German relations. Jewish contributions (from Germany) can be found on all levels of the debate, ranging from positive appraisal of Goldhagen's thesis to severe criticism of his argument and methodology.[209] Jewish engagement was not as emotionally charged as German criticisms. This was particularly apparent in the public discussions where a panel of critics debated with Goldhagen. Where the panel was almost entirely Jewish, as for example in Frankfurt, the discussion was less heated.[210]

Scholars who were largely born after the war often had a more nuanced understanding of the book and the debates surrounding it. Their careful appraisal of Goldhagen's thesis was mostly part of the final stage of the debate. Ingrid Gilcher-Holtey suggests that the critics who dismiss Goldhagen's book refuse to be challenged by the questions he asks and concludes that

> Daniel Goldhagen's book is a methodological challenge – to push ahead, finally, towards a deeper historical debate on the mentality of German anti-Semitism and of National Socialism.[211]

---

[207] Ash 1997, 405.

[208] Aschheim 1997, 243. Cf. also the letters addressed to Goldhagen (Goldhagen 1997). Johannes Heil and Rainer Erb argue that "dieser 1997 nachgereichte Band [...] bildet aber gerade das Beziehungssystem zwischen Goldhagen und seinem Publikum ab" (Heil/Erb 1998, 21). They also note that ironically this is not recognised by Goldhagen himself, as indicated in his response: "Daß er in der 'Antwort an seine Leser' so unbekümmert das Verdikt gegen die böswilligen, ihr Herrschaftswissen monopolisierenden Kritiker ('die Zunft') mobilisieren würde (ibid. 240f. passim), war selbst nach 18 Monaten durchgestandener Goldhagen-Debatte noch eine Überraschung" (ibid. 21).

[209] For the former cf. Julius Schoeps' contribution and for the latter the contributions of Michael Wolffsohn and Zimmermann in Schoeps (ed.) 1997.

[210] Cf. Ullrich 1998, 200.

[211] Gilcher-Holtey 1998, 107.

In agreement with this, Reemtsma and Habermas interpreted the publication of the book as a welcome contribution to the German debate on the memory of the Holocaust which could initiate a change in the patterns of discussion for which Goldhagen should be thanked.[212]

The change of pattern in the discussion of Holocaust memory indicated by the Goldhagen Controversy appears to be closely related to a change of generations among scholars. Members of the first generation who have to account for personal actions during NS or whose formative years are closely associated with years between 1933-1945 no longer dominate the debates. Still connected to NS through the biographies of their parents, members of the second generation influence the debate with no less a sense of immediacy, but often without the need to defend their academic territory as part of their identification as Germans. In particular, younger members of the audiences at the panel discussions on *Hitler's Willing Executioners* appeared to find answers in Goldhagen's book to questions that largely had remained taboo in the discourses on NS memory they inherited from their parents' and grandparents' generations. In this sense the Goldhagen Controversy can be compared to the effect *Holocaust* had on the previous generation. Whereas *Holocaust* opened the way to a – tentative and often still marginal – representation of Jewish victims of NS as part of German discourses, *Hitler's Willing Executioners* generated questions regarding the representation of NS perpetrators in Germany. As Reemtsma argues

> The fear of a study of the average man and the possibility of recognizing in him one's own grandfather, father, or uncle (or aunt or mother) has finally been replaced by the willingness to take the risk of such a recognition.[213]

4. Conclusion

The discussion indicates parameters which dominate debates on the memory of the Holocaust in Germany. Firstly, for Germans the memory of German suffering in the war and its aftermath continues to take priority in the formulation of identity, although the victims of Germans are no longer excluded from the discourse. Thus memories of German suffering and of the Holocaust exist in a dialectical relationship to each other. Moeller argues that since the end of the war, the German public was searching for a "usable past". The debates surrounding the relationship between history, memory and politics in Germany were and continue to be constructed around competing versions of history.[214] German public debates show that "pasts of German victims and pasts of the victims of Germans were [and are] still vying for space and

---

[212] Cf. their contributions in Shandley (ed.) 1998.

[213] Reemtsma 1998, 257.

[214] Cf. Moeller 1996, 1044ff.

recognition in public consciousness."[215] A "usable past" can be constructed much more easily if the memory of crimes against members of one's own society can be silenced. Arguably the Holocaust is not remembered as part of a German national narrative, but is understood to enter German memory from the outside in the form of narratives of survivors. Hanno Loewy goes as far as to argue that the Holocaust does not exist in German memory,[216] an observation that is supported by Christoph Münz's doctoral dissertation *To offer a memory to the world*.[217] Münz shows that German historiography of NS paid almost no attention to Jewish historiography of the same era. Similarly, Jewish attempts to relate to the Holocaust in a variety of genres, including religious thought, are still hardly known in Germany.[218]

Secondly, then, debates on the memory of the Holocaust demonstrate that Germans have difficulty in recognising Jews as equal members of German society. The Holocaust is often not understood as a crime that Germans committed against members of their own society as well as against members of other societies. Rather it is seen as a crime that Germans committed against groups of people who were excluded from membership in German society by definition. Jewish memory of the Holocaust was hardly recognised in the German public until the 1980s which testifies to the continuing definition of Jews as Other, as alien to German society and thus not part of the communities of memory of post-war Germany which have come to represent German public memory of NS and the Holocaust. In the present Jewish Holocaust memory is articulated in the majority by non-Germans, and the understanding that Jewish memory does not belong to German memory applies also in retrospect.[219] This suggests that post-war German self-understanding continued NS and pre-NS definitions of a contradiction between being German and being Jewish. Jewish memory, even memory of German Jews of the pre-war period, was hardly recognised as part of German discourses on the Holocaust.

Thirdly, with the Goldhagen Controversy the generational change in public representations of NS and the Holocaust from eye-witnesses to their descendants indicates a shift from communicated memory to enactments of historical memories without a necessary biographical link to the events represented. Geyer and Hansen formulate the set of questions confronted by Germans of the second and third generation after the Holocaust as follows:

> How would *you* remember and mourn *your* genocide – coming from the land of the murderers? This question, not meant to solicit sympathy but to acknowledge the problem, has

---

[215] Ibid. 1045.

[216] Cf. Loewy 1995.

[217] Münz ²1996.

[218] Cf. however the anthology Brocke/Jochum (eds.) 1982.

[219] Cf. the assumption that one cannot be Jewish and German at the same time, unless one gives up one's allegiance with the Jewish community and becomes a "Jewish individual" (cf. for example Scholem 1964/1976, 62f.).

tied Jews and Germans together. Jewish memory cannot be considered separate from the German one. One memory will be implicated in the other's story, as long as there is a German and a Jewish identity, and as long as both sides are able to tell their stories, and there are, again, Jews living in Germany *as Jews*.[220]

Thus, the challenge for subsequent generations is to create a historical discourse on NS and Holocaust memories that preserves the relevance of these memories for their respective communities.

What became already apparent in the analysis of the Rhineland statement – namely the difficulty with which German Protestants reflected on Jewish memory and responses to the Holocaust in their own right – also prevails in German society as it is represented in public debates on Holocaust remembrance. The Rhineland synod recognised the need to approach the memory of the Holocaust "with the help of Jews",[221] and as such attempts to break the pattern of constructing German (Protestant) identities in an antagonism to what is perceived as Jewish. However, the separation of German and Jewish communities of memory since the Holocaust and the perception of Jewish Holocaust memory as a threat to German identity, evident in attempts at *Vergangenheitsbewältigung*, have made it difficult to include memories of the "Jewish other" into narratives of German identity. The brevity of the Rhineland statement sufficed to indicate awareness of its social-historical context of post-Holocaust Germany, but could not provide a context analysis. However, the responses the statement received did not focus on the German context of Holocaust remembrance either, nor did they include reflections on Jewish contexts of Holocaust remembrance and cultural identification. Here the lack of reflection on one's own context as well as on the situation of "the other" is apparent.

For the theologian Friedrich-Wilhelm Marquardt, however, this communally defined memory of the Holocaust and NS has assumed extraordinary theological relevance. His systematic theology addresses the context of the FRG as a country which has inherited a responsibility to remember the failures and crimes of its historical predecessor. Perceiving this legacy as a challenge threatening theological assumptions which have thus far been taken for granted, Marquardt sets out to explore these threats. He intends to facilitate possibilities for Christians in Germany to confront the challenge posed by the criminal nature of NS and the atrocities of the Holocaust to their identities as Germans and Christians.

---

[220] Geyer/Hansen 1994, 176. Cf. also Dan Diner's the concept "negative symbiosis" (Diner 1990).
[221] Cf. EKiR (ed.) [2]1985, 9, 18.

III. Friedrich-Wilhelm Marquardt – Re-centring Christian theology on Jews

Friedrich-Wilhelm Marquardt is arguably the most distinguished systematic theologian associated with Christian-Jewish relations in Germany. He is the only theologian in Germany who has offered a dogmatic theology which grounds itself in Christian-Jewish relations and takes the Holocaust as its starting point. His theology can be regarded as exemplary in the sense that it takes up and further develops ideas from other theologians active in Christian-Jewish relations.

Born in 1928 and aged seventeen at the end of the war, Marquardt was too young to be directly responsible for the injustices of NS. However, his formative years were the 1930s and 1940s, and thus he was himself exposed to NS as a child and adolescent. He studied theology under Rudolf Bultmann and Karl Barth and worked as a minister to students in Berlin. He began his academic career in 1967 with a doctoral dissertation on the place of Israel in the theology of Barth,[1] supervised by Helmut Gollwitzer.[2] Today he is professor emeritus for systematic theology at the Freie Universität Berlin.

Marquardt first encountered Jews when travelling to Amsterdam in 1949 where he attended a theological conference and was invited to stay with a Jewish family.[3] According to his recollections these meetings with Holocaust survivors set him onto his theological path: "Not to be welcome as a German, in particular to stir terrible memories with the German language, has been a lesson for my entire life."[4] Marquardt agrees when a Dutch colleague, Coen Wessel, associates Marquardt's theology with the Holocaust memorial in the Wertheim Park in Amsterdam, and he reflects as follows:

> For I really experience this memorial of the broken mirrors as a material image of the shattering thoughts of my theology – [...]. When you look at yourself in the many mirror-fragments which surround the urn with the ashes of Dutch Jews from Auschwitz, you see the dark clouds of rain of the sky of Amsterdam in September in the broken mirror image: in between the broken branches of the trees of the park which are mirrored there as well – and in particular you see your own face which is fractured in the sharp edges of the fragments and here you are unable to see yourself "complete and uninjured". "Never again will the sky be mirrored intact in this place." Not the sky – but neither you Christian.[5]

---

[1] Marquardt 1976.

[2] Cf. Wessel 1998, 12.

[3] Cf. Marquardt 1998b, 97.

[4] Ibid. 98.

[5] Ibid. 101f. NB I translated *Himmel* as sky. However, the German *Himmel* can mean both sky and heaven.

Marquardt's dogmatic theology presents the first outline of a Christian systematic theology in the context of Christian-Jewish relations which is written in Germany. His work is written in the context of Christian theology in Germany which addresses Christian-Jewish relations. Influential theologians, Protestant and Catholic, of Marquardt's own generation are Bertold Klappert, Hans-Joachim Kraus, Hans Küng, Johann Baptist Metz, Jürgen Moltmann, Franz Mussner, Peter von der Osten-Sacken, Rolf Rendtorff, Martin Stöhr and Clemens Thoma. In the international context, Marquardt's dogmatic theology is comparable only to the effort of the American scholar Paul M. van Buren in his three volumes of *A Theology of the Jewish-Christian Reality*.[6]

Marquardt's aim is educational. He wants to influence the writing of theology and the life of the Protestant church in Germany. Hence his theology is contextual to the FRG, taking seriously the post-Holocaust context of German society. Therefore he develops his theology as part of the efforts to remember the Holocaust in the FRG. Prefigured in articles and monographs since the 1960s,[7] Marquardt began to publish a systematic theology at the end of the 1980s which at present numbers seven volumes.[8] Marquardt's theology moves forward from the Rhineland statement and addresses Christian-Jewish relations on the level of systematic theology.

This analysis focuses on the first part of his dogmatic theology, entitled *About the misery and affliction of theology (Prolegomena)*.[9] Further volumes are concerned with Christology and eschatology and will be considered where appropriate.[10] Marquardt's systematic theology is the fruit of a lifetime of teaching and active involvement in Christian-Jewish encounters in Germany.

Prolegomena justify and determine the structure of the whole of a dogmatic theology. Therefore, the understanding of Jews and the Holocaust as presented here is crucial to the further development of Marquardt's theology. The interpretation of these issues is meant to reflect the self-understanding of Christians in the context of Christian-Jewish relations. In the *Prolegomena* Marquardt reflects on the possibilities of faith and

---

[6] Buren 1981/1987/1988. In recent years younger theologians have presented dissertations concerning the impact of the Holocaust on systematic theology, cf. for example Jüngst 1996 analysed in chapter V.; Petzel 1994 and Reck 1998.

[7] Cf. in particular Marquardt 1979 as well as Marquardt 1983.

[8] Marquardt [2]1992 (first edition 1988); Marquardt 1990/1991; Marquardt 1993/1994/1996 and Marquardt 1997.

[9] Marquardt [2]1992.

[10] In particular in the *Eschatology*, Marquardt addresses the Holocaust and its significance for the possibility of any eschatological hope as well as for the relationship between Christians and Jews with a view to the hope for the future and redemption of this world. Cf. also Marquardt 1980; Marquardt 1986.

theology after the Holocaust, and tries to develop criteria for a new beginning of Christian theology.

Marquardt's theology can be characterised as a "dogmatic theology as a form of repentance" ("*Dogmatik in Bußform*")[11]. He understands it as an "experiment in biblical theology"[12] with which he intends to uncover the failures of Christian faith in history, to repent and to rework the Christian-Jewish relationship, so that, with its renewal, Christianity may again relate to the truth of the Bible.[13] Marquardt emphasises the biblical orientation of his dogmatic theology. He intends to gain new theological insights through a recovery of "the biblical order of reality" ("*biblische Wirklichkeitsordnung*").[14] According to Marquardt, "the biblical order of reality" is defined by the relationship between the Jewish people and G-d narrated in biblical texts and enacted in history. Marquardt claims that this relationship must shape the Christian worldview and understanding of the Christian relationship with G-d as well as of the relation of Christians and Jews.[15]

1. Theology after the Holocaust – Reading the "signs of the times" and (re)discovering Jews

Thesis: The murder of Jews in this century and its presuppositions and consequences for which theology and church have to be held responsible are the signs of our times which question every theology in an unprecedented radicality.[16]

The "signs of the times" – derived from Mat 16:3 – becomes the theological metaphor for Marquardt with which he attempts to understand the situation of contemporary Christian theology. Marquardt claims that in their biblical meaning, "signs of the times" imply a *kairos*, a time of events that change the course of history in opposition to "normal time". According to Marquardt, "signs of the times" are given by G-d to each generation, in a way quite different from what can be detected in an analysis of events in history.[17] In the Gospel of Matthew Jesus leaves the question about the "signs of the times" unanswered which leads Marquardt to interpret the question as one that needs to be asked again and again, continually accompanying the work of the theologian.[18] However,

---

[11] Funke 1991, 78.

[12] Marquardt [2]1992, 8.

[13] Cf. ibid. 124; § 3.8 is entitled "Denken aus der Umkehr heraus".

[14] Cf. ibid. 8.

[15] For overviews of his theology cf. Henrix 1989; Wessel 1998 and Liß-Walther 1999.

[16] Marquardt [2]1992, 74.

[17] Cf. ibid. 32.

[18] Cf. ibid. 33. Cf. also the importance of this concept in Rahner's and Tillich's theologies.

"Signs" can only be seen by someone who has been given eyes to see; they are an experience of faith. Therefore any generalisation to a theological statement communicable to everyone is difficult.[19]

Consequently, "signs of the times" become tautologies which can only be read by people who affirm the presuppositions which allow their recognition. According to Marquardt for contemporary theology "signs of the times" are the Holocaust and the conditions which made it possible. He thereby grounds his theology in the context of recent German history which continues to influence German society.

Following dialectic theology as expressed in the works of both Barth and Bultmann,[20] Marquardt describes the situation of any theology as existing in uncertainty. He claims that the Holocaust has questioned theology in a way that may make its continuation impossible. The uncertainty of theology after the Holocaust, then, becomes the most important presupposition of Marquardt's theological thought.[21] Before Marquardt can say where and why theology is radically uncertain after the Holocaust he needs to give a definition of theology in the first place.

Prior to all thought Marquardt affirms his trust in Christ: "That Christ teaches also today is the foundation of all theology. What and how Christ is teaching is its law."[22] From this it follows that: (a) theology is radically dependent on G-d-self; G-d is its reason and its life, therefore prayer predates theology; in its thinking theology participates in G-d's own thoughts, thinks according to G-d (*theologia ektypos*).[23] (b) G-d who wants to be known by human beings and therefore can be known in G-d's communications with people; discovering where G-d makes G-d-self known is the task of theology (*theologia archetypos*).[24] Thus theology remains dependent on G-d in all its thought. At the same time it is an unfinished business which is radically contextual and bound to historical situations, because G-d realises G-d-self in encounters with human beings and is dependent on human beings to be able to be known among them. Humans partake in and are able to influence G-d's life and knowledge of G-d-self.[25] Therefore "Theology is an effort to gain insight which is fundamentally determined by situation and time. Thereby it partakes in the historicity of God."[26] Marquardt sees this

---

[19] Marquardt 1986, 132.

[20] Cf. Marquardt [2]1992, 70f.

[21] Cf. Marquardt [2]1992, p. 7.

[22] Ibid. 52 (both sentences in italics in original).

[23] Cf. ibid. 13-17.

[24] Cf. ibid. 18f.

[25] Cf. ibid. 26.

[26] Ibid. 31. That Marquardt understands his theology to be radically contexual is made clear from the outset. He recognises that theology has different *Sitze im Leben*, depending on where theology is produced. Whereas according to Marquardt the Christian dependency on Jews will remain a presupposition wherever theology is produced, the Christian-Jewish relationship itself may not always need to be at the forefront of theological reflection. A guerillero in Nicaragua would,

contextuality operating in the Bible where a multiplicity of theologies coexist with each other so as to witness to the diversity of ways in which G-d relates to the Jewish people and the nations.[27] As a framework for his theology Marquardt chooses the metaphor of the way (derived from *Halachah*) to express his understanding of theology in the contemporary situation, because it corresponds to his analysis of the biblical interpretation of reality in Genesis which, according to Marquardt, is continued in the Gospel of Matthew and in the development of *Halachah* in rabbinical Judaism.[28] However, to Marquardt the concept of "the biblical order of reality" becomes normative and thus loses its immediate contextuality. Thus Marquardt's theology is built on a dialectic between the need to be contextual to each historical situation – a principle derived from the Bible – while at the same time inscribing a particular contextuality (of Genesis) as normative. The dialectic between contextuality and "the biblical order of reality" are what Marquardt understands to be the foundation and boundaries of theology of which theology can only speak in the affirmative.[29] This he sees as the part of theology which is received by humans and which, because of its source in G-d, does not need any justification. It is a given.

The other part of theology is the human side which needs to be humanly justified, namely the question about the necessity of theology. Marquardt is influenced by the tradition of dialectic theology, the "theology of crisis" of Barth and Bultmann. Their questioning concerned the right and ability to speak about G-d. This is where Marquardt sees theology after the Holocaust in a crisis which is not comparable to the crisis inherent in theology nor any particular crisis encountered by theology before. Marquardt goes one step further than Barth and Bultmann in questioning the possibility of theology altogether. He understands the possibility of theology to be questioned in an underlined unprecedented way. The reason for this is the Holocaust and the "signs of the times" it presents to contemporary theology.

> We are convinced that this "random truth of history" [the events of the Holocaust] has the power to disavow every "eternal truth of reason", because no power of reason has become known, not even a power of theological reason, which interfered with the murder of the Jews with the intention to stop it. Therefore this faith trembles, because also the divine revelation confessed by it may have lost its truth, that is its recognisability as well as its expressability.[30]

Marquardt imagines, if he was a theologian, be involved with a different set of questions than Marquardt at the university in Berlin, Germany (cf. ibid. 68). However, Marquardt claims that the Christian-Jewish relationship carries universal significance, in particular for the development of ecumenical theology (cf. ibid. 454f.).

[27] Cf. ibid. 32.

[28] Cf. Marquardt [2]1992, 287ff., 313ff., 179ff. For a different use of the metaphor of the way cf. Buren 1981.

[29] Cf. Marquardt [2]1992, 54.

[30] Ibid. 75.

The relationship of the Jewish people with G-d, and thus the relationship of Christianity and Judaism, is the reason why in Marquardt's thinking the crisis initiated by the Holocaust is unprecedented for Christian faith and theology. Because, according to Marquardt, the Holocaust aimed at the destruction of Judaism,[31] the failure of church and theology to interfere and try to stop the murder of Jews meant that the Holocaust also targeted the essence of Christianity.[32] Marquardt claims that the failure of faith, church and theology was (and still is) to understand that the relationship of G-d with the Jewish people is fundamental for Christian faith.[33] Similar to other Holocaust theologians Marquardt interprets the Christian-Jewish relationship as *sui generis*: "Because their [the church's and theology's] relationship to Judaism is neither a random truth of history nor an abstract eternal truth of reason, but choice of the living God in Jesus Christ."[34]

Marquardt locates the relationship between Jews and G-d – and as a consequence the Christian-Jewish relationship – at the centre of Christianity. He justifies this with an analysis of "the biblical order of reality" which understands the relationship between the Jewish people and G-d to be mutually reinforcing so that the future of G-d is intrinsically bound to the life of G-d's people. Marquardt understands the relationship between G-d and the Jewish people as presented in the Bible to be the paradigm of the history of all people with G-d and therefore the paradigm of world history.[35] Thus the Jewish people are the centre of world history in an exemplary way. Therefore if the life of Jewish people is endangered, then so is the future of G-d.

> Biblically this means first and foremost, that in fact the extinction [sic] of the *Jews* wanted the death of *God* at the same time and wanted – even more – *to get rid of God's loving recognition of all people, who looks at humankind through Israel, and with that: the death of any love whatsoever.*[36]

Marquardt rejects a rabbinical notion that even the divinity and (inner) life of G-d is dependent on the worship of the Jewish people.[37] He argues that such a notion is not supported by the Bible, because G-d is unchangeable; but G-d can lose faith in human beings – who are G-d's likeness – and can no longer recognise G-d-self in this

---

[31] Marquardt often uses Judaism and Jews interchangeably.

[32] Cf. ibid. 77.

[33] Cf. ibid. 144f.

[34] Ibid. 77.

[35] Cf. ibid. 263. This paradigm developed later into the trias of G-d-People-Land which Marquardt understands *sui generis*.

[36] Marquardt 1994, 47.

[37] Cf. Marquardt ²1992, 26. He refers to Midrash Rabba on Ps 123:1 which reflects on Isa 43:12.

likeness.[38] However, the assault on Jewish life presents the most serious assault on the recognisability of G-d in this world.

Arguably the "life of G-d's people" and "G-d's recognisability" describe two different things. The logic of Marquardt's argument suggests that if there are no Jews, G-d cannot be recognised by humans. In its result this conclusion is not that different from the rabbinical argument, since both argue that G-d can be G-d without being acknowledged by humans. However, the rabbinical suggestion that G-d's divinity is dependent on the Jewish people is part of an inner-Jewish argument about the task of the Jewish people. If this task is witnessing to G-d then, as a consequence, if this witness ceases, G-d, as witnessed to by Jews, would no longer be G-d. This conclusion is far from being a universal principle of theology, rather it is spoken to a particular community. It is thus questionable whether Marquardt's use of this rabbinical argument is appropriate. It is unclear why he thinks he can make a principle of inner Jewish thought mandatory for Christians – or even for humanity.

Marquardt argues that theology may have a future only if it recognises a twofold dependency of Christian faith and theology on Jews as its presupposition.[39] This implies a self-limitation of the church:[40] (1) through a biblical bond of a relationship of faith which understands the primacy of the Jewish people in historical terms (the Jewish people were chosen first) and ontologically as a criticism of the church ("God is born in Israel"[41]) and (2) because of the "signs of the times" which bind Christians particularly to contemporary Jews. Marquardt justifies this presupposition biblically and historically, the two dimensions which, he argues, need to be embraced by faith and theology if theology wants to be able to claim any relevance in the contemporary world. Marquardt appears to decide single-handedly which historical events are theologically relevant according to biblical-theological paradigms which are formulated as tautologies and as such are neither open to discussion nor accessible to outsiders to this circle of thought. Thus it is not clear why he feels able to assume the authority to make such assertions.

Marquardt wants to begin his reorientation of theology by going back to the point where the church left and rejected the Jewish people: "the biblical order of reality".[42]

---

[38] Cf. Marquardt [2]1992, 26.

[39] Cf. ibid. 31f. A similar demand is made by Metz (cf. Metz 1984, 26-33).

[40] Cf. Marquardt [2]1992, 427.

[41] Ibid. 427.

[42] Cf. ibid. 8. Marquardt's understanding of the Bible follows the principle *sola scriptura* of the Reformation which intended to safeguard the authority of the Bible for the formulation of theological insights. He therefore vehemently rejects any *Sachkritik* of biblical texts, because this would assume that human authority is greater than the authority of the text, the theologian would become judgmental and would no longer need continually to question her/his method of interpretation and

By rethinking the biblical interpretation of reality he hopes to be able to reformulate theology and arrive at a Christian theology which is faithful to G-d, G-d's relationship with the Jewish people and G-d's promises, and which is contextual to Germany. At the same time it also becomes a theology of reorientation which wants to orient itself towards the victims of previous theology. It wants to think from the perspective of the victims of traditional theology, it wants to orient itself in a relationship to Jews.[43]

Marquardt argues that, despite the shattering of Jewish and Christian faith in the Holocaust, the biblical testimony still extends a calling to Jews and Christians. He therefore intends to learn to read the Bible "from the perspective of the victims of traditional Christian interpretation of the Bible"[44], i.e. from a Jewish perspective. Marquardt believes that "the Bible as the testimony of the living God's word and will can, through its worldview, teach us to prevent inhumanity."[45] Hence, the scriptures are almost a kind of refuge where a renewal of faith and theology becomes possible: "Nowhere is the *Schriftprinzip* more relevant than in the situation after Auschwitz."[46] Therefore the Bible becomes the teacher of the theologian and is to be read under the guidance of Jewish victims of traditional Christian theology. In this context in particular Marquardt emphasises the character of his theology "as a form of repentance". Marquardt's dogmatic theology is an attempt to confront honestly the crisis the Holocaust presents to Christian faith. Klappert summarises Marquardt's interpretation of the relationship between biblical testimony and (contemporary) historical developments, which follows the framework of the "witness-people myth" in its positive post-Holocaust definition:

> According to Marquardt it has to be asked, to what extent the continuing history of Judaism and thus the periods of Jewish history up until today represent an adequate configuration of the messianic history of Jesus Christ. In Jewish terms adequate configuration means: Israel as God's sign of election amongst the nations.[47]

To create a Christian reading of the Bible from a Jewish perspective Marquardt develops the notion of "Evangelical *Halachah*"[48]. From Judaism Marquardt derives the understanding that *Halachah* describes the "science of finding the way of faith"[49]. He wants to develop an Evangelical *Halachah* in closeness to and distinction from Jewish *Halachah*. A close reference to Jewish understandings of *Halachah* is necessary

---

prevent the possibility of the theologian being educated further by the text (cf. ibid. 89f.). However, in a sense his tautological approach contradicts this principle.

[43] Cf. ibid. 124ff.

[44] Ibid. 151.

[45] Ibid. 151.

[46] Ibid. 151.

[47] Klappert 1994, 35.

[48] Cf. Marquardt [2]1992, 166ff.

[49] Ibid. 166 (phrase in italics in original). Marquardt does not define to which Jewish approach to *Halachah* he wishes to relate his "Evangelical *Halachah*".

because Marquardt intends to assume the perspective of Jewish victims of Christian theology and the most important Jewish form of interpreting Torah has traditionally been *Halachic* discussion. Marquardt locates the distinction of Christian from Jewish *Halachah* in Jesus Christ "who alone can lead us towards biblical texts of a binding Evangelical *Halachah*."[50]

Halachah describes the context of reflection particular to rabbinical or Jewish tradition while Marquardt is explicitly placing his "Evangelical *Halachah*" in a Christian context. As such Marquardt is in danger of misappropriating a Jewish concept to a Christian context. A consequence of this misappropriation would be the imperialistic treatment of Jewish tradition and a "Christianisation" of Judaism. Evangelical *Halachah* develops as discerning the way of faith/life from the gospel of Christ from which G-d's call extends through Christ. *Halachah*, then, should lead Christians from the place where they first responded to the calling onto the way of discerning G-d's will in debate with others. Evangelical *Halachah* thus begins with the calling of Christ which brings Christians out of their previous existence. Marquardt entitles §6 of the *Prolegomena* "Abraham, our Father: concerning vocation (*De Vocatione*)"[51], which he links to the story of Abraham as the paradigm for a person who responds to the calling of G-d and as a paradigm for the calling G-d extends to Christians.[52]

It is the history beginning with Abraham with which Marquardt shapes his theology. He chooses Abraham as a paradigm, because of the importance Abraham assumes in the New Testament (and subsequent Christian theology), to interpret the contemporary relationship of Christians with G-d.[53] Because of Abraham's significance to both parts of the Christian Bible, describing the Jewish people's and the church's relation to G-d, his story becomes the biblical paradigm *par excellence* which, according to Marquardt, can help Christians reconstruct their faith and reinterpret the relationship between Christians and Jews.[54]

> The goyim who are called to become children of Abraham, are thereby also called to become the brothers and sisters of the "physical" children of Abraham, of the Jews and the friends of the Jews. Only in this sibling relationship to Judaism can the identification as Abraham's children assume any meaning. [55]

He argues that the *toledot Abraham* (translated as "generations of Abraham") develops in three phases, which he intends to mirror in the structure of his dogmatic theology. Further parallels can be found in the structure of Jewish history and Christian faith.

---

[50] Ibid. 166 (italics in original).

[51] Marquardt [2]1992, 263.

[52] Cf. ibid. 263ff.

[53] Cf. Marquardt 1998a, 88.

[54] Cf. Marquardt [2]1992, 281.

[55] Ibid. 339.

The *toledot Abraham* begin with Abraham's calling by G-d out of his country with the words *lech l'cha* (enforced imperative "go") (Gen 12:1). Abraham is called out of the context of his life onto a way. Marquardt calls this event "Abraham's disruption"[56] and it describes the first phase of the *toledot Abraham* as well as the entirety of the three stages of the story.[57] Abraham cannot return – the second phase of the story – but he has also not arrived anywhere yet. He is on the way to the promised land – the third stage of the story. The *Prolegomena* and the three parts of Marquardt's dogmatic theology parallel "Abraham's disruption". §1-3 of the *Prolegomena* describe the situation theology finds itself in after the Holocaust, §4-6 represent the calling and indicate the present stage of theology which cannot lapse back into the previous existence, and §7 shows the first fruits of the rethinking of Christian faith towards a promised future by analysing recent attempts to rethink the Christian-Jewish relationship within the boundaries of Christian theology. In terms of the three parts of Marquardt's dogmatic theology, the *Prolegomena* form the call out of the existence of theology after the Holocaust, the second part – the Christology – spells out the implications of the calling in the present on the way towards a promised future and the third part – the eschatology – is concerned with understanding the meaning of the hope for the promised future in the present. All three parts combine listening to the biblical testimony with listening to the witness of contemporary Jewish experience.

Jewish history, too, can be understood in parallel to the scheme Marquardt discovered in the *toledot Abraham*. Being called out of an existence in the Diaspora which was destroyed in the Holocaust and which cannot be recreated (phase one), the Jewish people now live in the Diaspora and the State of Israel (phase two) discerning the way towards a promised future (phase three).

According to Marquardt, the Holocaust first and foremost questioned Jewish life physically as much as spiritually. Marquardt emphasises that Christian faith is affected by the Holocaust only secondarily. Christians are affected, because the Holocaust was an assault on <u>Jewish</u> life and consequently also on the possibility of Christian faith: "Christians are also affected by the Jewish experience in Auschwitz and should face the shattering of the fundamental biblical-Jewish-Christian categories of theological thought."[58]

To gain any insight about the Holocaust Christians must listen to Jewish testimony. The questions asked by Jews about the Holocaust are not the same as the questions faced by Christians. But Christians need to identify with the questions of Jews with regard to the Holocaust because, according to Marquardt, the Jewish witnesses to

---

[56] Ibid. 349ff.
[57] Cf. ibid. 353.
[58] Ibid. 130.

G-d are indispensable for the ability of Christians to recognise G-d.[59] Jewish testimony from the Holocaust, then, becomes normative for Christian theology as an expression of the contemporary historical experience of the Jewish people. Discussing Jewish efforts to grapple with the experiences and questions of the Holocaust, Marquardt refuses to draw any (theological) conclusions from the material. He claims that the Holocaust remains inaccessible to Christians, because of the incomparable nature of the event and because, he asserts, Christians did not have their own witnesses among the victims.[60] The Holocaust is part of Jewish experience that cannot be penetrated by Christians.

> We stay with the testimony of the victims. We neither question nor check it. Any opposition to it would presume a place outside or inside of this experience, none of which we can assume: as people who have been spared we are neither affected nor unaffected.[61]

This understanding of Holocaust testimony expresses Marquardt's interpretation of Jewish experiences in history. He characterises the Jewish outlook on history as that of the perspective of victims, Jews suffer history.[62] Jews have developed traditions which express these experiences in history without ceasing to hope for the future and the fulfilment of promises received in the past.

However, as much that may be true of aspects of Jewish history and however this has become visible in Jewish understandings of history and developments of tradition, it is by no means the only form of Jewish self-expression. As much part of Jewish tradition are expressions of Jewish power and resistance in the face of powerful enemies.[63] To suggest Jewish victimhood as the normative mode of Jewish self-expression is to inscribe Jews as victims into Christian theology, thereby limiting the extent to which different Jewish identities and self-expression can be recognised by Marquardt's theology.

Marquardt argues that the present day reality of the State of Israel has to be taken seriously by Christian theology as part of contemporary Jewish experience in history. He agrees with Barth that the life of the Jewish people is grounded in the nature of G-d and that G-d and the Jewish people form an indivisible unity,[64] and interprets the State

---

[59] Cf. ibid. 144f.

[60] Cf. ibid. 118ff., 131.

[61] Ibid. 124. Arguably, there is a difference between directing questions at an experience and opposing it. And there are ways of relating to an experience that do not imply a judgement.

[62] Cf. ibid. 191.

[63] Cf. Biale 1986. Cf. also for example the festivals of Purim and Chanukkah present narratives of Jewish power in the face of adversity, and the development of Zionism includes movements of Jewish political and military empowerment.

[64] Cf. Marquardt 1986, 127.

of Israel as a sign of the faithfulness of G-d to his people and his promises.[65] According to Marquardt, the land is the goal of the *toledot Abraham* and its promise together with the promise of many descendants to Abraham is the guarantee of Jewish survival.[66] However, he does not wish to confuse the political entity of the State of Israel with a manifestation of the hope for a messianic kingdom in the land of Israel. Marquardt argues that the promise of the land to Abraham implies a self-criticism:[67] because the promise of the land is bound to the observance of Torah (the precondition for entering the land and the condition for staying, because only in the land can the Torah be observed completely), this promise implies an obligation of the Jewish people: G-d has given the land for the observance of Torah.[68] Therefore, Marquardt concludes that the biblical foundation and the obligations implied in the promise of the land to the Jewish people cannot be used to justify theologically any political situations in the State of Israel.[69] The State of Israel and the reassertion of Jewish life after the Holocaust are interpreted as signs of G-d's continuing faithfulness to the Jewish people and to the promises of the Bible, but these signs are not to be confused with a fulfilment of eschatological hopes. Thus all that can be learned from Jewish survival is a manifestation of G-d's presence.

This understanding of the State of Israel is based on Marquardt's positive version of the "witness-people myth", which interprets Jewish history as a parallel to the relationship of G-d with Christ and relies on a measuring of historical reality with what is understood as the authority of biblical promises and standards. There appear to be certain standards, which can be derived from "the biblical order of reality" and then be directly applied to contemporary political situations. Because the relationship of the Jewish people with G-d is *sui generis*, Marquardt cannot recognise claims by any other people to such an intimate relation with the same G-d. He accuses traditional Christian and Muslim theologies of treating their relationship to the Jewish people as a dispute over an inheritance and, by falsifying genealogies (cf. Paul on Isaac and Ishmael in the letter to the Romans and similarly in the Koran), of rebelling against G-d's choice made in the election of the Jewish people.[70] Marquardt argues that G-d is free to choose and that "God's election is unambiguous and does not tolerate legacy-hunting nor falsification of family trees."[71] Thus to Marquardt the political situation of the conflict between the State of Israel and the Palestinians always has a theological dimension, because of the nature of the Jewish people and the way Muslims and

---

[65] Cf. ibid. 132.

[66] Cf. Marquardt 1994, 187-189.

[67] Cf. ibid. 274.

[68] Cf. ibid. 208-212.

[69] Cf. ibid. 274.

[70] Cf. ibid. 278. Marquardt does not provide any references to the Koran or any other Muslim sources to substantiate his claims.

[71] Ibid. 278f.

Christians interact with this. The primacy of the Jewish people becomes the criterion in Marquardt's dogmatic theology which can be used as an argument in political situations. When considering the contemporary situation in the land of Israel/Palestine Marquardt argues accordingly.

The Palestinian claim to the land of Israel/Palestine is of secondary importance to Marquardt, since they cannot lay claim to the same continuity of attachment to the land as can Jews. To Marquardt, the very name "Palestinians" is already confusing, because it is (1) connected with the Roman period and is thus a derogatory name for *Erez Israel*, and (2) because Palestinians are Arabs, who themselves only became an identifiable community with the beginning of Islam, so that the ancestors of "the people who *understand themselves as the Palestinian people*"[72] really are "Arabic Palestinians".[73] However, Marquardt has difficulty identifying the G-d he encounters in Jesus Christ with the G-d who decrees the primacy of the Jewish people with regard to this particular land in a way that at best degrades other people living in the land to second class citizens and at worst has them expelled or killed.[74] He almost suggests a parting of Christians and Jews on this issue, but then goes on to identify the positive effect the biblical claim of the Jewish people to the land should/could have on the victims of this decree, on the others already living there – since even in biblical times the land was not empty.[75] Because the promise of the land is bound to so many specific conditions, which are intended to guarantee the welfare of all its inhabitants, Marquardt's analysis attempts to keep a balance between an emphasis on the necessity of the fulfilment of Torah for the Jewish people to enter and remain in the land (the land is not a possession of the people but given only for the purpose of devoting space to Torah) and the affirmation of the State of Israel as a sign of G-d's faithfulness to the Jewish people. In this analysis, Palestinians must remain second class citizens, as Marquardt indicates in developing the notion of a "theology on the far side of God"[76] with regard to the Palestinians. Marquardt suggests John the Baptist as a figure of identification for Palestinians. John the Baptist demanded justice, relied on the identification of G-d with the Jewish people and confessed: "After me comes a man who ranks ahead of me because he was before me" (John 1:30). Imagining himself in the position of a Palestinian Christian, Marquardt interprets the Palestinian situation with the help of the Christological statement of the identification of Jesus with the Jewish people:

---

[72] Ibid. 198.

[73] Ibid. 198.

[74] Cf. ibid. 200ff.

[75] Cf. ibid. 202ff.

[76] Ibid. 285. Marquardt makes a reference to Psalm 130:1 about the possibility of calling to G-d out of the depths, and maybe of even praising G-d from this position (cf. ibid. 276).

> I would think, by thinking in a "Christ-centred" way about Jesus, about Jesus the Jew, about *Jesus not without his people*, whom he represents. Thus I would hear this word of John not only as a word about this particular "man", but also as a word about his people. After me comes his Jewish people. Before me was his Jewish people. It was the First before me and my Palestinian people. I would hear this surely with trembling, even with horror. I would hear it reluctantly.[77]

Marquardt knows about the danger of assuming a position which is so far from his own context and calls his suggestions immediately into question.[78] Nevertheless he is able to suggest the possibility and even viability of a "theology on the far side of God" to Palestinians.[79] Thereby Marquardt's argument about the mutual dependence of biblical testimony and historical experience for the development of theology disintegrates. His understanding of the relationship between G-d-People-Land as a given appears unable to take into account different interpretations of the relationship of Jews to the land of Israel/Palestine – and the State of Israel. Tobias Kriener summarises Marquardt's position poignantly:

> The permanent measure for the behaviour of the nations – for the assessment of international politics and thereby also for Middle Eastern politics – is solely their behaviour towards Israel: "Israel the measure with which God judges the nations."[80]

Marquardt's (re-)orientation of his theology towards the Jewish people, born out of the need to address the challenge the Holocaust presents to Christianity, has the potential to lose its humanity towards people whose existence and cause conflicts with his interpretation of the Jewish people and what he sees as Jewish needs and well-being. Arguably Marquardt's contextual theology loses sight of its context which is the FRG and makes universal assertions. A consequence of these universal assertions is the danger of substituting one form of discrimination for another.[81]

Marquardt's theology presents a courageous attempt to confront implications of the murder of Jews in the Holocaust for Christian theology in Germany. His theology remains continually threatened by the possibility that after the Holocaust any theology may become an impossibility, because he interprets the Holocaust as an assault on G-d's witnesses. With the murder of G-d's witnesses G-d's divinity becomes uncertain. However, Marquardt assumes a *sui generis* relationship between G-d-People-Land to which, he claims, Christian faith has to relate if it wants to be true to the revelation of the Bible and which has been confirmed by Jewish survival and the founding of the State of Israel. Thus he appears confident in arguing that Christian theology can

---

[77] Ibid. 285.

[78] Cf. ibid. 285.

[79] And he finds support for this position cf. for example Pfisterer 1992, 83-100.

[80] Kriener 1999, 222.

[81] Cf. also the criticism in Fuchs 1997, 168ff. and Brumlik 1998b, 185.

overcome the antisemitism built into it since its beginning.[82] As a consequence of this modification of the "radical paradigm" (Stephen Haynes), he suggests that

> In Judaism I reach my "biblical" self-understanding – in fact not through identification but through the discovery of my Christian identity in the Jewish roots which have not died and which carry me (as a Christian), and through the significance of the existence and endurance of the Jewish people for my (gentile) Christian heart and "being" which cannot be lost. [...] You *will* no longer kill Jews if you recognise how much you owe your Christian identity to their life alongside you, and if you acknowledge that you would loose yourself if you do not do everything to protect their "difference", their identity and the integrity of their life.[83]

2. Representing the Holocaust and Jews – Consequences

This brief introduction to Marquardt's dogmatic theology demonstrates how deep a crisis the Holocaust constitutes for his thought, as well as his struggle to renew Christian theology by redefining its relationship to Jews and Judaism. Marquardt's theology has received widespread recognition from theologians engaged in Christian-Jewish conversations in the FRG.[84]

Drawing on some of these responses Marquardt's representation of the Holocaust will be explored in more detail as well as his representation of Jews and Judaism. This will suggest consequences for Holocaust remembrance implicit in Marquardt's theology against the background of efforts at remembering the Holocaust in German society outlined in the previous chapter.

2.1. The Holocaust

As outlined above, because of Christian dependence on Jews for Christian faith, Marquardt interprets the crisis the Holocaust has brought for Christianity as unprecedented. According to Marquardt, the attempt to wipe out Jewish life on earth meant an attempt to deny the reality of G-d, because Jews are the prime witnesses to G-d's reality. Assaulting G-d's witnesses ultimately means denying the possibility of Christian faith.

> Together with the Jews the election, the covenant and faithfulness, of the God of Abraham, Isaac and Jacob, of the father of Jesus Christ, were abandoned, was God attacked and denied in the centre of his self-expression as true, living God. With this, then, Auschwitz has a

---

[82] Cf. also Marquardt 1998a, 86f.

[83] Marquardt 1998b, 120f.

[84] Cf. Hennecke/Weinrich (eds.) 1998 and Lehming/Liß-Walther/Loebroks/Veg (eds.) 1999. Cf. also Funke 1991; Henrix 1989; Henrix 1993 and Klappert 1994.

theological dimension of its own. Alongside the category of destroyed reason steps the category of guilt and of a blindness of Christian faith, its theology and the church.[85]

To Marquardt the Holocaust appears to assume a function beyond "the signs of the times". Marquardt argues that the Holocaust questions whether G-d can still be G-d:

> But *of what use is the word "God"*, when [...]six million Jews and after that millions upon millions of other people are gassed and decayed to death? With them God could have lost his divinity: because he did not *save*; first and foremost (and this is the epitomisation of his forlornness): because he did not *hinder* those people who were baptised from murdering [...] and because he did not motivate these to life-saving acts and rather to die themselves than to tolerate the crimes. But my problem is not that thereby God could have made himself impossible, but my problem is that people who have been rescued from the ovens, survive alongside me, people who have lost God in there with the aid of Christians. Not God, but *their* godforsakenness challenges me and this is the problem I cannot solve. [...][86]

Although Marquardt shifts the focus of his inquiry away from G-d to the people traumatised by the Holocaust, the Holocaust takes on the status of an additional revelatory event. Marquardt himself denies that his interpretation of the Holocaust and its consequences introduce the Holocaust as a revelatory event, by pointing to the fact that he focuses on the human dimension of survival and the need as Christians to take responsibility for the atrocities.[87] However, it is the fundamental nature of the relationship between the Jewish people and G-d, and hence the *sui generis* nature of the Christian-Jewish relationship, which afflicts theology in the Holocaust – and centuries of failing to recognise in faith and theology the importance of this relationship. The history of the Jewish people is understood as the normative paradigm of human history, where G-d shows G-d's concern for humanity in the particularity of G-d's concern for the Jewish people. Consequently, Jews are interpreted as the witnesses to G-d's concern for humanity. Thus Christian action in the Holocaust has challenged G-d's concern for the world: "If we lose our humanity towards Israel, he [G-d] loses the witnesses of his humanity towards us."[88]

From this it can be concluded that (1) the Holocaust (if understood as encompassing Marquardt's assumption of a revelatory dimension) could only happen to the Jewish people because of the unique nature of their relationship with G-d. Had the same assault been committed on any other people, it would not have been an assault on G-d-self and consequently would not have challenged the possibility of Christian theology; (2) where other genocide continues to happen it is related to the failure of Christians to understand their relationship with the Jewish people and the relationship of the Jewish people with G-d. How Christians relate to Jews, then, indicates how

---

[85] Marquardt [2]1992, 77.
[86] Marquardt 1998a, 83f.
[87] Cf. Marquardt 1998c, 162f. as well as Marquardt 1998a, 87.
[88] Marquardt [2]1992, 145.

Christians relate to all other peoples. If they fail to recognise the humanity of Jews and of G-d's humanity to the Jewish people in their unique relationship – which is interpreted as signifying G-d's intentions for all humanity – they will fail to understand the humanity of all other peoples.

Consequently, to Marquardt, the primacy of the Jewish people becomes an <u>ontological</u> statement without which Christian faith has no foundation. Because of the ontological dependence of Christian life and faith on the Jewish people theology has been questioned by the Holocaust – where the life of the Jewish people and therefore, according to Marquardt, the recognisability of G-d in this world was endangered and with this the possibility of Christian life and faith – in an unprecedented radicality. Therefore any future theology has to make the dependence of Christian faith on Jewish people a precondition for <u>any</u> theological thought. Thus, Marquardt's theology relies in every aspect on Jewish life past and present.

The consequences of Marquardt's definition of the Holocaust and Jews for the understanding of humanity are severe. Introducing an ontological difference between Jews and other people carries the danger of denigrating the victims of other genocides and atrocities, because these can never have a theological significance similar to the Holocaust. Marquardt demonstrated this potential denigration of victims of atrocity in his "theology on the far side of God" as a suggestion for Palestinian self-understanding in relation to Israel. The theological justification given for this privileging of Jewish life could be read as contextual to Germany where it is the mass murder of Jews that questions the viability and ethic of Christian life. However, Marquardt claims that the dependence of Christian life on Jews is a universal principle for theology.

Having defined the Holocaust as an event in the history of the relationship of G-d with the Jewish people, Marquardt addresses the Holocaust with the help of survivor testimony and Jewish religious responses from the USA and Canada.[89] Marquardt writes detached from the events of the Holocaust, hardly ever naming these in any detail. He interprets "Auschwitz" as an event that has impacted on theology in a particular way and asserts that it is the task of theology to discover how it has changed the nature and condition of theology.[90] While not making the Holocaust itself a subject of his theology, he nevertheless demands that theology thinks from the perspective of its victims. Thus his understanding of the Holocaust is implied in the terminology he uses and the testimony and religious responses he refers to in his reflections on the impact of the Holocaust on Christian theology.

---

[89] Cf. ibid. 118ff.
[90] Norbert Reck observes: "Ähnlich denkt auch Friedrich-Wilhelm Marquardt an Auschwitz nicht als ein 'Thema', mit dem sich Theologie beschäftigen müßte, sondern als ein Ereignis, von dem sie längst schon in ihrem Lebensnerv getroffen ist" (cf. Reck 1998, 87 note 156).

Marquardt begins with the presupposition that the Holocaust is unique[91] and that it is impossible to understand what happened in the Holocaust, that the world of the Holocaust is not accessible to people who have not witnessed it first hand. However, he believes that the experience of the victims can be articulated.[92] He then tries to approach this world of the Holocaust, the *l'univers concentrationnaire*, with reflections of a survivor on his time in Auschwitz. However, first a word on the terminology employed by Marquardt.

In his writing Auschwitz dominates as the term used to describe the events of the Holocaust. In the subject index at the end of the *Prolegomena* Marquardt lists "*Auschwitz – Holocaust –Schoa*"[93] as three interchangeable terms for the same event. However, in the text he invariably uses Auschwitz, except for a few changes to Holocaust in the latter part of the book. *Schoah* never occurs in the main text.[94] Only in the context of presenting Jean Améry's testimony does Marquardt refer to the Holocaust as *l'univers concentrationnaire*.[95] The names with which events are

---

[91] In volume 2 of his eschatology Marquardt explains uniquess following in part Eberhard Jäckel's understanding: "*Unvergleichlich* war und bleibt an der Schoah folgendes: 1. Die nationalsozialistische Judenvernichtung war anders als alle anderen Genozide, ein ideologisch und gesellschaftlich, also theoretisch allgemein universal konzipiertes *Ziel*, während andere Massenvernichtungen militärische oder politische *Reaktionen* in begrenzt gegebenen Verhältnissen waren [...] Dagegen sollten nur die Juden – u.zw. sie als *Juden* und sie *alle* – ermordet werden. 2. Bei anderen Genoziden bildeten die Verfolgten in irgendeinem Sinne eine politische oder gesellschaftliche oder militärische Gegenfront gegen die herrschenden Mächte oder ihre Ziele. Davon kann beim Judentum keine Rede sein . [...] 3. [...] Nur im Falle der deutschen Judenmorde stand *außerdem* das ganze *Gesellschaft*ssystem mit Recht, Religion, Kunst, Wissenschaft, seelischen Einstellungen von Bevölkerungsmehrheiten im Dienst der Mordmaschine. [...] Nur im Falle der Judenmorde gibt es eine zweitausendjährige Diffamierungs-, Verdrängungs-, Unterwerfungs- und Vernichtungs'kultur', damit auch ein kollektives Unbewußtes von Urteilen, Verurteilungen, die schon lange einen Lösungs- und Bereinigungsdruck im Bewußtsein von Generationen erzeugt hatten. 'Endlösung' war *geschichtlich* und kulturell lange möglich. [...] Nicht nur die *Zahl* der jüdischen Opfer, sondern *Ziel und System* ihrer Opferung sind unvergleichlich. [...] Für die Tötung anderer Bevölkerungen ließen sich immer irgendwelche Gründe nennen, nur Juden wurden grundlos, allein um ihres Todes willen getötet. Hier schlägt Zeitgeschichte um in Theologie [...] Es ist so auch das *Ende der Theologie*; und wir geben damit nicht einer Emotion im Denken nach, sondern drücken dessen Krisis aus, derer wir nicht Herr werden können und von der wir nicht einmal wissen, ob der an seinem Augapfel geblendete Gott ihrer noch einmal Herr werden will. Jedenfalls weist die Betroffenheit Gottes von der Schoah noch einmal auf den Systemcharakter der Todeswirklichkeit hin, und nirgendwo wie am Judenmord wird dies greifbar [...]" (Marquardt 1994, 45-47). That Marquardt sympathises with Daniel Goldhagen's views on German antisemitism is implicit in the text, he emphasises this explicitly in Marquardt 1998a, 86 and Marquardt 1998c, 164.

[92] Cf. Marquardt [2]1992, 119.

[93] Ibid. 472.

[94] This use of terminology is consistent throughout his dogmatic theology; only in the eschatology he repeatedly uses *Schoah*.

[95] Cf. ibid. 118.

identified carry meaning for the group of people to whom an event is relevant. Naming an event is the first act of owning it as part of one's own relevant memory. To Marquardt, Auschwitz has become the most powerful symbol of the Holocaust which he privileges over any other term available. He writes that no other concentration camp was "like Auschwitz"[96]. What are the implications of this statement? Given that Marquardt intends to communicate Jewish experience and history and the challenge these bring to Christian faith and theology, I would argue that he understands Auschwitz to name a place and a series of events that are particular to Jewish experience and which have become revelatory to Christians.

"Auschwitz" was the name for the largest complex of camps and has the largest number of survivors.[97] Thus testimony from Auschwitz is more frequent than that from other camps or sites of the Holocaust. However, in a theology that wants to privilege the voices of victims and argues that Christian theology has silenced Jewish voices throughout history, such a focusing of language and testimony on Auschwitz appears incongruous with the aims of the theology. There are more "Jewish" names for the Holocaust and Auschwitz may not be the most "Jewish" camp. The number of non-Jews present at Auschwitz, the use of the camp complex for slave labour and hence selections for work or death etc. arguably make Auschwitz an "untypical" Jewish experience of the Holocaust.[98] "The large majority of Polish Jews fell victim to Operation Reinhard in the three camps at Belzec, Sobibor, and Treblinka"[99], more than 1.5 million people. The sole purpose of the camps associated with "Operation Reinhard" – Belzec, Sobibor and Treblinka – was murder and these camps were operational only in the short time between February 1942 and November 1943.[100] There are few testimonies available from these camps, given the small number of survivors. After 1945 the sites of these camps were located in the sphere of influence of the Soviet Union and in the West these sites of murder were almost forgotten. Arguably, by not addressing the murder of Polish Jewry in particular, the circumstances of their murder, their testimony and the absence of testimony as well as the culture that died with them, Marquardt contributes with his theology to the silencing of their voices – the voices of victims he wishes to privilege theologically.[101]

---

[96] Ibid. 131.
[97] For an introductory overview cf. Benz 1999, 131ff.
[98] Cf. also Gutman/Berenbaum (eds.) 1994.
[99] Benz 1999, 151. Cf. also Benz (ed.) 1991,.
[100] Cf. for example Benz 1999, 143-152. Cf. also Yahil 1990, 356-375.
[101] Cf. also Levi 1988, 83f.: "we, the survivors, are not the true witnesses [...] We survivors are not only an exiguous but also an anomalous minority: we are those who by their prevarications or abilities or good luck did not touch bottom. Those who did so [...] have not returned to tell about it, or have returned mute, but they are the 'Muslims,' the submerged, the complete witness, the ones whose deposition would have general significance."

A theology which wants to privilege the witness of victims would also have to pay attention to the diversity of Jewish experience in the Holocaust and take care in naming different Jewish approaches to these experiences.[102] To name but a few that spring to mind immediately: hiding, ghettos, partisans, mass shootings by the *Einsatzgruppen* ("mobile killing squads"), Eastern and Western European Jews, different religious and ideological orientations of Jews murdered, Jewish men, women and children, etc. The list could easily be continued. This is not to say that Marquardt would have to include reflections on these experiences in his *Prolegomena*. However, if he is serious about grounding his theology in the voices of victims, then he needs to show awareness of who these people were, and are.[103]

A further implication of using Auschwitz as the key term for the events of the Holocaust is its connection with Polish history. Marquardt claims Auschwitz as Jewish, bemoaning the fact that few Christian witnesses became martyrs in Auschwitz and that the Christian martyrs in other concentration camps were few.[104] He does not specify whether he thinks about Christians from Germany, but this seems to be implied in the context. However, while the victims of Auschwitz-Birkenau were in the majority Jewish, the prisoner of the *Stammlager* Auschwitz I were in the majority non-Jewish. Auschwitz I, in particular, was the place of Polish suffering and death, where many resistance fighters of the Polish intelligentsia, priests and slave labourers were murdered. These were Christians who are remembered by Poles as martyrs. The importance of the sites of Auschwitz to both Jews and Poles is subject of a number of controversies about the use of religious symbolism at the sites.[105]

The implications of Marquardt's use of the term Auschwitz as an exclusive name for the events of the Holocaust suggest that its use is problematic. By using Auschwitz he contradicts his own intentions in approaching Christian theology from the perspective of victims of the Holocaust, because his terminology excludes many places of NS atrocity. These observations concerning Marquardt's terminology extend to his understanding of "victim" which in Marquardt's texts never loses the ambiguity implied in its other meaning of "sacrifice". The understanding of the dead Jews of the Holocaust as "sacrifices" is particularly strong in the passage defining the uniqueness of the Holocaust, where he states that "Not only the *number* of the Jewish victims

---

[102] Such a theology does not necessarily need to adopt Jewish terminology. Reck argues that "auf die im Judentum gängigen Begriffe glaubte ich verzichten zu sollen, weil sie [...] religiöse Deutungen aus der Opferperspektive enthalten, die einem christlichen Autor nicht zustehen [...]" (Reck 1998, 27).

[103] For a recent suggestion how to incorporate perspectives of victims theologically cf. Reck 1998. Reck also includes reflections on the term victim and the different perceptions of "victim of the Holocaust" and "survivor of the Holocaust" which are part of Holocaust literature and discussion of Holocaust testimony.

[104] Cf. Marquardt [2]1992, 131.

[105] For an overview of the events and an introduction to issues of the discussion cf. Rittner/Roth (eds.) 1991.

[*Opfer*], but the *aim and system* of their sacrifice [*Opferung*] are incomparable."[106] The question arises as to who qualifies as a victim and a survivor and hence on whose perspective Marquardt wants to ground his theology. Are the victims the dead and the survivors or only the dead? Marquardt emphasises survival as the human condition after Auschwitz:

> For me it is not the world-historic event of Auschwitz as such that is the turning point, but rather the survival after Auschwitz, which divides humanity into surviving victims and surviving perpetrators; to me this abyss between the survivors is a theological provocation. [...] As I understand it [...] the issue is the suffering of survival [...][107]

Lawrence Langer describes the power of language to interpret challenging events in a manner that allows us to integrate them into our frameworks of interpretation and thus

> to change the impact of a disastrous event simply by renaming it. When we speak of the survivor instead of the victim and of martyrdom instead of murder, regard being gassed as a pattern for dying with dignity, or evoke the redemptive rather than the grievous power of memory, we draw on an arsenal of words that urges us to build verbal fences between the atrocities of the camps and ghettos and what we are mentally willing – or able – to face.[108]

The way Marquardt invests the notion of Jewish survival with meaning as the only hope for a future of Christian faith and theology suggests a renaming of the Holocaust in the sense that it provides a lifeline for Christianity, albeit an uncertain one. Does the perspective of the victims and survivors themselves matter? Does it matter that such an appropriation of the Holocaust would be offensive to survivors? Are the victims necessarily Jewish and if so, who determines who is Jewish?[109] Does it matter that there are comparatively few testimonies of the people who died in the Holocaust, so that it is close to impossible to gain their perspective on the events?[110] The impact of these questions become apparent when analysing the use of Améry's testimony in Marquardt's *Prolegomena*.

To Marquardt, Améry becomes the key witness, who is able to verbalise the conditions of Auschwitz and thus communicate them to people who do not share these experiences. Améry testifys to the situation of the intellectual in a concentration camp where any intellectual exercise becomes utterly meaningless, where what was taken for granted before no longer had any significance, where what had been learned could

---

[106] Marquardt 1994, 46.
[107] Marquardt 1998a, 87. Cf. also Marquardt 1996, 393, and also in the sense of hoping for a proof that G-d is alive (cf. ibid. 507).
[108] Langer 1995, 6.
[109] For an introduction to issues in defining Jewishness cf. Webber 1994, 3ff.
[110] Cf. for example the small number of survivors of the camps at Belzec, Sobibor and Treblinka and the subsequent amnesia about such places. Reck avoids the term victims in this context and instead speaks of witnesses, cf. Reck 1998.

no longer be applied.[111] Marquardt understands Améry to be a witness to the dehumanisation in a concentration camp which changes anything known thus far about the condition of reason and intellect. He concludes that

> This means: Auschwitz has become an anthropological condition which is indestructible in its surviving victims as well as in the people who have been spared and which changes intellect and reason, so that they are different from what they were before.[112]

Several issues arise from this portrayal of the destructive and dehumanising quality of the Holocaust. Marquardt does not give a reason for choosing Améry from the wealth of testimony available. Améry's witness does not include much narrative about the day-to-day life in Auschwitz, but can be read as a reflection on what the camp system does to the human mind and spirit. As such it corresponds to the level of reflection and language Marquardt is using and is thus easier to incorporate than a narrative testimony. In a way, Améry appears to point out what Marquardt himself has concluded from the Holocaust. Thus Marquardt's own interpretation of the Holocaust is confirmed by a survivor. However, Marquardt does not explore Améry's perspective on his experiences in Auschwitz. In this context, it is interesting to note that Marquardt introduces Améry as an intellectual and chooses not to reveal anything else about his biography.[113] If he did, Améry's analysis of the dehumanisation in Auschwitz might not read so well as a piece of intellectual work on the destruction of the intellect in the camp. Améry's biography and writing communicate a destruction of a person that goes far beyond what Marquardt is presenting in his exploration of Auschwitz.

Born as Hans Meyer in Austria, son of a Catholic mother of Jewish ancestry and a Jewish father, Améry was fully assimilated and began to recognise his Jewishness only after the proclamation of the Nuremberg Laws.[114] He fled to Belgium, joined the resistance movement and was arrested in 1943 and sent to Auschwitz when identified as Jewish. Liberated in Bergen-Belsen by the British, Améry moved to Brussels and for twenty years he refused to travel to Germany or speak to a German audience.[115] His Jewish identity was contested by Jewish intellectuals and religious leaders.[116] He understood his Jewishness only in terms of the Nuremberg Laws. Améry committed suicide in 1978. In his collection of autobiographical essays *At the Mind's Limits*[117] written in the 1960s for a German audience, Améry explores how his experiences in the Holocaust have affected his identity. He portrays how the Holocaust has alienated

---

[111] Cf. Marquardt [2]1992, 119ff.

[112] Ibid. 123.

[113] This lack of biographical information about Améry could also be attributed to the fact that Marquardt assumes that his readers are familiar with Améry's writings.

[114] Cf. Rosenfeld 1980, 106.

[115] Cf. ibid. 107.

[116] Cf. ibid. 109.

[117] Améry 1980.

him from what he considered home and how impossible it is to put anything into its place:

> We, however, had not lost our country, but had to realize that it had never been ours. For us, whatever was linked with this land and its people was an existential misunderstanding. What we believed to have been our first love was, as they said there, racial disgrace. What we thought had constituted our nature – was it ever anything else but mimicry?[118]

Even more pronounced is his perception of his separation from the German language, on which he as a writer depended:

> I was excluded from the fate of the German community and thus from its language. "Enemy bomber," fine, but for me these were the German bombers that were laying the cities of England in ruins, and not the flying fortresses of the Americans, which were attending to the same business in Germany. The meaning of every German word changed for us, and finally, whether we resisted or not, our mother tongue became just as inimical as the one they spoke around us.[119]

The Nuremberg Laws dissociated Améry from German culture in such a way that reclaiming it at any point became impossible. Referring to Thomas Mann's saying "Wherever I am is German culture", Améry writes

> The German-Jewish Auschwitz prisoner could not have made such a bold assertion, even if by chance he had been a Thomas Mann. He could not claim German culture as his possession, because his claim found no sort of social justification. Among the émigrés a tiny minority was able to constitute itself as German culture, even if there was not exactly a Thomas Mann among them. In Auschwitz, however, the isolated individual had to relinquish all of German culture, including Dürer and Reger, Gryphius and Trakl, to even the lowest SS man.[120]

The alienation described by Améry is more than the destruction of the intellect referred to by Marquardt. It is not intellect in the abstract that is destroyed, but a particular intellectual, cultural and linguistic identity of the community of Jews from Germany and German speaking countries which were part of the Third Reich. Reason and intellect are not destroyed for the SS man in the above quotation. His world remains intact. The rupture in Améry's identity is made even more apparent when considering that he writes in German to a German audience. He is writing in the language of the culture that has excluded him violently. He is producing an intellectual piece of writing about the failure of intellect and reason. Marquardt's reproduction of the results of Améry's inquiry cannot reproduce what Améry himself has experienced, but it could witness to Améry's sense of betrayal and loss. However, Marquardt's own work shows little signs of the change he claims has come about for intellect and reason. His combination of biblical and contemporary contextualities relies on reason and intellect

---

[118] Ibid. 50.
[119] Ibid. 53.
[120] Ibid. 8.

working as they did before. He relies on the work of religious thinkers and theologians of past centuries. His language displays the intellectual tradition of German Protestant theology without showing any discomfort at using it.[121] The discrepancy between what Améry writes and what Marquardt argues throughout his theology becomes even more apparent when considering Améry's understanding of his Jewishness:

> Society, concretized in the National Socialist German state, which the world recognized absolutely as the legitimate representative of the German people, had just made me formally and beyond any question a Jew, or rather it had given a new dimension to what I had already known earlier, but which at the time was of no great consequence to me, namely, that I was a Jew.[122]

According to Améry, he is only a Jew because someone else makes him into one and because he has lost all other forms of identification.

> To be a Jew, that meant for me, from this moment on, to be a dead man on leave, someone to be murdered, who only by chance was not yet where he properly belonged; and so it has remained, in many variations, in various degrees of intensity, until today.[123]

After the Holocaust Améry identifies as Jewish in an act of solidarity, a solidarity Améry did not choose, but which was produced by the circumstances of NS.

> Solidarity in the face of threat is all that links me with my Jewish contemporaries, the believers as well as the nonbelievers, the national-minded as well as those ready to assimilate.[124]

Améry does not associate a religious or national belief or identity with his Jewishness. Rather it is a condition of being which does not form his identity, but which stands in place of an identity that has been taken from him and cannot be substituted by anything else. He has no pre-NS Jewish identity to fall back on or to recover after the war, and therefore, he argues he cannot "become" Jewish, because "No one can become what he cannot find in his memory."[125] As such it is a negative definition of Jewishness. Hence

---

[121] This is evident, for example, in the titles Marquardt uses throughout his dogmatic theology which frequently employ Latin and Greek terminology which, by his own admission, is part of a longstanding antisemitic tradition: "Christus omnium magister", "theologia archetypos – theologia ektypos", "Damnando fit theologus" in the *Prolegomena* or "Christus: promissio omnium promissionum fons", "Praesens historicum oder praesens eschatologicum", "de adventu Domini et de resurrectione caris" and "de extremo iudicio et de vita aeterna" in the *Eschatology*. In his definition of the uniqueness of the Holocaust he does not appear to have any difficulties in using NS terminology, such as "Massenvernichtung", "liquidiert", "Ausrottung" cf. Marquardt 1994, 45-47.

[122] Améry 1980, 85.

[123] Ibid. 86.

[124] Ibid. 98.

[125] Ibid. 84.

If being a Jew means sharing a religious creed with other Jews, participating in Jewish culture and family tradition, cultivating a Jewish national ideal, then I find myself in a hopeless situation. I don't believe in the God of Israel. I know very little about Jewish culture.[126]

Marquardt's assertion that theology needs to think from the perspective of the victims of the Holocaust comes in conflict with his grounding of theology in the relationship between Christians and Jews. Marquardt derives his understanding of the Holocaust from the writing of a Jew who is not necessarily recognised by other Jews as Jewish, who is not Jewish of his own choice, but rather has been made Jewish by NS, who has been violently separated from his culture and language, who has permanently lost his name and who is not religious:[127] "I entered the prisons and the concentration camps as an agnostic and, on April 15, 1945, freed by the British in Bergen-Belsen, I left the Inferno as an agnostic."[128] Améry's writing is directly opposed to what Marquardt is trying to achieve. From its starting point Marquardt's theology cannot incorporate what Améry is saying, because this would undermine the ground on which he is basing his thought. Marquardt's thought is founded on the positive assumption of the ability of Jewish tradition to forge a link between biblical reality and the present context of theology, in spite of the Holocaust. In fact, Marquardt's theological enterprise bypasses the Holocaust and intends to redeem Christianity by interpreting the contemporary situation with the help of biblical contexts seen through the eyes of Jewish tradition. According to Marquardt, thinking from the perspective of the victims does not mean from the perspective of the victims of the Holocaust, but rather more generally from that of Jews and their traditions which have developed alongside Christian thought. Norbert Reck explores in his doctoral dissertation the possibilities for Christian theology to think from the perspective of survivors of the Holocaust and to make the narratives of survivor testimony the starting point for theological reflection.[129] He concludes in the context of reflecting on the use of testimony from the Holocaust in post-Holocaust theology that

However, the voices of the victims – if they gain a hearing at all – exist more on the fringes in an ornamental capacity, expressing a motto in the form of quotations which sometimes precede individual chapters. That thoughts and observations from the testimonies of victims have found entry into theological reflection as challenges can rarely be discerned [...]. However, even more significant is the fact that the epistemological question of what we are at all able to know about Auschwitz has largely not been recognised as a problem. In particular the above mentioned conglomeration of various references witnesses to a naivety which appears to assume that everyone at all times knows with precise clarity and without difficulties of access what

---

[126] Ibid. 83.
[127] Cf. also Rosenfeld 1994, 59-69.
[128] Améry 1980, 12.
[129] Cf. Reck 1998, in particular, 90ff.

happened in Auschwitz. In the theology after Auschwitz the question regarding the origin of knowledge about Auschwitz is generally not asked.[130]

The fact that Marquardt chooses a survivor testimony only as an illustration and that he does not include reflections on testimony of dead and surviving victims of the Holocaust in his theology becomes clearer when he reflects on Jewish religious writings on the Holocaust. He presents the approaches of Richard Rubenstein and Emil Fackenheim, but does not comment. Regarding Rubenstein he concludes as follows: "We listen. We forgo any criticism which could be directed at this model theologically, historically and psychologically."[131] Similarly, he does not comment on Fackenheim. In effect this represents a refusal to engage with the thought of these two Jewish thinkers. In Marquardt's reflection the Holocaust becomes a symbolic event, a canvas which can be inscribed with meaning and which leads directly to the reflection on Christian identity after the Holocaust.[132]

> It is our task to understand the murder of one third of world Jewry in its shocking quality which moves God and accuses us and to estimate what it means that God was not witnessed to in Auschwitz. It teaches us: the Jewish witnesses to God are irreplaceable for the Christological integrity of his [G-d's] being, to enable us to recognise him in his unity as the true God and the true human and the Holy Spirit which is poured out over all flesh to revive it. If we lose our humanity towards Israel, he [G-d] loses the witnesses of his humanity towards us. Put differently: the life of the Jewish witnesses to God is indispensable for a Christian faith that wants to confess the living God. And if there is any task at all for theology after Auschwitz then it is this: to think about what is missing in God if we give up Israel.[133]

However, the question arises how Marquardt can arrive at the conclusion that G-d was not witnessed to in Auschwitz. With whose authority can he make such a decision? He quotes that "the dead don't praise God" (Ps 115:17) and concludes that

> In Auschwitz they [Jews] could no longer be his witnesses, there they died as his witnesses, there he was not witnessed to, there he was at least no longer their God, the God of their witness.[134]

Marquardt confuses different statements. There is a contradiction between saying that Jews could not be witnesses any more in Auschwitz and that Jews died as witnesses to G-d. If Jews die as witnesses to G-d, then they must have witnessed. Further how can Marquardt be the judge of Jewish witness anyhow? Metz, for example, makes the

---

[130] Ibid. 95f.
[131] Marquardt [2]1992, 127.
[132] Cf. ibid. 138f.
[133] Ibid. 145.
[134] Ibid. 144.

opposite assertion that prayer after the Holocaust is only possible, because Jews prayed, and thus witnessed, in Auschwitz.[135]

Marquardt appears confused as to who Jews are – *Halachic* and other definitions of Jewish identity are not even mentioned – while at the same time having firm ideas as to what "Jewish witness" constitutes – as for example in his characterisations of what he understands as the relationship of Jews with G-d. The Jewish responses to the Holocaust Marquardt refers to are written by scholars who are either religious but not orthodox and hence approach Jewish tradition differently from orthodox Jews (Fackenheim and Rubenstein) or they are agnostic and have difficulty in identifying themselves as Jewish and being identified as Jewish by others (Améry). It strikes me as ironic that Marquardt does not address orthodox Jewish responses to the Holocaust, some of which deny his understanding of the Holocaust in terms of "rupture" (of a Jewish relationship with G-d) and which could be said to reflect the standpoint of the majority of Jewish victims of the Holocaust.[136] Arguably, Polish Jewry was the most traditionally religious and would draw on Jewish tradition to interpret their experiences in the Holocaust – a tradition which, at other points, Marquardt is keen to appropriate to Christian theology (cf. "Evangelical *Halachah*).

Marquardt wishes to introduce an awareness of victim perspectives on the Holocaust into the context of German Holocaust remembrance and its separation of German from Jewish memory of NS and the Holocaust. However, he appears unable to consider Jewish positions in their own right. Hence his appropriation of Jewish tradition and Holocaust memory for Christian theology and its "Christianisation" contributes more to the silencing of Jewish memory in a German Protestant context, than it allows to listen to Jewish self-expression in the context of Christian theology.

The confusion in Marquardt's understanding of Jews and his appropriation of Jewish tradition to Christian contexts is further apparent in his interpretation of "the Christian-Jewish relationship".

---

[135] Cf. Metz 1984. Reck notes that this does not imply that contemporary believers do not carry responsibility for their own faith, also in confrontation with the victims of the Holocaust (cf. Reck 1998, 139).

[136] Cf. for example Berkovits 1973; Schindler 1973 and more recently Rosenberg (ed.) 1992. Cf. also Wollaston 1995.

2.2. The Christian-Jewish relationship

In chapter seven of the *Prolegomena* entitled "How does Christian theology speak about Israel?"[137], Marquardt traces the history of Christian theological understanding of Jews and indicates possibilities for its future. According to Marquardt, Christian theological talk about Jews has focused traditionally on exegesis and dogmatic theology, ignoring the historical dimension of the task, "the relationship to the history and the witness of the Jewish people."[138] Only recently have theologians in Germany considered alternatives to this thinking. Marquardt locates a new theological beginning especially with Kraus' biblical theology.[139] According to Marquardt, Kraus identifies the existence of the Jewish people as the only proof for the existence of G-d.[140] He understands Jews and Judaism in the continuing history of the covenant of the Jewish people with G-d as revelation of G-d's relationship with humanity.[141] Thereby he defines Jews and Judaism in positive theological terms, positive also in the sense that they direct questions to the church "about the actual redemption of the world, about the completion of creation in the kingdom of God in this world and about the future of creation."[142] Marquardt wants to develop the kind of theological self-criticism implied in Kraus' understanding of the meaning of Jews and Judaism for Christian theology into dogmatic theological terms and make it an intrinsic part of his theology.[143] Therefore he links scripture and history and claims that "Judaism in its history needs to become the subject of a Christian *Israellehre*"[144], because

> The Hebrew Bible links Christians and Jews, but neither is it the theological basis of their mutual relationship – that is for the Christian Jesus Christ and the history of his influence – nor is it the code of law for the derivation of Christian definitions and judgments of Jews and Judaism.[145]

Marquardt introduces a parallelism of Jews with Christ. Both Jews and Christ refer to the same set of scriptures to explain their identity. By aligning Jews and Christ (and by extension Christ's followers) Marquardt introduces a Christological dimension to Judaism. Without asking whether Jews could appreciate a similar parallelism, Marquardt's argument interferes with Jewish self-definition. However, this interference with Jewish self-understandings introduces a contradiction into Marquardt's argument given that he wants to avoid Christian interference with Jewish identity.

---

[137] Cf. Marquardt [2]1992, 374-459.
[138] Ibid. 388.
[139] Cf. ibid. 385ff.
[140] Cf. Marquardt [2]1992, 386.
[141] Cf. ibid. 386.
[142] Kraus quoted in ibid. 386.
[143] Cf. ibid. 387.
[144] Ibid. 393.
[145] Ibid. 392.

The term "relationship" assumes extraordinary importance in Marquardt's theology. Relationship Marquardt understands to mean "relation of encounter" in opposition to a power-relationship where Christians subject Jews to their Christian definitions.[146] This new relationship of Christians and Jews should be based on the self-limitation of the church which determines that the role of the Christian should essentially be one of the learner and listener.[147] If definitions are offered at all they are self-definitions which limit the church rather than define and judge someone else.[148] Jews encounter the church as Other and challenge the church with their understanding of reality. Theology needs to understand what this challenge entails and how it should relate to it.[149] It cannot define Jews but has to relate to them.[150] Marquardt defines the Christian-Jewish relationship here in terms of a theology of reorientation, of a theology which tries to think from the perspectives of the Other, of the victims of theology.

> We hope to gain from this relationship a sensitivity and an ability to be moved, which we have lost in the intellectual alone. Physical wholeness of life prevents us from speaking about Judaism – and not thinking about dead and living Jews at the same time.[151]

Marquardt's understanding of the Christian-Jewish relationship is, then, a modification of the "witness-people myth". His approach intends to leave space for Jewish self-expression and wants to make this an essential part of his theology. That Christians cannot define Jews is an important presupposition of Marquardt's thought. Thereby he tries to prevent Christians from ever again understanding Jews as "signs for the church" in the sense of the negative models of the "witness-people myth". For Marquardt Jews can only be "signs for the church" when their significance as signs is learned through listening to Jews. Thus the historical and contemporary identity of Jews as expressed by Jews themselves becomes part of the "sign"-character Christians attribute to Jews. Only as "real" people can Jews be the signs the church understands them to be. And only if Jews are "real" people in the eyes of Christians can antisemitism be counteracted and avoided. Marquardt has adopted the framework of the "witness-people myth" not only as a theological safeguard against potential antisemitism, but also as a presupposition for his theology. To him this framework of thinking arises from the relationship between Christians and Jews constituted by the "Hebrew Bible" and is as such part of the foundation of his Christian faith. What Haynes understands to be common to all Christian Holocaust theology applies to Marquardt's approach to theology after the Holocaust in particular.[152]

---

[146] Cf. ibid. 393.
[147] Cf. ibid. 428.
[148] Cf. ibid. 428.
[149] Cf. ibid. 428f.
[150] Cf. ibid. 429ff.
[151] Ibid. 155.
[152] Cf. Haynes 1995a.

What emerges from Marquardt's understanding of the Christian-Jewish relationship from a biblical and historical perspective is the need to define – however limited – who the Jewish people are and what they are meant to be in G-d's world. Marquardt follows the theologies of Calvin and Barth and bases his theology on the reality of the election of the Jewish people into the covenant with G-d.[153] He concludes that there are theological statements Christians need to make about Judaism,[154] although Christians can by no means define what constitutes Judaism and Jewish identity.[155] Contrary to Marquardt's own intentions this constitutes a power-relationship in which the possibilities of Jewish self-definition are limited from the outset.[156] To be in a relationship with the Jewish people means that there must be an understanding of who Jews are and what they are meant to be. This amounts to a definition of Jewish identity which needs to be part of Christian faith and theology. Furthermore this definition needs to be <u>prior</u> to and even apart from any encounter with Jews. That this definition can be modified in the encounter and has to learn from Jewish self-expression, does not alter the fact that Christian theology needs a <u>Christian</u> understanding of Jews and Judaism to be able to function as Christian theology. If Christians need to know what the election of the Jewish people means to them, the "election of the Jewish people" is already a statement of faith which has to be believed about Jews. If Jews disagree with this, Christians can choose not to express their own belief about Jews as the chosen people. But since, according to Marquardt, the election of the Jewish people is fundamental for even the <u>possibility</u> of Christian faith, they have to continue to believe that Jews are the chosen people – or give up Christian faith. Although Marquardt's theology needs Jewish self-expression and self-definition, it implicitly has to limit the extent to which Jewish identities can inform Christian beliefs about Jews.

By particularly linking Christological statements so closely to Jewish thought, even if they could only be acknowledged in a potential, hypothetical way, Marquardt wants to make sure that theology cannot possibly develop without thinking of Jews first. Before formulating any theological statement, a detour via Judaism has to be taken, as a continuing reminder of Christianity's ontological dependence on Judaism and Jewish life. That this detour has to be taken is further guaranteed by the truth of faith that the relationship between Jews and G-d is <u>normative</u> and <u>a given</u> which has to be acknowledged by Christianity. From a Christian perspective this appears to be a watertight system against any possibility of antisemitism in theology which could be acted out in society. This Christian understanding of Judaism and contemporary Jewish life might render the negative elements of the "witness-people myth" invalid for positive reasons of faith. The traditional "witness-people myth" ambiguously united positive and negative elements with regard to contemporary Jewish life. By claiming

---

[153] Cf. Marquardt [2]1992, 132.
[154] Cf. ibid. 97.
[155] Cf. ibid. 429.
[156] Cf. ibid. 393.

that Christian faith is continually dependent on Judaism and Jewish life in history as well as today, Marquardt aims to abolish the need for the negative aspects of the myth.

Henrix's analysis of Marquardt's Christology demonstrates well how much Marquardt relies on the positive aspects of the "witness-people myth".[157] Henrix locates Marquardt's theology as a biblical theology which explores the "G-d-in-relationship" of the Bible:[158] "Whoever wants to get to know this God needs to look at the relationship between the God of Israel and the Israel of God and strive to participate in it."[159] With reference to Jn 4:22 – "salvation is from the Jews" – Marquardt's Christology finds its *Sitz im Leben* quite literally in the context of the contemporary Christian-Jewish relationship.[160] The aim of Marquardt's Christology is to

> work out a Christology which is no longer anti-Jewish in its substance, even more than that: a Christology which is so unambiguous that it also cannot be misused in an anti-Jewish way in practice.[161]

Marquardt wants to make Christological statements only if they could potentially be acknowledged by Jews which, according to him, is only possible if they can be argued in "biblical-Jewish" terms:

> *Among the norms that can today make recognisable the word of God in the word of humans belongs therefore the acknowledgement through Israel.* And it [this norm] is in my eyes also normative to the extent, that I am, in return, no longer really convinced by something as a commandment, a promise, a thought of God which lacks Israel's: "so be it" or which prevents Israel's appreciation right from the start or is not at all interested in it.[162]

The fact that G-d has chosen to bind G-d-self to a particular human community (the Jewish people) and is faithful to this union until today can be learned from Jews; the "repetition" and "recurrence" of this choosing of G-d and G-d's faithfulness in Christ can only be recognised when its first time occurrence has been properly learned from Jews.[163] This leads Marquardt to entitle the central paragraph of the second volume of the Christology "Israel as 'formal Christology'", thereby referring to Hans Urs von Balthasar's notion of "Israel as formal Christology".[164] If the relationship of G-d with human beings can be exemplarily learned from G-d's relationship with the Jewish

---

[157] Cf. Henrix 1993.

[158] Cf. ibid. 141.

[159] Ibid. 141.

[160] Cf. ibid. 141.

[161] Marquardt 1990, 105.

[162] Marquardt 1993, 162.

[163] Cf. Marquardt 1990, 44f. By employing the terms "repetition and recurrence" Marquardt tries to overcome the traditional structure of "promise and fulfilment" in which the relationship between G-d's election of the Jewish people and the election of Christ has been understood (cf. Henrix 1993, 143).

[164] Cf. Henrix 1993, 137.

people and if this relationship is repeated in Christ, then, Marquardt concludes, the Jewish people have a Christ-like relationship with G-d and must therefore be able to develop a Christology without actually referring to Christ.[165] This can only be stated from a Christian perspective which can recognise "in Judaism a world-historical witness to Christ outside of her [the church's] boundaries."[166] Marquardt's criterion for the possibility of this statement is that it must be possible to think Christology in "biblical-Jewish" terms; it is formal in the sense that it is a Christology without Christ, a Christology which relies on the structures of the relationship between humans and G-d as reflected in the history of the Jewish people.[167] The church needs to listen to the manifestations of Christology within Judaism, without interfering with it, since the church cannot develop a Christology without Christ.[168] But this Christology of Judaism can be understood by the church as an affirmation of its own Christological confession.[169] Here, again, the dependency of Christian theology on Jews becomes relevant.

Marquardt establishes a primacy of the Jewish people as the presupposition for his theology. This has consequences for his understanding of the relationship of Christians and Jews. That Christian faith is dependent on Jewish existence implies that Jews are ultimately responsible for Christian life. According to Marquardt's theology, Christian faith (and therefore life and theology) would be impossible without Jews. Furthermore, Marquardt's theology has to define Jewish identity to be able to assume Christian dependence on Jewish life. As a consequence Jewish disagreement with Marquardt's understanding of Judaism and Jewish identities is capable of endangering Christian faith. If Jews and Christians cannot agree on a basic religious definition of Jews and Judaism, Christian-Jewish conversations are in serious difficulty, because Christians will have to dispute Jewish self-understandings. The situation becomes even more complicated when Marquardt argues that Christians should be interested in Jewish acknowledgement of Christian theology, because Jewish approval is an indicator for discerning G-d's word in human speech.[170] Although Christian theology cannot ask for Jewish approval, it must always orient its thought towards what can be seen as potentially acceptable to Jews. This constitutes potential for antisemitism, although Marquardt is surely far from intending such.[171]

---

[165] Cf. Marquardt 1990, 58.

[166] Marquardt [2]1992, 429.

[167] Cf. Henrix 1993, 143.

[168] Cf. Marquardt [2]1992, 429.

[169] Cf. ibid. 429.

[170] Cf. Marquardt 1993, 162f.

[171] However, this appears to contradict his hermeneutical decision: "Ich binde das Verstehen der Bibel an die jüdische Zeitgenossenschaft meiner Generation. Nicht daß ich es ihrem Urteil unterwürfe und also das Judentum zur Wahrheitsinstanz der christlichen Lehre machte; das schüfe nur neuen Antijudaismus und würde auch dem christlichen Eigen-Bau nicht gerecht" (Marquardt 1998c, 167).

Similarly, the exclusion of contemporary Jewish experiences and theologies and the privileging of particular Holocaust testimonies and rabbinical theology is problematic. By making these forms of Jewish self-expression an indispensable part of Christian theology, Marquardt integrates a heritage into Christian thought which is traditionally not part of Christian discourse. That Christian theology draws on sources outside of Christian thought to reinterpret the Christian Bible and develop theological ideas is not new. However, how Christian theology does so warrants justification. Marquardt explains his use of rabbinical sources and Holocaust testimony by reference to the nature of the Christian-Jewish relationship which makes Jewish heritage also part of Christian heritage, since Christians can only rightfully exist in a relationship with Jews. Thus corrupted and sinful Christian tradition can be confronted and then be substituted by Jewish ideas, because these are part of a tradition Christians should always have learned from. However, in the chapters dealing with the land of Israel, Marquardt does not take into consideration contemporary Jewish religious literature on the land of Israel/Palestine, neither Orthodox Zionist positions, nor for example, the controversial writings of Marc Ellis.[172] This contradicts his presupposition that contemporary expressions of Jewish experience matter to Christian theology and that Christian self-understanding has to be learned in an encounter with Jews, however controversial their positions may be. Marquardt is not prepared to allow the same in the context of the State of Israel, where he gives hardly any space to contemporary Jewish writings – Martin Buber (1878-1965) and Franz Rosenzweig (1886-1929) being among the few 20th century Jewish authors referred to in this context.[173] Referring to post-Holocaust Christian definitions of Christian-Jewish relations, Ellis argues that

> If the Holocaust symbolizes the demonization of the Jews and in this way represents the alienation of Christianity from its source, by recovering the beauty of the Judaic faith and by realizing that Israel is chosen and that the gentiles are grafted onto that chosenness, the history of Christianity can be confessed *and* jettisoned. [...] In light of the Holocaust, it is almost incongruous that it is by relationship with the Jews, past and present, that salvation for the non-Jew is approached. Though it is an understanding reached through critical appraisal and soul-searching, it also functions to relieve Christians of a history that is difficult to identify with in a positive manner.[174]

While appreciating Marquardt's positive intentions, the Jewish philosopher Victor Kal criticises this Christian use of Jewish tradition. Referring to Marquardt's idea of an "Evangelical *Halachah*" he suggests that Marquardt inappropriately broadens Jewish particularity to a universality not implied in Jewish tradition and thereby uses Jewish tradition to legitimise his Christianity:

---

[172] Cf. for example Ellis 1990 and Ellis 1994.

[173] Cf. Marquardt 1994, 187-285. Others are Yehoshua Amir, Walter Benjamin and Robert Rafael Geis. Marquardt prefers Yehuda Halevi, Moses Mendelssohn, Moses Hess, Samson Raphael Hirsch and Moritz Lazarus as sources.

[174] Ellis 1997, 51.

> Surely, the gesture of following a Jewish offer implies the noble intention in future no longer to ignore the Jew. But in Marquardt's work this gesture also implies the attempt to justify oneself, thus it is also a form of conformity and normality. One's own *universal* partaking in the doing of Torah is justified with reference to a Jewish, *particularistic* practice of the doing of Torah. One could perhaps say [...] that the Christian justifies himself by referring to the Jew.[175]

In partaking in Jewish *Halachah*, Christians can legitimise themselves, because they can refer to a Jewish authority which offers *Halachah* as a way of approaching life. However, Kal argues that by binding themselves to Jewish authority Christians transfer the responsibility for the expression of their faith to Jews, because "Here the Jew is acting solely on his own authority – or on the authority of G-d (which is one and the same). A universal justification is missing."[176] Consequently Marquardt needs the victims – who have been betrayed by Christian theology – to justify his (new) theology. Kal concludes that even if Marquardt's understanding of Christian-Jewish relations envisages the Christian in the position of the listener, his theological model nevertheless usurps Jewish tradition in its particularity and thereby betrays Jews again.[177] Therefore Kal suggests that Christianity should not look for a justification outside itself.

> The particularism, which we are concerned with, implies *vulnerability*. If vulnerability is delegated the vulnerability has already been betrayed. The conclusion of my analysis is that a Christian who seeks an encounter as intended by Marquardt, needs to stand *on his own* two feet [...][178]

---

[175] Kal 1998, 28. Even stronger reads Christoph Münz's assessment of the "Christian-Jewish symbiosis", a concept which is often referred to in post-Holocaust German writings on German/Christian-Jewish relations, as a shared heritage of Christians and Jews, and used as an excuse for Christians to draw on Jewish tradition: "Im Blick auf die fast zweitausendjährige Geschichte des Christentums gegen das Judentum, die ihren Höhepunkt – präziser: ihren Tiefpunkt – nicht zuletzt im Holocaust fand, erinnert dieser Euphemismus an jemanden, der seinen Mitmenschen erschlägt und ihn anschließend seinen Bruder nennt. Man verfolgt, diskriminiert, entrechtet und mordet ihn, um im gleichen Atemzug von seinem Namen zu profitieren. Der Dieb rühmt sich seines Diebstahls und schämt sich nicht einmal dafür" (Münz [2]1996, 479).

[176] Kal 1998, 28.

[177] Cf. ibid. 29f.

[178] Ibid. 31. In his response to criticism Marquardt discusses Kal's suggestions, but he does not conclude that he needs to alter his theological focus. He understands learning from Judaism in the sense of appropriating Jewish tradition not as an act that seeks to legitimise Christianity, but rather as a criticism against Christian tradition which ignored Jewish readings of the scriptures. While recognising the potential danger this form of theology presents to Jews, Marquardt emphasises that he writes for the church and does not ask for Jewish approval (while welcoming Jewish readership), (cf. Marquardt 1998b, 105-121). Cf. also his recognition that the idea that Christians have entered into the covenant of G-d with the Jewish people may not be welcomed by Jews as well as an acknowledgement of the need for recognising distance and difference between Judaism and Christianity in Marquardt 1993, 161ff.

Despite its morally honourable intentions, the implications of Marquardt's theology for Holocaust remembrance and Christian-Jewish relations in Germany are worrying. Marquardt's theology builds on the assumption of an unquestionable continuity of biblical Israel with contemporary Jewry. His biblicism hardly takes into account thousands of years of interpretation and the Bible is allegedly free from crisis in Marquardt's "biblical order of reality". His historiographical arbitrariness in deciding single-handedly what event in the history of humankind is revelatory is based on a *sui generis* understanding of the relationship between G-d-People-Land adopted from Judaism. His combination of revelation and history excludes the majority of humankind, in particular the non-Western part of Christianity not involved in the Holocaust, and the way he is importing Christian theological terminology into Judaism deforms it into a parallel to Christology. To a certain extent it appears as if Marquardt is not prepared to think the categories established by his own theology to their conclusion. A biblical theological framework has been suggested by theologians of the "reformist" as well as "radical paradigm" in efforts to construct a theology which is not antisemitic. Marquardt, however, goes a step further and argues for a continuing (ontological) dependency of Christians on Jews. In the present this relationship is expressed in the assumption of a dependency on Jewish victims and survivors of the Holocaust. I would suggest that this dependency may cover up a failure of theological nerve to conclude that the challenge of the Holocaust indicates the possibility of G-d's inaccessibility to Christians after the Holocaust as well as the possibility of G-d's loss of divinity and as such might point to the end of Christianity (in the German context). Although Marquardt claims that he takes seriously this possibility, his writing of seven volumes of systematic theology and numerous articles suggests otherwise.

3. Conclusion

Reck suggests that a theology which is situated in a particular historical context and encourages communication has to take seriously the fact that biblical texts and contemporary witness are each bound to particular contexts which have to be brought into contact.[179] He concludes that

> Therefore it is not permitted to impose onto a later historically developed situation, in an authoritarian and static fashion, as a guideline a biblical situation which is understood as an ideal: with this method the people of the later constellation with their history and its specific conditions would not be listened to, i.e. they would not be communicated with.[180]

Marquardt's theology aims to hold the balance between the two contexts, biblical and contemporary Christian in post-Holocaust Germany, so that a communication can take place. However, he fails to adhere to this principle of communication, because he

---

[179] Cf. Reck 1998, 225.
[180] Ibid. 225.

inscribes both the "biblical order of reality" and his understanding of the Holocaust as normative and assigns the former the quality to help contemporary Christians regain their identity. As a consequence, communication between the two contexts as well as communication inside either context is limited. Curiously, the fact that Marquardt writes his theology as addressing the context of the FRG in particular finds very limited expression in his theology. Thus contemporary Christians in Germany and Jews who live in the FRG are not given any space to voice their understanding of the historical situation they find themselves in. While aiming at the context of the FRG, and understanding himself to be rooted in this context, events that shape German public cultural life hardly appear in his theology. However, the Catholic theologian Johanna Kohn reminds her readers that

> The reality of the anxieties, insecurities, aggressions and injuries should not be avoided in Christian-Jewish dialogue. These pose questions for the content and reasoning of the dialogue itself which need to be taken seriously. Further these are hindrances to communication which need to be worked through. I think it is important in the interest of such a working through first of all to understand the historical and psychologically-concrete as well as the political characteristics of the reality which shapes us.[181]

What Marquardt appears to take as read and obvious to his readers – namely an understanding of the "nature" of the post-Holocaust context of life in the FRG, his younger colleague has to examine before she feels able to proceed to an analysis of Christian and Jewish theological responses to the Holocaust.

Interestingly Marquardt suggests that a generational difference in the approach to the Holocaust by Germans should not be permitted; rather the immediacy of the encounter with the dead and surviving victims of NS atrocity should be safeguarded in the following generations.[182] However, this approach does not take seriously the different relationship subsequent generations need to assume to NS history and the Holocaust, because of their temporal distance to the events and their dependency on transmitted narratives of memory and continuing historical research. Further, the consequences of this form of immediate identification in a society which tends to identify with narratives of German victimisation, strike me as counterproductive to Marquardt's aim, given that it would obliterate victimiser perspectives. He argues further that

---

[181] Kohn 1986, 17.

[182] Cf. Marquardt [2]1992, 403: "[...] einen Generationensprung im Verhältnis dazu nicht zuzulassen, – jedes Präsens als Gegenwart, die aus *dieser* Vergangenheit kommt, zu erfahren [...]. Im Grunde hätte jeder Christ sich mit dem Namen eines gemordeten Juden zeichnen sollen (wie Juden vom nationalsozialistischen Gesetz gezwungen wurden, Zusatznamen anzunehmen) und das 'Nachleben' dieses Juden, die Folgen seines Gelebthabens und Gemordetseins übernehmen sollen: von materiellen Konsequenzen bis zu seelischen und geistigen Exerzitien der Erinnerung und Repräsentation, eines gelebten Requiem. [...] Gericht ist Erleben dessen, was folgt: was nachfolgt, hinterherkommt, und es läßt uns Konsequenzen erleben, generationenüberschreitend."

To us the preceding generations are not honourable in their death, are not worthy of remembrance, because they were not only victims of death but accomplices and virtually masters of killing.[183]

However, as has become clear in the previous chapter, the amnesia of the victimisers regarding their roles as victimisers is at the root of many conflicts of memory in Germany. The difficulty of owning victimiser heritage, and the willingness to cast oneself in the role of the victim, for example, initiated protest at the screening of *Holocaust*, prompted the production of *Heimat*, drove *Nasty Girl* Anna Rosmus out of her hometown, lingers in Nolte's suggestions of the renewal of national history, and greets the audience in the "good German" in *Schindler's List*. The victimisers are "worthy of remembrance" if only for reasons of historical honesty.

In a theology that is so intent on addressing the concreteness of the historical context, the category of remembrance appears in Marquardt's theology largely in the form of Jewish approaches to history and memory and in the need of non-Jewish Germans to remember the victims of the Holocaust. The difficulties Marquardt has in identifying victims of the Holocaust and portraying Jewish perspectives on Holocaust memory suggest that his theology makes at best an ambiguous contribution to the inclusion of perspectives of the "Jewish other" into the collective memory of German Protestants. Even the attempt to recall in his theology the tradition of the victimisers of Jews, before as well as during the Holocaust, as the heritage of German Protestants, does not prompt a reflection on how to address memories of NS and victimiser narratives that are part of German collective memory. As a consequence, second and third generation Germans and their relation to the events of NS and the Holocaust can hardly be addressed in a theology which does not reflect on victimiser heritage and does not acknowledge generational difference. How the different generations have come to remember (or failed to remember?) and discuss the Holocaust is not part of Marquardt's theology, rather it forms its background which is not clearly defined. However, it remains to be asked whether relating the narratives that shape the theologian's and the audience's understanding of their community's relation to NS should be a necessary part of writing a dogmatic/systematic theology.[184] Such a reflection would then need to include a discussion of victimiser heritage as well as obliterations of this heritage in the formulation of collective memory and theologies.

Therefore, issues particular to the third generation of Germans after the Holocaust need to be considered next. These form the patterns which shape their narratives of NS as distinct from the previous two generations of Germans. This is yet another set of issues that shapes the remembrance of the Holocaust and NS in Germany and which

---

[183] Marquardt 1996, 133.
[184] Marquardt's own few autobiographical comments (as well as the data provided by others) address his encounter with Jews, but hardly relate memories of NS.

begins to be taken seriously by a new generation of theologians. The doctoral dissertation of the Christian-feminist theologian Britta Jüngst, subject of the final chapter, explores the transmission of trauma from the first generation of Germans and Jews to their descendants.

IV. Generations of memory

An overview of recent research concerning the third generation of Germans and Jews after the Holocaust enables the concretisation of issues raised in preceding chapters concerning Holocaust remembrance in the Protestant community in Germany. Focusing on particular communities of memory, i.e. groups of third generation Germans and Jews who evaluate their self-understandings in relation to the Holocaust, demonstrates how this generation has inherited their respective cultures' patterns of Holocaust remembrance. In particular I will evaluate the exchange programmes facilitated by Björn Krondorfer and Christian Staffa since 1989. These programmes bring together non-Jewish Germans and in the majority Jewish Americans to explore relations to each other in a study programme on the Holocaust.[1]

My analysis aims to understand the challenges to the perception of the Holocaust and Jews when the German students encounter their Jewish peers and their memory of the Holocaust. The focus of my inquiry is the German participants in the exchanges. The underlying question is how challenges to the perception of the Holocaust and Jews initiated in third generation Germans by encounters with third generation Jews can inform Protestant theological reflections on the Holocaust and Jews. An understanding of dynamics between descendants of the community of victims and victimisers can inform Christian reflection on Christian-Jewish relations in Germany. It is likely that emotional issues concerning the memory of NS and the Holocaust will surface strongly in encounters of peers from historically antagonistic communities when both are invited to study the impact of the Holocaust on their own and on the respective other community. Hence an awareness of underlying group dynamics concerning the impact of the memory of the Holocaust in each community needs to inform contemporary Christian reflection on Christian-Jewish relations in Germany, if theologians wish to establish the Holocaust as a subject relevant to subsequent generations. Only if the impact of the transmission of memory of NS and the Holocaust on each community, including the concerns of Jews and Germans of the third generation, are reflected theologically can the Holocaust retain theological relevance.

---

[1] Source material concerning these programmes: Krondorfer/Schmidt (eds.) 1990; Staffa/Krondorfer (eds.) 1992; Staffa/Krondorfer/Jurgovsky (eds.) 1994; Staffa/Krondorfer (eds.) 1997. For evaluations of and comments on the programmes cf. Krondorfer 1991; Krondorfer 1995; Krondorfer 1997 and Krondorfer 1998.

1. Research on the generational transmission of Holocaust memory

The shock of the evidence of the Holocaust was followed by a long silence because "intense individual and collective defense mechanisms functioned to ward off preoccupation with, and memories of, traumatic experiences"[2] reflecting "the world's need to forget."[3] In the 1960s psychoanalysts in the USA and Israel began to be confronted with traumas connected with the survival of the Holocaust. The loss of an entire family and community, experiences in ghettos, camps and hiding, partisan activities, being a refugee and DP after the war, in addition to re-establishing a new life and home in another country without being able to relate the experiences of the Holocaust, surfaced in therapy sessions.[4] Only a small number of survivors had begun to seek help in therapy. However, the work that was published concerning the traumas related to Holocaust survival generated research on the so-called "survivor syndrome"[5] and initiated a literature concerned with the study of the impact of the experiences during the Holocaust on the development of identity.[6]

In the wake of the Eichmann trial in Israel, and in particular since the 1980s, a more pronounced interest in testimonies of Holocaust survivors emerged.[7] This process of recognition was facilitated by the changing national ethos of Israel which now began to celebrate survivors as national heroes rather than dismissing them as naive victims who had been led "like sheep to the slaughter" without any resistance. Psychoanalysts who worked with survivors had also included their families in the therapy and from the mid-1980s onwards their interest begun to include children of survivors.[8] Important for this psychoanalytical research rooted in family therapy is a direct family relation of the client to the Holocaust. Age and socialisation become relevant only as secondary factors. Thus the second generation holds together people of different ages, the common denominator being that one or both parents are survivors of the Holocaust. Judith and Milton Kestenberg summarise issues relevant to the children of Holocaust survivors in relation to their parents as follows:

> For example, the question of how a parent survived – whether he or she was guilty, base, betrayer, or hero – becomes a central theme in the analysis of survivors' children. Another central theme is the preoccupation with specific experiences of the parents, such as starvation, details of persecution, and loss of family members. It is almost universal for a child of a

---

[2] Bergmann/Jucovy 1982, 5.

[3] Ibid. 6.

[4] Cf. Bergmann/Jucovy (eds.) 1982.

[5] Niederland 1968.

[6] For references to this research cf. Bergmann/Jucovy (eds.) 1982.

[7] Cf. for example Segev 1993, 323ff.

[8] Cf. for example Bergmann/Jucovy (eds.) 1982 as well as Epstein 1979; Hass 1990; Hass 1995 and Wardi 1992.

survivor family to grapple with the conflict of whether one should dwell on the Holocaust or whether to forget it.[9]

In Germany, psychoanalysts began to recognise that the trauma of NS, the war and the Holocaust was transmitted to the children of the victimiser generation and had to be addressed in therapy.[10] Jürgen Müller-Hohagen describes psychoanalytical research in the FRG and its ignorance of social-historical conflicts as determinants in the interaction between client and analyst.[11] The fact that psychology became an independent discipline at German universities only in 1941 highlighted a complicity of the entire discipline in NS, as well as in the post-war tendency to ignore (transmissions of) traumas connected with NS.[12] Judith Kestenberg concludes in her essay that

> The first analyses of Nazis' children in Germany were done mostly in isolation. European analysts who are working with Nazis' children are courageously looking within themselves and undergoing a new analysis, a self-analysis, as they conquer what can be generally subsumed in the heading of "countertransference," [...][13]

In 1985 the Israeli psychologist Dan Bar-On interviewed children of high-ranking Nazis and perpetrators of the Holocaust who live in contemporary Germany, thereby initiating cross-cultural research on second generation German and Jewish relations to the Holocaust.[14] The important criterion for second generation research remains the direct family relation to NS and the Holocaust. Second generation in the German victimiser context means that the fathers of the interviewees had been involved in the perpetration of the Holocaust. Women were, and largely still are, not regarded as possible perpetrators themselves, but only appear as people who defined themselves in relation to their husbands or partners and their involvement in the NS regime.[15] Since the end of the 1980s, children of both survivors and perpetrators of the Holocaust have begun to meet separately and together in second generation groups initiated by Bar-On.[16]

---

[9] Kestenberg/Kestenberg 1982, 44.
[10] Cf. Kestenberg 1982, 161. Cf. also Ehlers 1994; Müller-Hohagen 1988 and Westernhagen 1987.
[11] Cf. Müller-Hohagen 1988, 22ff.
[12] Cf. ibid. 49ff.
[13] Kestenberg 1982, 163.
[14] Cf. Bar-On 1989.
[15] However, more recently feminist scholars have taken up the subject of women's responsibility during NS, cf. for example Ebbinghaus (ed.) 1996; Gravenhorst/Tatschmurat (eds.) 1990 and Rommelspacher 1994.
[16] Local groups are established in Britain by the organisation Second Generation Trust (http://www.secondgeneration.org) which addresses the concerns of the children of Holocaust survivors, and the first public meeting of a child of a survivor and of a perpetrator took place in a public dialogue in the summer of 1996 in London. Cf. also the work of Samson Munn and the group To Reflect and Trust: http://www.toreflectandtrust.org.

Research concerning the second generation of both Jews and Germans shows that the traumas which the children have inherited from relationships with their parents centre on the silences in survivor as well as perpetrator families. Both sets of parents and the wider families censored the narratives that were related to their children and concealed information about their lives, experiences and actions. Thus the children grew up with the knowledge that some things could not be talked about in their families, that there are secrets which threaten their parents and the development of themselves. However, the reasons which motivated parents to censor the experiences they relate to their children are different for survivor and perpetrator families.[17] Survivors acted out of concern for their children so as not to burden them with the knowledge of the horrors they experienced, they found language to be inadequate to express what had happened to them and the social climate in both Israel and the USA for a long time did not encourage them to tell their stories. In perpetrator families the reasons for concealing information were a means to exculpate and forget the crimes family members were involved in. Children of survivors sense the pain behind their parents silences and would not ask questions in order to protect their parents and themselves from more pain.

> Children and grandchildren of survivors do not want to imagine their parents and grandparents in situations where attempts were made to rob them of their human dignity and where they were helpless to prevent the humiliation and murder of other people, such as their parents, siblings or even their own children.[18]

Children of perpetrators omit questions about their parents' involvement in NS because of fear of discovering that the father was a murderer, shame, or for the sake of keeping the family peace:

> descendants of Nazi perpetrators are protecting themselves from having to realize the cruel deeds, lack of guilt feelings, emotional coldness, racism and antisemitism that continue unabated to this day in their closest reference individuals. And they are also trying to defend themselves against both guilt feelings and fear that their grandparents or parents will murder them or classify them as *lebensunwert*.[19]

While themselves refusing to confront the enormous crimes in which their family members had been involved, they also protected their parents from having to confront and thus relive their actions and omissions.[20] Gertrud Hardtmann argues that

> The conspiracy of silence, which has not been broken by the perpetrators is followed by the conspiracy of burial – of memory and of its traces. The more this conspiracy is enacted in the political sphere, the more we are repeating mentally what happened concretely during NS: we

---

[17] Cf. Rosenthal 1998a, 9ff.
[18] Ibid. 9.
[19] Ibid. 9.
[20] Cf. Hecker 1993, 89.

exclude the dead and the injured, as if they were not our dead and our injured, as if the wounds we inflicted on them were not also our wounds.[21]

In an everyday life that is invested with "normality" the suppression of memories still affects the children, who, as Müller-Hohagen argues, are burdened with this "normality".[22] He suggests that this "normality" had its roots in NS which silenced groups of the population, who could not conform to the ideal of "superiority" developed in NS ideology, in order to establish a "normality" resting on the assumption of superiority.[23] Thus the disruption of communication initiated by NS in the name of a "normality" continued in the FRG serving a different invention of "normality". Hence subsequent generations became complicit in the "solidarity of silence"[24] of the first generation which to subsequent generations became a "conspiracy of silence" (Krondorfer)[25] or a "second guilt" (Giordano)[26].

Hence, for different reasons, the communication between parents and children in survivor and perpetrator families was severely disrupted.

While the real perpetrators attempt to deflect responsibility from themselves by blaming the victims [...], survivors continue to be plagued with guilt for having survived [...]. Their children take on these feelings of guilt at having survived, too [...].[27]

Regarding the third generation the situation of defining its membership is different from the previous two generations. Members of the third generation of both Jews and Germans do not have to be directly connected to either side of the Holocaust through family members to be defined as part of this generation. If there are direct connections these can be considerably less straightforward than one's grandparents. Members of the wider family who have survived or who have been involved in NS actions that contributed to the Holocaust are still common in this generation and establish a personal entry to the issues involved in Holocaust memory and the impact this can have on the formulation of identity. However, more important in relation to the third generation is a shared cultural context and age group. Both Jews and Germans have grown up with established discourses in their communities regarding the memory of the Holocaust.[28] Thus regardless of whether there is a family connection to the crimes of the Holocaust, the third generation is asked by their respective cultures to relate to the memory of the Holocaust. How this relationship is negotiated is part of the research interest in the third generation. Particular to this generation is their temporal distance from the Holocaust. While they do not have to

---

[21] Hardtmann 1988, 60. Cf. also Rosenthal 1998b, 240ff.

[22] Cf. Müller-Hohagen 1988, 147ff.

[23] Cf. ibid. 221.

[24] Hecker 1993, 75.

[25] Cf. Krondorfer 1995, 98-104.

[26] Cf. Giordano ²1990, 9ff.

[27] Rosenthal 1998a, 12.

[28] Cf. Krondorfer 1995, 31-46.

identify with their grandparents' fate or actions, they are nevertheless still able to make personal contact with members of this generation and thereby forge a historical link to the time of NS and the Holocaust. They are the last generation which is able to do this. Krondorfer argues that the temporal distance of the third generation of both Jews and Germans from the Holocaust puts them in a unique position to challenge current narratives of the Holocaust:

> Because they are distant enough from the trauma itself, but still affected by its repercussions, they can replace static discursive patterns with a more immediate and honest human bonding. They can formulate a new set of questions while still being rooted in history.[29]

The third generation is confronted with narratives on NS, the war and the Holocaust by official representatives of the state or community, in public culture and the media, and in the intimate setting of the family and friends.[30] The third generation after the Holocaust is in a position to confront the history of the Holocaust and to unearth some of the stories that have been censored by the first and second generations. As grandchildren of either victims or victimisers in the broadest sense, members of the third generation have the privilege of being able to address questions to the first generation their parents were unable to ask. The communication between the generations of grandparents and grandchildren is less fraught with the complex emotional relationship between parents and children which makes intergenerational communication difficult even without the additional trauma of the Holocaust.[31] The fourth generation will hardly have the possibility to speak personally to members of the first generation of Germans and Jews. For them the Holocaust will be a subject that is thoroughly part of history. However, as the third generation, the fourth generation and any subsequent generation will also inherit discursive patterns established by the preceding generations concerning the memory of the Holocaust. Thus, the questions the third generation asks of the first and second generations are vital in challenging existing discursive patterns and in creating new ones. Without the ability and willingness of the third generation to confront the challenge of the transmission of memories of the Holocaust and the legacies left to them by the first and second generations, subsequent generations will be deprived of chances to relate to the Holocaust and ask their own questions of this history. Or they can ask questions if they have learned to do so, but will be deprived of answers since the silences in families will have become so established that there is hardly any way of transcending them to challenge their assumptions about the lives of the first generation.

Before addressing the issues that arise in third generation research it is necessary to define more closely the membership of the third generation of Germans and Jews after the Holocaust.

---

[29] Krondorfer in Staffa/Krondorfer (eds.) 1997, 16.

[30] Cf. Winkelmann 1988, 194ff.

[31] Cf. Müller-Hohagen 1988, 176ff.

1.1. Defining generations[32]

In his influential essay on "The Problem of Generations"[33] Karl Mannheim analyses the difficulties in defining generations. Generations mark the passing of history and initiate new beginnings by enabling society to forget and recall from the past only memories relevant to the present.[34] He argues that

> Members of a generation are "similarly located", first of all, in so far as they all are exposed to the same phase of the collective process. [...] what does create a similar location is that they are in a position to experience the same events and data, etc., and especially that these experiences impinge upon a similarly "stratified" consciousness.[35]

Hence the fact that people are born in the same years is "sociologically significant only when it also involves participation in the same historical and social circumstances."[36] Mannheim argues that subdivisions in a generation, so called "generational units", signify closer bonds of identification as groups.

> Youth experiencing the same concrete historical problems may be said to be part of the same actual generation; while those groups within the same actual generation which work up the material of their common experiences in different specific ways, constitute separate generation units.[37]

Regarding the definition of generations as social groups in relation to the Holocaust, family history has been the criterion for the first and second generation. Family history does not necessarily coincide with political eras and thus there are a lot of grey areas when attempting to establish any kind of schema. I understand the first generation of Germans as those who were mature adults during the Third Reich and can thus be said to bear some form of responsibility for its development. Hence they are born not later than 1920, so that they reached maturity during NS. The second generation of Germans are their children, the third generation their grandchildren, largely born in the 1960s and 1970s.[38]

The identification of Jewish generations in relation to the Holocaust employs a different principle. Since survivors of the Holocaust involved all age groups, the first generation, i.e. the survivors, are even less of a homogenous group than the German first generation. Second generation Jews are understood to be the children of

---

[32] Sources for the following characterisation are Kohlstruck 1997, 75-92, 289-291; Krondorfer 1995, 12f.; Mannheim 1952 and Schuman/Scott 1989. Cf. also Greiffenhagen/Greiffenhagen (eds.) 1981, 49.

[33] Mannheim 1952.

[34] Cf. ibid. 294f.

[35] Ibid. 297.

[36] Ibid. 298.

[37] Ibid. 304 (italics in original). Scholars agree that the generation-creating experiences are shared in early adulthood (cf. Schuman/Scott 1989, 360).

[38] Cf. also Kohlstruck 1997, 75ff. For a different division of generational cohorts cf. Marcuse 2001, 292f.

Holocaust survivors, their children form the third generation. Thus the age difference in the Jewish second generation is much greater than in the German second generation.

However, many Jews do not relate to the Holocaust in this personal way, but rather through their identification as Jews, whether they have lost family in the Holocaust or not.[39] Similarly the identification as German (as well as socialisation in Germany) implies a relation to the history of NS, the war and the Holocaust. When identifying the third generation of Germans and Jews after the Holocaust I am therefore referring to a group of people that only in some respects can be said to form one generation. People who share common memories in terms of growing up and maturing can belong to different biological generations which influences the set of questions they will be confronted with concerning their family histories during National Socialism.

However, in the case studies I have accessed, the participating Jews and Germans are mostly born in the late 1960s and 1970s and are part of the third generation also in terms of their family backgrounds.[40] They are of the same age group and relate to similar cultural backgrounds, in particular they share in an international youth culture. However, in individual cases the Jewish participants in these studies are part of the second generation after the Holocaust.

1.2. Research on the third generation

In the last two decades scholars have shown an increasing interest in the third generation of both Jews and Germans after the Holocaust. This research developed as an extension of the work with children of Holocaust survivors for whom the term second generation was invented. Whereas the research on the second generation was at first confined to children of survivors and children of high-ranking Nazis, it has broadened for the third generation to include members of the same age group of both Jews and Germans whether they have a directly identifiable family connection to the Holocaust or whether they have simply grown up in a society which addresses the memory of the Holocaust as part of its self-definition (Germany, Israel, USA).

The study of the third generation after the Holocaust draws on a variety of disciplines and research techniques. Psychology, quantitative and qualitative sociology, as well as oral history projects, biographical research, and cultural studies are part of the

---

[39] Cf. Segev 1993, 323ff.

[40] An exception is Michael Kohlstruck's study. His definition of third generation is much broader. One criterion for choosing his interviewees was that their parents were born after 1930. The interviewees themselves were are all born between 1951 and 1967 (cf. Kohlstruck 1997, 100-102). Birgit Rommelspacher counts the generations differently and thus talks about a first and a second post-Holocaust generation of Germans and Jews which corresponds to the second and third generation after the Holocaust in most of the literature (cf. Rommelspacher 1994, 9).

discourse. As a result the field of third generation research is diverse and, by its very definition, cannot be homogenised. This makes it difficult to assess the achievements of third generation research and its insights. Interviews concerning the third generation involve (where possible) interviews with family members of the preceding two generations,[41] and exchange programmes which bring together young Germans and Jews.[42] Individual studies are concerned with a particular phenomenon such as forms of antisemitism in third generation Germans (Rommelspacher).[43]

However, none of the research projects can claim to have worked with a representative sample of the third generation of both Jews and Germans. The most comprehensive sample of third generation Germans and Jews is probably found in the fieldwork conducted by Bar-On, Konrad Brendler and their colleagues in a joint research project of the Bergische Universität Wuppertal and Ben-Gurion University of the Negev in Beersheva (1989-1994).[44] In questionnaires and selected follow up interviews they asked ca. 1,000 students in Israel and North-Rhine Westphalia, from all school types to university level education, about their relation to the memory of NS and the Holocaust. The conclusions that can be drawn from this research with regard to the relevance of the memory of the Holocaust to young people in Germany are limited.[45] North-Rhine Westphalia, the state (*Bundesland*) with the highest population in Germany, provides a diversity of population which is exemplary. On the other hand it has to be considered that education is in the authority of the different states (*Bundesländer*) and although Holocaust education is compulsory, its implementation varies.[46] In addition the sample refers to West Germany only.

Nevertheless, however limited the findings of third generation research are, they do indicate issues which are of importance for the development of Holocaust memory in Germany. Given that most participants in the research projects are volunteers who chose to examine their relationship to the Holocaust and their peers on the other side of the historical division of memory, the difficulties and challenges to their self-perception and the perception of each other are significant in that they reflect issues likely to be relevant to the wider communities of both Jews and Germans.

Regarding the third generation, the cultural divide between Germans and Jews, i.e. descendants of victimisers and victims, is largely also a national divide. For Germans, Jewish life is experienced mostly in American and Israeli contexts and thus involves

---

[41] Cf. for example Bar-On 1995; Kohlstruck 1997; Rommelspacher 1994; Rosenthal (ed.) 1998; Sichrovsky 1987 and Sichrovsky 1986.
[42] Cf. for example Bar-On/Brendler/Hare (eds.) 1997; Bergerson 1997; Krondorfer 1995; Roberts 1998; Rosenthal (ed.) 1998.
[43] Cf. for example Rommelspacher 1994.
[44] Cf. Bar-On/Brendler/Hare (eds.) 1997.
[45] Cf. Brendler 1997, 59.
[46] Cf. for example Schreier/Heyl (eds.) 1992. Cf. also Rommelspacher 1994, 15ff.

the crossing of international borders. Research on the third generation of Germans and Jews is often confined to either context, i.e. Jewish or German, or involves the analysis of organised cross-cultural encounters of Germans and Jews.

Cross-cultural research in comparison with research in a culturally homogenous context has the advantage that the assumptions of the participants, facilitators, researchers, interviewers and interviewees etc. can be challenged by the set-up of a programme or study. Thus the possibility of transcending discursive patterns pertaining to one cultural context is to a certain extent built into its format, so that the presuppositions with which the researcher approaches a scene can never be regarded as "safe". The difficulty of inadvertently becoming the object of one's own research can be beneficial as much as it can be obstructive to the learning process. However, by writing oneself into the research readers can be enabled to learn from the dynamic of the programme or study conducted.[47] A problem of research on third generation Germans conducted in homogenous settings is that the questions asked in interviews relate to NS and the Holocaust alike, often not specifying which memories the interviewees are supposed to focus on. Hardtmann, for example, speaks about the Holocaust and NS in interchangeable terms which appears to reflect her own relation to the subject and its definition, rather than the attitudes of her interviewees.[48] However, a strength of a culturally homogenous approach is highlighted by Michael Kohlstruck's study. He explicitly focuses on NS memories only (rather than on the Holocaust or using NS and Holocaust as synonyms) and is thereby able to explore the perspectives of young German men whose understanding of NS has not been challenged in cross-cultural encounters with Jews.[49]

All members of the third generation are historically distant from the events of NS and the Holocaust. They have no personal memories which frame their understanding of this period of history. While they are often still able to make the personal connection to the events through their grandparents' biographies, the historical distance enables them not to have to identify personally with their grandparents' experiences and actions. Germans and Jews come from different cultures with distinct patterns of remembrance which are constructed antagonistically.[50] Thus when Germans talk about Jews, they largely stick to stereotypes which have little to do with Jewish life as experienced by young Jews and when Jews speak about Germans their

---

[47] Cf. for example Bar-On 1989: on the one hand he tries to write himself out of the interviews he conducts while at the same time having a great awareness that his identity as a Jew and Israeli with family from Germany influenced the way his interviewees reacted to him and vice versa. As a concession to this situation he inserts comments into the text reflecting on his own (emotional) perception of an interview situation and raising questions. Krondorfer consistently writes his own story into his analysis of cross-cultural exchanges (cf. Krondorfer 1995) as does Bergerson 1997.

[48] Cf. Hardtmann 1997.

[49] Cf. Kohlstruck 1997.

[50] Cf. for example Krondorfer 1997, 6.

characterisations stereotype young Germans in the role of paradigmatic enemies, thereby ignoring the cultural context of post-war Germany. Krondorfer's definition of

> Holocaust memories as the intergenerational transmission of common motifs and sensitivities takes into account that the majority of third-generation Jews and Germans are no longer direct descendants of victims and victimizers but are still emotionally attached to the Holocaust – despite the growing temporal distance to it.[51]

For both Germans and Jews the areas in which they encounter memories of NS and the Holocaust involve the family, schools, and discourses in public culture. Each of these fields of discourse involves distinct patterns that have to be negotiated in the life of the individual. Krondorfer distinguishes between "discursive practices", describing patterns of publicly articulated forms of Holocaust remembrance and "ethos", expressing "what people deeply believe about their way of living and thinking" which are distinct for Germans and Jews.[52] He argues that the discursive practices of Jewish and German communities are characterised by a victim/victimiser dichotomy.

> Young Jews and Germans need to familiarize themselves with this history if they want to understand their present relationships. The scale of cruelties inflicted upon Jews has been so immense, and the impact of visual evidence of the genocide so strong, that the victim/victimizer dichotomy is not going to fade away. It has determined the discourse in the past and will continue to shape it in the future.[53]

The German public discourse on the Holocaust displays ambiguous forms of dealing with the historical role of victimiser, accepting it on the one hand as a historical reality, while at the same time trying to escape it by inscribing Germans in the role of victims (cf. the Bitburg Controversy and the *Historikerstreit*). In Jewish discursive practice the identification with the victims of the Holocaust serves as a force of integration of an otherwise divided community.[54]

> [...] Israeli society, by contrast, insists on specificity and identifies the Holocaust as a unique period in the history of Jewish suffering and exile. But critics of the Israeli construction of a "memory industry" charge that the Shoah has turned into a secular religion which functions as historical and ideological glue for keeping a fragmented society together. [...] Among Jewish Americans, the Holocaust similarly provides social cohesion. [...] To counter the trend toward assimilation and disaffiliation, the Jewish discourse on the Holocaust often serves as a reminder of the importance of remaining Jewish.[55]

Concerning the ethos of Jews and Germans in relation to the Holocaust, Krondorfer argues that Jews have created an empowering ethos of remembrance which moves from destruction to redemption, whereas Germans remain caught in an ethos of guilt

---

[51] Krondorfer in Staffa/Krondorfer (eds.) 1997, 14.
[52] Krondorfer 1995, 11.
[53] Ibid. 28.
[54] Cf. ibid. 38ff. and Segev 1993.
[55] Krondorfer 1995, 38f.

which strives for forgiveness.[56] This observation leads Krondorfer to conclude that remembering the Holocaust refers to different concepts in the community of Germans and the community of Jews. Both discourses rely on the need to remember the Holocaust while their enactments of memory express different purposes.

> American Jews cherish the memory of those who died in the Shoah, and they interpret remembrance as a means of Jewish survival. Remembrance is the marrow of Jewish identity. For Germans, informed by an ethos of guilt, Holocaust memory is more like a tumor that threatens their identity and belief in their own humanity. Remembrance seems to have no function other than to elicit unresolved emotions.[57]

The inherited discourse and ethos of each community is also fraught with stereotypes about the identities of the respective other. Whereas Germans largely encounter Jews as dead and surviving victims of the Holocaust, portrayed in black and white documentary footage, Jews often cast Germans in the role of the "bad German" and Nazi.[58]

When Jews and Germans meet in organised encounters, one dimension of these meetings is biographical work. The different patterns in which stories about the National Socialist period are transmitted in German and Jewish families allow the participants to challenge the self-understandings they have inherited from their families and cultures. The encounters facilitate an awareness of the omissions and silences in family stories. Regarding the context of contemporary Germany this involves, for example, the recognition that Jews as "real-life" persons remain absent from German narratives. German family stories often read as if there never had been Jewish communities in German towns and cities – an indication of how much history has been censored and of the depth of the divide between Jewish and German memory regarding the Holocaust. German narratives of the third generation centre on memories of the war and the involvement of fathers and grandfathers in NS activities. Gabriele Rosenthal argues that first generation Germans extracted their biographies from the political context of NS and, as such, from the context in which the Holocaust needs to be acknowledged as part of the collective history.[59] Subsequent generations are implicated in this "conspiracy of silence" and with the third generation the narratives transmitted in families are so well hidden that gaps and silences can only be detected by the grandchildren if these display an extraordinary "emotional openness, experience and historical knowledge."[60] Unless there was a direct participation of a family member in atrocities against Jews which is acknowledged in stories circulating in the family, Jews hardly figure in the narratives.

---

[56] Cf. ibid. 50ff.
[57] Ibid. 48.
[58] Cf. ibid. 68ff.
[59] Cf. Rosenthal 1998b, 240f.
[60] Ibid. 241.

> The glossing over of Nazi crimes in one's own life story and the family history goes hand in hand with the exclusion from the family "historiography" of the victims of the Nazi system, who neither feature as individuals nor as a collective.[61]

These findings suggest that Jewish memories and thus the perspective of the victims of the Holocaust has hardly entered German memories of NS and the Holocaust.[62]

However, Andrew Stuart Bergerson attaches significance to the fact that the participants in such encounters are young people who act their age in confrontation with facilitators of exchange programmes and at official events. He observed a week in an exchange programme for 16-20 year-olds from the cities of Hildesheim and Haifa. Regarding the prevalence of the victim/victimiser dichotomy and the efforts of the programme to transcend these, he writes

> They were also students in a school program, however. Enacting their generational identity required that they not respond when the teachers forced them into confrontations. They preferred to use their friendship to transcend the stale discourse of the intellectuals during those moments before, after, or in-between official events. Where public intellectuals may not sympathize with the historical other without invoking fears of relativizing the past, the younger generation transgresses difference simply by experiencing the world from the perspective of their new-found friends during cross-cultural encounters. In this, they differ from the second generation, preoccupied as it was with overcoming the repression of the first. Remembrance for the third generation is not the final destination, but the point of departure.[63]

While having to negotiate their identities, balancing an inherited discourse and ethos of their respective communities and the patterns of memory transmission in their families, young Jews and Germans can also enjoy the relative freedom of simply making friends across the historical divide of their communities. Bound together by their age and interests the German and Israeli youths in Bergerson's study shared a cultural context different from that of the previous two generations.[64] However, Bergerson argues that aspects of establishing such friendships are not without danger, because

> By attempting to overcome the past through friendship, the Exchange tried to circumvent the victim/izer metanarrative through the depoliticized habits of a modern global youth culture. Under the guise of consumerism, generational non-conformity, eroticism, and "normalcy," a mass culture potentially represses the past once again.[65]

This points to a change in the context of Holocaust remembrance from the first and second generation to the third generation after the Holocaust. I will explore this new context using examples from Krondorfer's study *Remembrance and Reconciliation*, as well as the exchange programmes facilitated by him.

---

[61] Ibid. 241.
[62] Cf. chapter II. as well as Diner 1990.
[63] Bergerson 1997, 147.
[64] Cf. ibid. 162ff.
[65] Ibid. 165.

2. Cross-cultural encounters of Germans and Jews – Challenging discourses of memory and facilitating remembrance

In *Remembrance and Reconciliation*[66] Krondorfer outlines how third generation Germans after the Holocaust have come to understand and challenge the attitudes of their families and society to the memory of the Holocaust.[67] Krondorfer approaches the ways in which young Germans of the third generation remember the Holocaust by observing how they enact their relationship to the Holocaust in encounters with young American Jews. He argues that a reconciliation of the antagonistic past and the divided memory of the two communities of Germans and Jews in the present, which defines them as descendants of victims and victimisers, can best begin in a space where it is safe to encounter each other while learning together about the Holocaust. He facilitates study programmes which bring together young non-Jewish Germans and Jewish Americans to explore their relationship to the Holocaust and each other in a month long encounter in the USA, Germany and Poland.[68] Organised by an American and a German organisation,[69] the programmes have run regularly since 1989. At the end of a month of study the participants are invited to write a reflective essay in which they grapple with what concerned them most of the issues raised by the programme and the personal consequences they draw from that. These essays are then compiled in documentations which are published in a bilingual version with the original texts printed alongside their English or German translation.[70] Krondorfer's book analyses these study programmes, as well as the work of the German-Jewish Dance Theatre.

Confronted with each other in a month long encounter of studying the Holocaust in the majority Jewish American and non-Jewish German students have to cope with the differences between the assumptions their respective cultures had taught them about each other and the identities of the actual people they encounter:

> Post-Shoah Jews and Germans have been taught historical facts and moral lessons but they have also learned to accept their culture's silences, omissions, and taboos. Germans may have learned never again to victimize Jews, but they do not know any; American Jews may have

---

[66] Krondorfer 1995.

[67] A strength of these programmes is that they focus on the Holocaust and as such allow young Germans to explore distinctions in the memory of NS and the Holocaust which are not easily identifiable in German discourses on *Vergangenheitsbewältigung* which speak about the NS past and mean NS, the war and the Holocaust, depending on what the speakers imply in a given situation.

[68] For an overview of the organisation, the programme offered and other details cf. Krondorfer 1998 as well as the documentations of each programme referred to earlier.

[69] The Philadelphia Interfaith Council on the Holocaust and the Evangelische Akademie Brandenburg, facilitated by Krondorfer and Staffa.

[70] Krondorfer/Schmidt (eds.) 1990; Staffa/Krondorfer (eds.) 1992; Staffa/Krondorfer/Jurgovsky (eds.) 1994; Staffa/Krondorfer (eds.) 1997.

learned not to be victimized ever again and to see "the German" as paradigmatic enemy, but they do not know the society in which young Germans grow up today.[71]

These cross-cultural meetings of Jews and Germans force both groups to question the narratives of their respective communities and tentatively begin to trust each other.

Most German participants reported that their families and friends supported their participation in the programme, while at the same time expressing their doubts about it (not using the term Holocaust, advice such as "don't let them make you feel guilty", indifference to experiences of the participants after their return).[72] The willingness of the participants to challenge their identity in relation to dominant German discourses on the Holocaust makes them different from the majority of young Germans. However, their rootedness in this discourse indicates the framework with which it operates and the distortions in the young Germans' perceptions of Jews indicate stereotypes created by the discourse in FRG society.

With three examples from Krondorfer's study and the exchange programmes I will illustrate conflicts young Germans encounter when their self-understanding in relation to the Holocaust is challenged in encounters with their Jewish American peers.

2.1. Guilt

After listening to a survivor testimony and participating in the following discussion, Dieter, a German student reflected in an essay on his feelings about the evening:

"Perhaps all emotions – anger, rage, strength – are dead. I no longer feel them vis-à-vis Germans. Therefore I can talk to you about my memories of the Warsaw ghetto without blaming you." This is how Edith Millman ended her report on the evening of March 26, 1987, in Philadelphia in front of us twelve students from the Rheinland. ... Ms. Millman spoke English although she was obviously capable of speaking German without an accent. How should we Germans react to such a report? Were we supposed to feel guilty again? ... We had mentioned our list of questions for this evening and repeated them again: How did Jews live in the United States during and after the war? What roles do Jews play in contemporary American society? Who in the States is printing neo-Nazi brochures both in English and German, and how do Americans react to that?
Our questions were not answered during this evening because an aggravating and strained discussion started with the young Jews. They had recorded Millman's story on tape and followed it with such intensity as if they were asked to transform it into internal and external movements. We, too, were touched, but rather stayed in a defensive position. ...
After one of us made a statement, which aimed at soliciting compassion but might have been insensitively phrased, the debate turned into open aggression. She had said: "... We see how difficult it is for you as descendants of victims of Germans to talk to us. But please also acknowledge that it is similarly difficult to live as the descendants of victimizers and to talk to

---

[71] Krondorfer 1995, 47.
[72] Cf. Krondorfer in Staffa/Krondorfer (eds.) 1997, 13.

you, especially now that you have arranged this evening in such a way that you make us guilty. But we are not guilty as individuals."

This juxtaposition greatly disconcerted Lisa, one of the Jewish dancers: "I reject such a juxtaposition. This is unacceptable for victims. The problems of victimizers and their children are exclusively yours. ... Everything has been taken from us by the Germans: history, culture, family. And we still suffer as the second generation. Do you, as young Germans, have similar problems with your identity? How can we talk to you and gain trust if this is your gift in return? ..."

In this strained situation, we (Germans) experienced that there are situations in which we are forced to be silent. This was difficult since we sensed the underlying accusations. But why talk if that would only worsen the situation and hurt the other even more? ...[73]

When the survivor Edith Millman said "I can speak to you without blaming you" it was apparently intended to prevent the emergence of feelings of guilt in the young Germans listening to her story. But the young Germans were extremely sensitive to anything involving guilt and so they misunderstood her and thought she wanted to make them feel guilty. They "stayed in a defensive position" writes Dieter. The audience seemed entirely unprepared for the intense emotions generated by the survivor's testimony and the possibility that young Jews identify with the survivor's pain and loss. The young Jews insisted on identifying Germans with the tradition of the victimisers and rejected the notion that young Germans see themselves as victims of their parents and grandparents who were sometimes the actual victimisers. Neither side in the conversation had thought about the ways in which the other would hear the testimony and reflect themselves in it. Therefore both sides left misunderstood and dissatisfied. This discussion exemplifies how differently the words "guilt" and "victim" can be understood by Jews and Germans. When Jews described their suffering, Germans heard that they were blamed, and when Germans identified themselves as victims, Jews felt that their fate was not being respected. Both words are loaded with the history and emotion of two antagonistic discourses, so that neither side heard what was actually said, but connected it with stereotypes about the other.[74]

These stereotypes are part of the public discourse on the memory of the Holocaust as was evident in the Bitburg Affair. There, the anger expressed by the Jewish community was not about blaming all Germans for the crimes of the Holocaust, but was rather a demand for historical accuracy. However, this was understood by Germans as an accusation of "collective guilt" for the Holocaust. Similarly, the blurring of the distinction between victims and victimisers in Bitburg politicised the word "victim", in the sense that it is understood to reflect the political aims of the speaker rather than historical facts. Therefore, if Germans identify Germans as victims, the mistrust of Jews towards Germans is reinforced.

---

[73] Krondorfer 1995, 62f.
[74] Cf. Krondorfer 1991, 132.

Guilt is an emotive subject in German debates on the Holocaust. In fact, the discussions on *Vergangenheitsbewältigung* can be understood as discussions on various conceptions of guilt. Kohlstruck's analysis of interviews with third generation German men evaluates the notion of guilt for NS in the context of *Vergangenheitsbewältigung* and intergenerational transmission of NS memory.[75] According to Kohlstruck "The question of guilt is the pivot of *Vergangenheits-bewältigung* and excludes [...] fundamentally different dealings with injustice."[76] He claims that guilt and feelings of guilt as transmitted between the first and second German generations after the Holocaust diffuse in the third generation, because the direct responsibility of the first generation and the indirect responsibility of the second generation through the relationship with their parents is no longer given. Kohlstruck argues that

> The connections of history and biography which thus far were historically possible and actually observable are not applicable any more for the third generation. [...] Certainly not everything can start anew with the third generation, however, the biographical and psychosocial burdens of the first and second generations are missing.[77]

Because of this distance, third generation confrontations with NS take a twofold form. On the one hand there is the confrontation with NS itself and, on the other hand there is the encounter with the history of its interpretation (*Wirkungsgeschichte*). Kohlstruck argues that because of a lack of personal memories, NS has to be encountered via eye-witness accounts of the preceding generations as well as via its documentation in the media. Thus NS is always encountered together with its history of interpretation in society.[78] In this context Kohlstruck observes that the young men in his interviews are reluctant to allocate guilt for NS to members of the first generation, regardless of whether these would be members of their families or not. He explains this by referring to the fact that he interviewed grandsons of bystanders and by arguing that the third generation has largely not experienced public allocations of guilt to members of the first generation who were able to establish a career during NS which was continued in the FRG. Thus although the discourse of *Vergangenheitsbewältigung* remains a discourse about allocation of guilt, the third generation lacks the personalised perspective that was characteristic for the first and second generations.[79] According to Kohlstruck, the fact that the third generation is twice removed from NS has as a consequence that young Germans can only be part of the discourse on *Vergangenheitsbewältigung* if they identify as German.[80] Beginning with the third generation NS becomes history. Kohlstruck argues that belonging to a national community now becomes a precondition for transforming the

---

[75] Cf. Kohlstruck 1997.
[76] Ibid. 39.
[77] Ibid. 91.
[78] Cf. ibid. 275.
[79] Cf. ibid. 281ff.
[80] Cf. ibid. 92.

history of NS and the Holocaust into relevant memory, because "To the third generation National Socialism is no longer a part of their biography, neither directly nor mediated via the discussion with their parents."[81]

Kohlstruck's analysis is based on research conducted in the cultural environment of Germany and does not involve cross-cultural encounters with young Jews of the same age. Whereas I agree that allocations of guilt necessarily become less and less personalised with the third generation, feelings of guilt may not be so easily resolved. Krondorfer's study demonstrates that feelings of guilt emerge in young Germans in confrontation with a survivor of the Holocaust. Birgit Rommelspacher's interviews with young German women regarding their perceptions of Jews and encounters with Jews show that simply the presence of Jews is associated with feelings of uneasiness and guilt.[82] This predominance of feelings of guilt in Germans of the third generation in encounters with survivors of the Holocaust in particular, and Jews in general, appears to be linked to the discourse on *Vergangenheitsbewältigung* in the FRG. Dieter writes about the "defensive position" the German students adopted in the encounter with a survivor of the Holocaust and a group of young Jews. This defensive attitude appears to arise from the confrontation with the testimony of the survivor and other Jews present, a situation in which the German students felt that they were looked at through the eyes of victims of the Holocaust and their community. They felt that they had no choice but to accept the tradition of the victimisers as theirs, in particular when they made the attempt to distance themselves and were rejected by the Jewish participants in the discussion. The discourse on *Vergangenheitsbewältigung* in Germany often omits direct confrontation with interpretations of the community of victims. Arguably this exclusion of victim perspectives is in itself a defensive strategy. When faced with people who understand themselves as representatives of the community of victims, the ways of allocating guilt and of distancing oneself from NS facilitated inside the community of victimisers appear to collapse, even for members of the third generation, to whom NS has largely become a subject of history. Brendler argues in this context

> Further it has to be recognised that the generation of the grandchildren is biographically so close to the perpetrators, fellow travellers and onlookers of the mass murders that they react to the facts of the crimes often with defence mechanisms and blows to their self-esteem which are very similar to the reactions of the generation of the perpetrators at the time after they awakened from their moral lethargy.[83]

However, Rommelspacher suggests that feelings of guilt or, as I would add, the refusal to name wrongs and failures in one's grandparents' actions, which are part of

---

[81] Ibid. 93.
[82] Cf. Rommelspacher 1994, 50ff.
[83] Brendler 1997, 54.

the defence mechanisms of the first, second and third generation have a protective function which needs to be challenged.[84] She argues that

> No matter how you look at it, in the end the crucial question is how the past is appropriated. As long as it remains alien and impersonal any meaning of the term "response"ibility [Ver"antwort"ung] stays empty, because it is unclear what needs to be responded to. And a confusing feeling of guilt protects from examining details. Such a repression is exactly the opposite of an answer, because in this way history is silenced. Thus this past is not understood as a history of one's parents and grandparents into which one is integrated through one's ancestors and for which one has to take responsibility, in the same way as one comes into the positive aspects of one's parents' inheritance. Neither does the relational aspect become clear, namely that in this past relationships have been destroyed which need to be restored.[85]

These feelings of guilt are challenged in the exchange programmes which can enable young Germans to face the legacy of their grandparents' lives as part of their own responsibility.

Another source of misunderstandings and mistrust between Jews and Germans concerns the silences in German family histories which are so difficult for Germans of the third generation to detect themselves.

2.2. "Conspiracy of silence"[86]

The silence in German families about the involvement of family members in NS still prevails today. Many young Germans know next to nothing about the personal history of their relatives during this time, because the few stories circulated in the family about the years 1933-1945 are censored and therefore "safe". Thus it is hard to know the extent to which information is withheld and distorted.[87] Reflecting on the beginning of the 1991 exchange, Anna, an American student with Polish-Jewish American and German-Christian parents, writes

> In order to get acquainted, we began the program by sharing our family histories. This forced us to face each other and ourselves as well. It was a remarkable experience to watch the Germans as the Jewish students told of the suffering and hardship of their relatives during the Nazi era. Just as moving was the struggle that the German students went through as they realized the holes in their family histories. Very few of them knew what their grandparents had been doing during the Nazi years. Some of the German students received no answers when asking their families; others did not ask at all.[88]

But the German participants in the exchange programmes were interested in the Holocaust and had obviously prepared for the session on family histories. Still it

---

[84] Cf. also Krondorfer 1991, 131f.

[85] Rommelspacher 1994, 125.

[86] For the following cf. Krondorfer 1995, 98ff.

[87] Cf. ibid. 98.

[88] Blau in Staffa/Krondorfer (eds.) 1992, 22.

proved difficult to find any detailed information, except for photographs of grandfathers sometimes in their Nazi uniforms. This lack of information and the inability or unwillingness of the German students to ask their grandparents about their lives and thus break the silence presented a stark contrast to the detailed stories provided by the Jewish students.[89] In the beginning, the Jewish students empathised with the Germans and tried to interpret the gaps in the Germans' family histories not as a real lack of knowledge but as information which would be shared eventually once trust had grown and the Germans had become accustomed to communicating in a foreign language. When the German students could not fulfil this expectation and simply continued to acknowledge the gaps, mentioning their parents' silence as an excuse for not knowing more, the Jewish participants were angry. In the ensuing discussion the German students slowly became aware that they were actively participating in the silence in their families.

Young Germans are implicated in a "conspiracy of silence". Krondorfer developed the notion of "third guilt" for the involvement of the third generation in this "conspiracy of silence". Presupposing the first guilt of the actual crimes of the victimisers in Nazi Germany, and a second guilt of post-war Germany in the repression and denial of the first guilt,[90] the third guilt, amongst other things,

> refers to the failure of post-Shoah generations to [...] understand their own cultural assumptions and emotional investments in regard to antisemitism, Jews, and the Holocaust; and the failure to motivate themselves and their families to discover the skeletons in their own closets.[91]

The fact that "Even to young Germans, the Germans of the past remain faceless figures, detached from any family they personally know"[92], reflects fears of what might be discovered in one's family. If young Germans decide to ask painful questions, then they have to prepare for the (rare) possibility that they may be confronted with murderers. Thus, often the fear of what might be discovered is greater than the interest in knowing the truth. Krondorfer describes this as the "fear of specificity" which is rooted in the silence of the family: if nobody admits their involvement with NS everybody is a suspect, parents and grandparents included.[93]

---

[89] The narratives provided by Jewish students about their families are also censored, but in ways that would not necessarily be obvious during such an encounter, cf. for example Bar-On 1995 and Rosenthal (ed.) 1998.

[90] Cf. Giordano [2]1990.

[91] Krondorfer 1995, 113.

[92] Ibid. 100.

[93] Cf. ibid. 119. Matthias Heyl argues differently, claiming that third generation Germans' images of Nazis are incapable of forging a link with living family members: "Movies, T.V. programs, documentaries, let them think that Nazis are tall, fair-haired young people with blue eyes, looking resolutely at the world, a breed of idiotic beings, constantly clicking their heels. [...] Nazis seem to be either victims of diabolic demagoguery, or inhuman beings, monster-like in a way that does not

The result of the "conspiracy of silence" and the "fear of specificity" is a generalising approach to the Holocaust. Rather than inquiring about details, the Holocaust is understood as a paradigm of evil which can teach us specific lessons.[94] This understanding is not necessarily wrong, but it is not the only possible and desirable one. Not asking questions, or not inquiring how and what to ask, generates ignorance about their families' connections to the Holocaust.

The implicit assumption in these exchanges is that every German family will have some connection with the Holocaust, however tentative. Whether this assumption is realistic or not, the underlying question is one of trust. The Jewish students' mistrust regarding the Germans' portrayal of their families sensitises the German students and makes them question whether they can take the narratives transmitted by their families at face value. It is unlikely that all members of any German family remained completely unaware of NS policies regarding Jews, whereas the extent of antisemitic atrocities in the Holocaust may well have not been known to them at the time. Arguably the Jewish students were not looking for an acknowledgement of detailed knowledge of the Holocaust from the Germans' family histories. Rather they wanted to find traces of knowledge about Jewish lives and history in their German peers' family histories.

Brendler's interviews with third generation Germans in the context of an exchange programme with students from Israel, notes four defensive reactions of both members of the third and first generation of Germans which enforce a "double-wall of silence" on conversations about NS:[95]

- Subsequent generations suppressed their need to ask questions to avoid further aggressive rejections or family conflicts.
- Contemporary witnesses evaded conversations about NS, because they had repeatedly experienced accusations and criticism from younger generations for their political naivety and selective memory.
- Burning questions were suppressed out of consideration for relatives, because the children were aware or were made aware in a fashion that asked for sympathy, that being reminded is awkward or painful for the contemporary witnesses.
- Some children or grandchildren abstained from the outset from finding out about biographical data or personal experiences of their relatives, because they feared a loss of self-esteem in the case of uncovering guilty entanglements.[96]

Cross-cultural exchanges of Germans and Jews can help to recognise the implications of this "double-wall of silence" and enable members of the third generation to

---

allow any links to their grandparents, who are infirm, weak, grey-haired, and elderly" (Heyl 1996, 282).

[94] Cf. also Kohlstruck's conclusions regarding third generation German approaches to NS which have not been challenged in cross-cultural encounters (cf. Kohlstruck 1997, 273-288).

[95] Cf. Brendler 1997, 84ff.

[96] Ibid. 84.

challenge their family's and individual relationship to NS. However, Bergerson notices that the liminal space created by the spontaneous *communitas*[97] in Krondorfer's exchange programmes resists integration into the contexts to which each of the participants returned. Regarding the performances of the Jewish-German Dance Theatre Krondorfer was part of, Bergerson argues that

> He [Krondorfer] wants to believe that such performances offer a possibility for escaping the metanarrative of victim/izers. Yet he fails to describe what the new public discourses are in fact (and not in dance), nor how antistructural transformations might be integrated into them. In dealing with their families, their non-involved friends, their audience after performances, and their society at large, the third generation participants seemed to return to old habits of non-confrontational silence [...] Constructed in the space of transgression, this synthesis of remembrance and reconciliation resists being transplanted back into *societas*.[98]

The partial transgression of boundaries in cross-cultural exchanges points to issues particular to Holocaust remembrance in Germany. These need to be further explored outside of the liminal space of the exchanges if their transgressions are to influence public discourses on the Holocaust in Germany.

Feelings of guilt and recognition of silences are two issues addressed in Jewish-German encounters. A third issue arises in particular when Jewish students visit Germany, often for the first time, and painfully experience the absence of Jewish communities.

2.3. A town "free of Jews"

Beth, a Jewish student participating in the 1993 exchange programme, writes about a visit to Halberstadt, a picturesque town in East Germany with a thriving Jewish community before the war. The yeshiva building has been restored and now displays an exhibition about the history of the Jews of Halberstadt. A memorial to the Jews of the town has been erected in front of the cathedral and two overgrown Jewish cemeteries can be visited. Beth reflects in her essay:

> Never before had I actually thought Hitler might have won. My family lives in an area of Los Angeles filled with Jews. Just about everywhere I look, from television, to newspapers, to the faculty at distinguished universities, I see Jewish names and faces. We won, I thought. We Jews conquered Hitler and proved to the vicious anti-semites who cheered for our defeat that we cannot be beaten.
> Then I went to Halberstadt. [...]
> After the cemetery we visited a building that was for hundreds of years a famous yeshiva [...]. We climbed to the top of the stairs until we reached a small room where six or seven thin, wood panels were standing alongside one another. German writing was printed on each one accompanied by several black and white photographs. Together, the panels functioned to give

---

[97] Krondorfer uses Victor Turner's ritual theory to frame his interpretation of cross-cultural encounters of Germans and Jews, cf. in particular Krondorfer 1995, 89-91.
[98] Bergerson 1997, 169.

a chronological history of Halberstadt's now extinct Jewish community, from the time they arrived in the 1250s, to their ultimate annihilation in the early 1940s.
It was these panels [that] made me realize for the first time the stunning success of Hitler. [...] I felt like a living ghost in Halberstadt; almost as though I were visiting that famed museum Hitler was trying to make of a vanished people. I had always prided myself that Hitler never succeeded in finishing that museum, because we Jews survived. But standing in that room this past summer, I felt the enormity of Hitler's success. I was a visitor. I do not live there. With the Jewish community gone, erased, and vanished, Halberstadt is exactly like the way generations of non-Jews would have liked it: devoid of any Jewish presence. [...]
I wish I could feel the same sense of gratitude so many other people felt on our program towards Halberstadt for what it has done to remember the Jews. But I cannot. My inability to do so is rooted in the deep suspicion I have that so little in Halberstadt has changed. To put it more bluntly, I remain unconvinced that something like what happened fifty years ago would not happen again. [...] Even if people profess to have "changed", it is rather easy to make such claims when there are no Jews left, thereby allowing one's prejudices and beliefs to remain intact. As Matthias, a German student, commented, "The only Jews Germany loves are its dead Jews." Never have I heard a statement that more adequately sums up the feeling I got in Halberstadt.[99]

That Jewish life is largely absent in most German towns is known to young Germans. Most places have their memorials and plaques, pointing to buildings of a (former) Jewish community, and their history and destruction or repossession for a different use. But really missing the presence of Jewish communities is only possible when one knows what their presence entails. Hence Beth's emotional trauma when experiencing the absence of people she could imagine as present, and her scepticism towards the museum which appears to be a painless way for Germans to remember former Jewish communities. Her suspicion "that so little in Halberstadt has changed" might be a little exaggerated. However, the point she is making regarding prejudices remaining intact while Germans are fond of "their dead Jews" is echoed in testimonies of Jews living in contemporary Germany.[100] The exchange programmes did include meetings with Jews living in Germany and thus Beth's interpretation of Jewish life in Germany was challenged by Jews who made the FRG their home. However, the testimonies of Jews living in Germany can be read as neither confirming nor rejecting her suspicion, but exploring the context of Jewish life in Germany.[101] Whereas for first and second generation Jews in Germany the shadows of the Holocaust were much more pronounced, because they lived for a long time in a society in which Germans of the first generation assumed public positions and thus shared in the personalised forms of German attempts at *Vergangenheitsbewälti-*

---

[99] Silverberg in Staffa/Krondorfer/Jurgovsky (eds.) 1994, 70-74. Similar comments have been made by other participants, cf. Krondorfer/Schmidt (eds.) 1990, 18ff. and Guertin in Staffa/Krondorfer (eds.) 1992, 55f.
[100] Cf. for example Brenner 1997; Brumlik/Kiesel/Kugelmann/Schoeps (eds.) 1986; Stern (ed.) 1995 and Brumlik (ed.) 1998.
[101] Cf. for example Brumlik (ed.) 1998 and Stern (ed.) 1995.

gung,[102] third generation Jews affiliate with Germany in different ways. Tracing communal identification of Jews in Germany, Michael Brenner demonstrates that since the 1980s the dissociation of Jews living in Germany from German society has shifted toward a greater identification with Germany as homeland.[103]

> As the community increasingly came to be dominated by a "second" generation that was born and grew up in Germany, a stronger affirmation of life in Germany was also introduced. People who were still living in Germany after three or four decades and went on talking about the need to migrate hardly sounded credible any more. Next to the Israeli flags and the posters of Jerusalem, documents about the local Jewish past and present were slowly making their way into the community halls; the German-Jewish heritage took center stage.[104]

In particular, since the 1990s a revival of Jewish culture and religion has been taking place in Germany which is actively trying to re-establish a plurality of Jewish life. Whereas it remains a reality that many among audiences and participants in this wave of learning and exploration of Jewish culture, history and religion are non-Jewish, there is nevertheless the desire of young Jews in Germany to (re-)kindle a relationship with their communal heritage.[105]

Regarding the influence of Holocaust memory on the Jewish community in Germany in the second generation, Lynn Rapaport argues that

> What is really at issue here is determining the different meanings that Holocaust memory generates for the lines of distinction Jews draw between themselves and Germans, and the role these meanings play in their interpersonal relations. I show how second-generation Jews in Germany draw on Holocaust memory as the ultimate tool for constructing identity and community. They form a community of memory that does not forget its past. They draw on collective memory in daily interactions as they raise and erase group boundaries. The Holocaust provides the framework for representing the past, understanding the present, and envisioning the future. It is their ultimate metaphor, a part of their roots, the source from which the meanings they bestow to daily life are constituted.[106]

Even if the third generation of Jews and non-Jews in Germany is able to begin to transcend the antagonistic patterns of transmission of Holocaust memory dividing Jews and non-Jews in Germany, the strong division of Jewish and non-Jewish memories in Germany is likely to determine German-Jewish relations for the foreseeable future. Hence this deep division in identity formation and memories needs to be addressed also in the context of Christian reflection on Christian-Jewish relations in Germany. When Peter Sichrovsky conducted his interviews with children of Nazis in Germany and Austria he did not anticipate that the reality of family-life

---

[102] Cf. for example Broder/Lang et al. 1979; Fleischmann [5]1996; Jacoby/Schoppmann/Zena-Henry (eds.) 1994; Rapaport 1997 and Sichrovsky 1986.

[103] Cf. Brenner 1997, 143ff.

[104] Brenner 1997, 144.

[105] Cf. for example Brumlik 1998a.

[106] Rapaport 1997, 24.

described by his interviewees could be so very alien to him. He had grown up and gone to school with children of Nazis and considered them as different (Other) to him but did not think of them as strangers. However in interviewing these young people he discovered that they did not share experiences, that there was no overlap in their identities. He concluded that they had lived alongside each other rather than shared in the same reality.[107]

3. Conclusion

Research on the third generation of both Germans and Jews has begun to outline issues that are particular to this generation. The development of an identity which integrates the history of NS and the Holocaust and transcends approaches of identification chosen by previous generations and public discourses is the challenge faced by members of the third generation. What can thus far only be enacted in the liminal spaces of *communitas* needs to be translated into the social and cultural contexts of everyday life of Germans and Jews.

Three issues have become dominant in the evaluation of research on the third generation of Germans. Firstly, Germans grow up with silences in their families who censor narratives relating to the Holocaust and NS. The lack of insight into the lives of the victims of NS before and during the Holocaust is particularly evident in research that does not explicitly focus on the Holocaust, but rather asks questions concerning the interviewee's relationship to NS in general.[108] In particular all three generations tend to avoid questions of guilt regarding their own families and identify victims among their relations or communities, rather than explore the perspective of victims of NS which they understand as Other, such as Jews.[109] As such, research results on the transmission of memories of NS and the Holocaust in German families correspond to the conclusions reached about the reluctance of representing victims' perspectives on NS and the Holocaust in German public culture.

Secondly, Germans lack knowledge of contemporary Jewish life and the contexts in which Jews have grown up. They identify Jews via discourses common to their communities. Thus the stereotypes they have learned about Jews are evident in the encounters. Krondorfer notes that "young Germans are repeatedly surprised that Jews of the same age have feelings towards them and hold (pre-)judgements about them."[110] Rommelspacher's study on young German women's relations to antisemitism and Jews concludes that the stereotypes transmitted about Jews are so strong that if Jews in their self-expression do not correspond to these stereotypes they

---

[107] Cf. Sichrovsky 1987.
[108] Cf. for example Kohlstruck 1997.
[109] Cf. Rosenthal 1998b, 244.
[110] Krondorfer 1991, 136.

will not be acknowledged as Jewish.[111] Thus although the interviews demonstrate that many of the interviewees have contact with Jews as acquaintances and friends they still deny knowing any Jews, since their friends do not exhibit characteristics they can identify as Jewish, such as for example orthodox garb and religiosity. Rommelspacher regards these non-recognitions of Jews as strategies to avoid any confrontations with challenging histories.[112]

Thirdly, the emotional weight the memory of NS and the Holocaust carries for Germans is evident in all third generation testimonies. To negotiate one's relationship to the Holocaust, bearing in mind the involvement of one's family and/or community in the events and thereby developing one's own independent identity remains the task encountered by Germans who confront the Holocaust and NS. As evident in the challenges cross-cultural encounters with young Jews posed to Germans, this task includes the need to transcend the discourses of their own community in order to gain a better understanding of their community's history. Conflicts regarding the ownership of NS and Holocaust history evident in German society, as well as in the cross-cultural encounters, can only be addressed if Germans are willing to understand Jewish memory and history as related to their own history and no longer have the need to suspect Jewish memory of undermining German narratives.[113] Implicit in this "appropriation" of Jewish history and memory is the rejection of a usurpation of primarily dead and victimised Jews who can conveniently be claimed as part of German history, because they can no longer protest and challenge German assumptions about Jews with their own expressions of identity. What needs to be included are Jewish narratives precisely in their difference and inconvenience for Germans.

The exchange programmes from which the examples discussed in this chapter are taken are one contribution to facilitate understanding between young people who grew up with the memory of an antagonistic past. These programmes rely on an inherited antagonism of Jews and Germans as a result of NS and the Holocaust. During the encounters boundaries of self-definition and identity formation are challenged and, ideally, the participants have begun to transform their identities when they leave the programme. What is supposed to happen, i.e. what determines a successful programme, is a sharing of memory, not an agreement on forms and content of Holocaust remembrance, but an exchange of "memory material", so that narratives previously owned exclusively by one community can now be shared in by both communities. Krondorfer argues that

---

[111] Cf. Rommelspacher 1994, 51ff.
[112] Cf. ibid. 51ff.
[113] Cf. ibid. 189.

Genuine reconciliation [...] is a communal and experimental practice in which third-generation Jews and Germans remember the Holocaust, but also creatively engage in overcoming the limitations and deceptions of the currently cultivated discourse.[114]

Thus the third generation of Germans and Jews after the Holocaust can challenge the patterns of remembrance of the Holocaust in Germany. Their ability to read the discourses of their parents' and grandparents' generations on the memory of the Holocaust, and their historical distance from NS and the Holocaust, increases the chances to transcend these discourses through encounters with each other and thus to move the debate in Germany onto a less personal but still involved level.

Christian-Jewish relations can be understood as cross-cultural encounters and can as such be interpreted with the categories developed in third generation exchanges. In the context of the Rhineland statement as well as Friedrich-Wilhelm Marquardt's theology, the need to examine German perceptions of and behaviour towards Jews was recognised as a necessary condition for Christian-Jewish encounters. Nevertheless, in the Rhineland statement, the responses it received, as well as Marquardt's theology and the discussion surrounding it, active inquiries into these perceptions were only carried out on the level of Christian antisemitism apparent in theology. Thus it concerned the analysis of written texts and ideas rather than the personal lives of the contributors to the discussions. Hence the emotional entanglement of theologians in the context of their theologies has not yet become part of the theologies themselves.

Both the Rhineland statement and Marquardt's theology claim Jewish tradition as part of Christian religious resources to develop their theologies. Both appear to understand this sharing in Jewish cultural and religious resources as an extension of their conversations and encounters with Jews. However, the fragile transgression of boundaries in the *communitas* of the exchanges programmes cautions against such imperialistic behaviour. Debates regarding the ownership of memory and the right to the representation of a shared history are strong in the third generation. Suspicions about each other's motivations to represent a particular perspective on the Holocaust are illustrated in debates on the USHMM during the exchange programmes.[115] A German student writes perceptively on the dangers inherent in German representations of Jewish culture in Germany:

In the past years, a certain kind of memory culture is spreading through Germany, focusing on restoring cemeteries and synagogues. The result is displayed in every decent bookstore: large volumes with neat pictures of tombstones. This is a deadly embrace, directly connected to the difficult relations Germans have to their own identity. One claims that the Nazis thoroughly

---

[114] Krondorfer 1995, 16.
[115] Cf. Krondorfer 1991, 138f. as well as Krondorfer 1997, 13.

destroyed part of one's "own" culture: the taking care of remnants of the Jewish culture then becomes part of one's own life – they are appropriated posthumously.[116]

In a sense, Christian appropriation of Jewish tradition in Christian theology which grows out of Christian-Jewish encounters after the Holocaust reads like such a posthumous appropriation which bypasses the questions the memory of the Holocaust addresses to German self-understanding. Usurpation of another community's memory and cultural texts, so that one does not have to face one's own history and memory, once again silences Jewish voices on the memory of the Holocaust and NS.

The idea of looking at one's own context and self-understanding through the eyes of another, which Marquardt's theology aimed at, has thus far not been realised. Without considering the patterns of identification on the background of the memory of NS and the Holocaust particular to the communities of Germans and Jews such a crossing of boundaries is unlikely. Pseudo-identification with Jewish culture and tradition in the context of Christian-Jewish relations is not helping Christians to understand their own nor Jewish entanglements with the history of NS and the Holocaust on emotional, biographical and intellectual levels.[117]

However, impulses of generational research are beginning to be considered in German Protestant theology which addresses Christian-Jewish relations after the Holocaust. Britta Jüngst's theology takes experiences of second generation Jews and Germans as its starting point. Analysing how her theology represents the Holocaust and Jews may indicate how testimonies of descendants of victims and victimisers might influence representations of the Holocaust and Jews in German Protestant theology.

---

[116] Kandiorza in Staffa/Krondorfer/Jurgovsky (eds.) 1994, 27f.

[117] Rosenthal suggests that this pseudo-identification which avoids confrontation with one's family's German history during NS can also be found in expressions of philosemitism, as well as marriage to a Jewish partner or even conversion (cf. Rosenthal 1998b, 245; cf. also Heyl 1995, 34ff.).

V. Britta Jüngst – Conversational theology

In *In the realm of death there is life*[1] Jüngst develops a theology that is part of both feminist and Christian-Jewish discourses in the FRG. Her theology is part of a recent development among young theologians in Germany, both Protestant and Catholic, who have written their (doctoral) dissertations on subjects pertaining to post-Holocaust Christian theological thinking about Jews. Theologians such as Jüngst, Birte Petersen, Paul Petzel and Norbert Reck, for example, take their starting point from the work of the previous generation of theologians in the field of German post-Holocaust Christian-Jewish relations such as Bertold Klappert, Hans-Joachim Kraus, Hans Küng, Friedrich-Wilhelm Marquardt, Johann Baptist Metz, Jürgen Moltmann, Franz Mussner, Peter von der Osten-Sacken, Rolf Rendtorff, Martin Stöhr and Clemens Thoma. In her MA dissertation Petersen evaluates Christian theological responses to the Holocaust in the context of West German Christian-Jewish relations and Jewish religious responses to the Holocaust from the USA, asking for renewed approaches to the subject which take seriously questions posed by the historical reality of the victim-perpetrator dichotomy, Christian guilt and responsibility for the Holocaust, and the use of theological language.[2] Petzel's dissertation explores the significance of Jews for the development of Christian theology,[3] and Reck examines theological possibilities of portraying the rupture caused by the Holocaust in history and theology.[4] Reck takes seriously the demand of Christian theology to think from the perspective of the victims of the Holocaust and approaches theology with the help of survivor testimony. These theologians from Germany share a concern for Christian-Jewish relations in the present which is rooted in its historical and theological context after the Holocaust. Their own biographical distance from NS allows them to address questions which have been posed before, but which the previous generation of theologians has not been able to consider in detail.

Jüngst describes both feminist theology and Christian-Jewish relations as existing on the margins of academic theology and church practice in Germany and sometimes in conflict with each other as the debate on anti-Judaism in feminist theology demonstrates.[5] Influenced by feminist debates on the relevance of women's experiences for the formulation of theological statements, she makes these the centre of her inquiry into the possibilities of writing Christian theology which is sensitive to the context of women's lives while locating it firmly in the context of post-Holocaust Germany.

---

[1] Jüngst 1996. The title is derived from Ingeborg Bachmann's poem "Dunkles zu sagen".
[2] Petersen [2]1998.
[3] Petzel 1994.
[4] Reck 1998.
[5] Cf. Jüngst 1996, 13. Cf. also the analysis of post-war feminist theology in the FRG in Siegele-Wenschkewitz 1988.

The necessity to frame itself as a theology after Auschwitz does not confront Christian-feminist theology from the outside as a secondary principle, as a task it is free to address or not. The historical, spiritual and social condition (in particular in the FRG) "after Auschwitz" is always also a theological condition, whether it is reflected on as such or not. [...] The meaning of the Shoah for the thought and life of Jewish men and women has since been truly listened to by comparatively few Christians; as a disruption of *Christian* faith the Shoah has been well repressed. But the Shoah has invaded our thinking, emotions and actions as a fact which has exposed previous securities – such as for example the reign of reason, the understanding of human beings (criticised by feminists anyway) – as fantasies.[6]

As a consequence of employing the concept of experience as developed in feminist theory and theology as her hermeneutical key, Jüngst includes reflection on social realities of contemporary Christian and Jewish life into her theological investigation. Thus space is devoted to testimony of Jews and Germans on the Holocaust and NS as well as generational research on the transmission of Holocaust and NS memory. Her dissertation is a search for a Christian-feminist theology

[...] which does not want to cover-up its insecurities, but rather accepts these as part of its context, for a theology which does not only avoid anti-Judaism, but rather does not need it at all as part of its structure and understands itself from the beginning as being in conversation with Jewish women even if everything appears to stand in its way. Walking like Ruth with Naomi, without calling and promise, but not alone.[7]

1. Difference and equality – Formulating experiences theologically

The preoccupation with experience in the history of Christian theology above all revolves around the uncertainty with which Christian men and women can give information about themselves being in a state of grace.[8]

Jüngst argues that, as such, the relation of revelation and experience is always controversial.[9] The nature of the relation between revelation and experience concerns not only the reliability of experience as a confirmation of revelation and an inclusion of experience in or exclusion from theology. Rather it concerns the question of whose experiences are recognised as valid experiences in the first place and as such it is a question of power.[10]

---

[6] Jüngst 1996, 19.

[7] Ibid. 14.

[8] Ibid. 31.

[9] Cf. also the influential articles Ebeling 1975 and Ebeling 1978.

[10] Cf. Jüngst 1996, 31f. and 58: "[...] der grundlegende Unterschied zwischen herrschender und feministischer Theologie in bezug auf die Rede von Erfahrungen [ist] letztlich eine Machtfrage. Strittig ist nicht, ob sich Theologie auf menschliche Erfahrungen bezieht, strittig ist, *wessen* Erfahrungen thematisiert werden und *wer* das tut."

In the course of its early history the church has abandoned people, because/provided that they were Jewish and/or female and/or poor. They were deprived of the opportunity to define themselves in opposition to the church or by ignoring the church or as part of the church community, and thus they were deprived of originally shaping the face of the church. Rather they were turned into objects of church teaching and church action.[11]

Jüngst refers to the theology of Karl Barth as a helpful contribution to the discussion about which experiences can be linked to G-d's revelation. She argues that Barth's scepticism towards drawing theological conclusions from human experiences provides a critical element which allows the questioning of experiences about their meaning when brought in relation to the word of G-d.[12] Liberation theologies in particular have taken up the interpretation of experiences.

The discourse on experiences in the context of the various liberation theologies provides a framework of interpretation which articulates, takes seriously and interprets theologically the various contexts in which groups and individuals find themselves, i.e. political, biographical, gender, sexual, spiritual/intellectual, work-historical, educational-historical, family-historical ... The discourse becomes theological speech by being measured against the history of God with his people Israel and with Jesus Christ.[13]

In particular, the second women's movement elevated the experiences of women to a hermeneutical principle.[14] Because patriarchy is the context in which men and women live and learn to express themselves, all experiences are articulated within the framework of patriarchy.[15] Jüngst understands feminism as a response to patriarchy, as a liberation movement of and for both women and men: "Feminist theology has made it its business to pick out women's experiences in patriarchy as a central theme and to make them theologically effective."[16] Stretched between accepting dominant cultural attributes of what it means to be a woman and the danger of being unable to find viable categories outside of these, Jüngst argues that the experiences of women can provide a measure of reality at which all theory and theology has to be constantly verified.[17] Thus a counter-narrative to patriarchy is supposed to be produced which is able to transcend the constraints of patriarchy. Surveying the work of French feminist philosophy, Jüngst concludes as follows concerning the representation of women in patriarchy and feminist discourses:

- statements about the nature of women are normally attributes which pretend identity where identity is in fact systematically denied. The condition of non-identity and the denial of attributes is hard to tolerate. Here Christian-feminist theology is required to hold on to the Christian vision of identity, wholeness and redemption without concealing reality.

---

[11] Ibid. 32.
[12] Cf. ibid. 36f.
[13] Ibid. 37.
[14] Cf. ibid. 41f.
[15] This understanding would be challenged by non-white feminists.
[16] Ibid. 59.
[17] Cf. ibid. 38f., 42.

- images of women, attributes as well as attempts to become a subject in all its contradictions have to be viewed in a differentiated way. "The woman" does not exist, rather there are different women with very different experiences.[18]

Thus feminism as a liberation movement from the limitations of patriarchy encourages and celebrates not only the difference of women from men, but also the differences between individuals as men and women. However, this conceptualisation relies on a unity of all women as well as men which underlies the differences displayed in their individual and communal lives.

Hence "difference" (*Differenz*) and "equality" (*Gleichheit*) are the two dialectically opposed concepts which Jüngst analyses in three feminist debates on racism in the USA, the debate on the roles of women during NS, and finally the discussion on anti-Judaism in feminist theology.[19] She argues that the feminist category of experience carries the danger of generalising women's experience with the result of suppressing differences between women so as to highlight the "greater" difference of all women's experiences in patriarchy from men's experiences. However, recently the articulation of differences between women has begun to be celebrated as a privilege rather than as a loss of unity.[20] Concerning Christian-Jewish relations Jüngst claims that because the differences between Jewish and non-Jewish women are real and not imagined, these need to constitute the basis of Christian theology.[21]

> A feminist theology which does not only choose women's experiences as the starting point for its reflection and speech, but women's experiences in their different shapings, in their discrepancy, needs to perceive this discrepancy also in its respective historical perspective.[22]

To recover this historical perspective of difference between Jewish and non-Jewish women for the context of the FRG, Jüngst portrays artistic representations of Jews in German caricatures since the 18th century and the history of the women's movement in Germany since the turn of the 20th century.[23] The fact that the written history of the women's movement in Germany has largely excluded the history of Jewish women, indicates how little, even in this in itself marginal history, Jewish history is understood as part of German history.[24] Jüngst writes that

> This is all the more astonishing, given that feminism intends the liberation of all people from any kind of oppression, also from antisemitism, which, however, in contrast to, for example,

---

[18] Ibid. 70.

[19] Cf. ibid. 76-127. Regarding the translation of the terms *Differenz* and *Gleichheit*: *Differenz* can be translated as difference, discrepancy and variance; *Gleichheit* has the connotations of equality, homogeneity and uniformity.

[20] Cf. ibid. 118f.

[21] Cf. ibid. 92.

[22] Ibid. 92.

[23] Cf. ibid. 93-102.

[24] Cf. also Siegele-Wenschkewitz 1988, 12ff., 32ff.

racism, is rarely specifically mentioned. Antisemitism is a taboo – also in the feminist movement.[25]

In particular, the debate on anti-Judaism in Christian feminist theology, which in the middle of the 1980s occupied feminist theologians in the FRG, illustrates the suppression of issues pertaining to Jewish identities in Christian feminist theology. Jüngst argues that this ignorance concerning Jews and Jewish lives in history and today also prevails in Christian-Jewish encounters in Germany. According to Jüngst

> Making the Shoah the central subject is the key to conversations; Christian and post-Christian feminists in Germany are completely unprepared for a conversation with Jewish men and women without awareness of their own history and their place therein, even if they have noticed and assimilated Jewish traditions now and then.[26]

According to Jüngst, feminist insights regarding the articulation of differences in women's experiences are helpful to Christian-Jewish encounters, in particular in the FRG, because Jews and Christians approach the conversations with very different backgrounds and experiences as well as from different places in German society. However, Jüngst characterises the debates on anti-Judaism as the "*Gretchenfrage*" of Christian-feminist theology in the FRG, thus locating her criticisms and the issues this theology needs to address in the context of antisemitism. The Holocaust thus becomes the extreme example of antisemitism. The question arises whether subsuming the Holocaust into the debate on antisemitism narrows the focus of (theological) issues that can be addressed and hence ignores particularities of Holocaust experiences.

To articulate difference theologically, Jüngst refers to biblical images of community and argues that the "Hebrew Bible and Jesus-scriptures clearly advocate the idea of reconciling difference and equality of people with each other".[27] Borrowing the idea of "community in diversity" from the Jewish feminist Judith Plaskow, Jüngst develops this concept of solidarity with the help of 1 Pet 2:9 and 1 Cor 12 and Lk 9:1-10:42. She concludes with an illustration of the fact that Jews and Christians can share in this concept of community which celebrates difference. Quoting Plaskow she argues:

> But high regard for differences in a community, i.e. the experience of not being made to conform, but to be in good hands particularly because of one's differences – like the different limbs in the one body of Christ – is not a genuinely Christian invention. "This relationship between universality and particularity (regarding experience, BJ) ... also characterizes the biblical message of sin and grace which is conveyed through the story of a particular people living in a particular place and in a particular situation."[28]

---

[25] Jüngst 1996, 102.

[26] Ibid. 106.

[27] Ibid. 121.

[28] Ibid. 123.

According to Jüngst the *toledot* of Genesis open the biblical narratives of difference in a community of equals. She follows the interpretation of the Dutch theologian Frans Breukelman.[29] Breukelman translates *toledot* (from the verb *yalad*, "to beget" and "to give birth to") as "begettings" ("*Zeugungen*"). Jüngst adds the translation "birthings" ("*Gebärungen*") to capture the double meaning of the Hebrew which refers to both male and female roles in the process of producing a child.[30] Genesis narrates the stories of individuals and their relationship with G-d.[31] Jüngst argues that their rivalries and different roles depending on their position in the hierarchy of the family are stories of conflict, jealousy, reconciliation and acceptance.[32] Regarding the representation of difference and equality Jüngst concludes that

> Thus the structure of Genesis raises our awareness of the experiences of the Other, teaches us to listen to them, to acknowledge them as experiences which are different from one's own, but have the same value. I am not asked to tolerate them, because this implies hierarchy and a restraint to use it. Not to place myself *above* the experiences of others, but to *relate to* them, to come close to them, to understand them and to question myself about this experience which is foreign to me, to discover it as meaningful for my own life and my own experiences – this corresponds to the biblical understanding of reality.[33]

She refers to the various ways in which the stories of Genesis negotiate the tensions caused by the experience of difference.

> Power struggle and war (Sarah-Hagar, Jacob-Esau), flight from the experiences of the others (Lot), alternating between solidarity and antagonism (Leah-Rachel), murder (Cain-Abel), recognition after long struggle and the experience to be saved and blessed through the other (Joseph and his brothers).[34]

Jüngst concludes that

> The Bible can be read as history of rehearsing life with differences, the rehearsal of difference in the search for community, in community, asking for community, leaving the community and endangering it.[35]

Similar to Marquardt, Jüngst claims a "biblical understanding of reality" as the foundation of her theology, the measure with which to assess experiences. Experiences influence the reading of the biblical text, but can only do so, because that is what the Bible is asking of its reader. Jüngst hopes that her theological framework will be able to incorporate everyone's experience in their own right without a

---

[29] For references to Breukelman's work cf. Jüngst 1996, 124, 230.

[30] Cf. Jüngst 1996, 124.

[31] Jüngst refers to feminist interpretations of the *toledot*, however these are not her focus since she reads the narrative as an illustration of how difference and equality inside a community can be represented (cf. ibid. 126 note 234).

[32] Cf. ibid. 126.

[33] Ibid. 127.

[34] Ibid. 127.

[35] Ibid. 127.

hierarchy, the only criterion being that these experiences must be related to the Bible to partake in the formulation of theology. Like Marquardt's biblical hermeneutics, Jüngst binds her principles of reading the Bible back to the *toledot* of Genesis.

However, feminist theory has since moved on from the privileging of women's experience to questioning the concept of "woman" and that of experience. While the second women's movement focused on the difference of women's experiences arising from the social-historical context of their lives their theories still relied on belief in an underlying essence shared by all women. Difference could be articulated on the basis of a unity of all women (and by extension of humanity). This movement away from an essentialist understanding of femininity towards concepts which recognise the constructed nature of gender still acknowledged an underlying essence common to all. Hence any representation of "other" women still recognised their similarity to one's own interpretation of what it means to be a woman. The criticism of post-structuralist feminist theory is levelled against this assumption of a shared essence, because of the inability to create meaning outside of the systems which people operate to identify ourselves.[36] Regarding feminist theology Mary McClintock Fulkerson argues

> that feminist theology has failed to offer theories of language, social location, power, and gender capable of displaying difference. When it relies upon appeals to women's experience as the origin of or evidence for its claims, feminist theology cannot account for the systems of meaning and power that produce that experience.[37]

Hence McClintock Fulkerson suggests a "change of subject" so that we better understand the "role of our own definitions in constructing the other, as well as make us understand that we have no access to the real outside of our own power-laden constructions."[38] As a consequence of this argument, Jüngst's way of describing difference remains in the realm of liberal pluralism which aims to integrate the Other by adding its description to the multiple voices which make up society, however, without changing the structures of the established social order.[39] Such integrations of the Other that do

> not take seriously the radical instability of discourse and the intimate connection of power/knowledge are tempted to ignore the ways in which our definitions of the other do not allow us to really have an "other." Our definitions continually domesticate that which is outside and give it a name that may appear to be other, but is actually a process of objectifying or saming.[40]

---

[36] Cf. Cady 1997, 18.
[37] McClintock Fulkerson 1994, vii.
[38] Ibid. 7 (italics in original).
[39] Cf. ibid. 5 as well as Cady 1997, 18ff.
[40] McClintock Fulkerson 1994, 382.

Hence Jüngst's interpretation of difference against the background of concepts of community derived from biblical texts may in fact be in danger of continuing the process of Christian "domestication" of Jews for the purposes of Christian theology.

To Jüngst, the story of Naomi and Ruth as a story of "loving solidarity of two who became home for each other and made a home for each other"[41] becomes a paradigm for the exploration of Christian theology in the context of Christian-Jewish conversations. According to Jüngst, Ruth represents a female perspective on history complementary to the *toledot* of Genesis which narrates history according to the succession of men as heirs to G-d's promises.

> This story here confronts the story of the *toledot* of Genesis with the story of women. Genesis was concerned with the election of the male firstborn and the efforts and difficulties of the others to join in the praise of the firstborn's experiences with God. Here we are challenged by the experiences of two women to praise with them their experiences of God and their birthings [*Gebärungen*].[42]

She argues that the presuppositions of her theology demand attention to the historical context in which women formulate theology. Therefore she focuses on exploring the context in which Jews and Christians in Germany learn to develop their identities before moving on to read the book of Ruth as an experiment in Christian-Jewish conversation.

2. Representing the Holocaust and Jews – Traditions of victims and victimisers

Jüngst's theology takes as its starting point the experiences of Holocaust survivors and their descendants.

> In the context of Jewish-Christian conversation in the FRG the experiences of survivors of the Shoah and their descendants become audible to Christian-feminist theology – this is an attempt to give the witnesses the chance "to keep their word", to listen to the "suffocated words", as articulated by Sarah Kofman's question: "Mon père est mort à Auschwitz. Comment ne pas le dire? Et comment le dire?"[43]

To Jüngst the category of experience becomes the organising principle for her theology. Experience functions as the hermeneutical key to recover material not previously recognised. Similar to the use of (collective) memory in the context of communities of memory, experience enables a description of the context in which people come to understand themselves. The category of experience makes audible silences and facilitates communication. Thus Jüngst is able to portray various

---

[41] Jüngst 1996, 127.

[42] Ibid. 194.

[43] Ibid. 14.

narratives that fight for space in the articulation of post-Holocaust Jewish and German identities. However, she privileges Jewish experiences as interpretations of reality from the start. Focusing on German memories she aims to understand their silences with the help of Jewish experiences as the experiences of victims whose articulation is supposed to enable the liberation of Germans as well as Jews.

Jüngst is one of the first theologians in Germany who allows the testimony of survivors and their descendants as well as of victimisers and their families to enter theological reflection as a necessary component of Christian theology after the Holocaust. Devoting space to testimonies of survivors of the Holocaust and their children, as well as to the children of victimisers, enables her to focus on issues particular to the groups of victims and victimisers and their descendants.[44] She concludes that the Holocaust challenges Christian-feminist theology, because

> as any theology it is bound to Jewish thought and life and needs to understand itself from the perspective of Jewish tradition, together with this tradition and alongside it in historical and theological terms. And it needs to work through its anti-Jewish and antisemitic past and present in a critical fashion.[45]

According to Jüngst, the Holocaust should be the centre of Christian-Jewish conversations in Germany, because it challenges the participants to examine their understanding of their own place in the context of this history.[46]

> In the rare encounters of Jewish and Christian women in Europe, especially in Germany, it matters that Christians are able to communicate in an informed manner about their own tradition and its difficulties and values as well as about the meaning of the Shoah for their own life and their theology. Learning about Jewish history and contemporary Jewish life is indispensable, but cannot substitute for the self-criticism which asks about the meaning of the study of Judaism for my personal life and what happens emotionally (and theologically) when I come into contact with real-life Jewish women.[47]

Thus the reason Jüngst grounds her theological reflections in the experiences of Holocaust survivors and their families is twofold. One the one hand she argues that the social-historical context of Germany as post-Holocaust is a condition of theology, and on the other hand she understands Christian theology to be fundamentally dependent on Jews. Following Christian post-Holocaust theology, she argues that if Christian theology negates its intrinsic dependency on Jews, it violates its own essence.[48] Consequently, the experiences of survivors of the Holocaust and their descendants take priority for the formulation of theology, for two reasons. On the one hand the dependency of Christians on Jews has Christians partake in Jewish experiences in the same way as the *toledot* teach that others partake in the blessings

---

[44] Cf. also Reck 1998.

[45] Jüngst 1996, 93.

[46] Cf. ibid. 106.

[47] Ibid. 183.

[48] Cf. ibid. 19.

promised to the Jewish people via the firstborn.[49] On the other hand, she argues that only the theological recognition of the testimony of Jewish victims can facilitate the liberation of both German and Jewish women in a feminist theological context that aims to adopt the perspective of the people whose experiences were previously silenced by the dominant theological tradition.[50] With this twofold binding of Christian theology to Jewish experience, Jüngst wishes to make antisemitism an impossibility in the formulation of theology, and at the same time avoid the imperialism with which post-Holocaust theology tends to approach Jewish testimony of the Holocaust. Her theological framework intends to ban Christian identification with Jewish experiences while at the same time facilitating Christian recognition of Jewish perspectives.

However, by accepting the presupposition of post-Holocaust theology which understands Christians to be dependent on contemporary Jews she also accepts the imperialistic structure of post-Holocaust theology. If Christian theology is dependent on Jews, then the definition of the "Jewish other" in terms of Christian theology is already part of the presuppositions which make Christian theology possible in the first place. Furthermore, with the introduction of a hierarchy of experiences which privileges the testimony of Holocaust survivors, the articulation of experiences of subsequent generations is measured against the voices of survivors which are understood as normative. As such it may be difficult to hear the experiences of victimisers and their descendants, as well as testimony of descendants of survivors.

2.1. The Holocaust

Jüngst presupposes that her readers are familiar with "the Holocaust". She chooses not to explore the events she is referring to. In contrast, Reck suggests that post-Holocaust theology needs to specify what it is talking about when referring to "Auschwitz":

> To qualify the situation "*after Auschwitz*" and to derive specific conclusions from it, one would need to think first of all *about* Auschwitz, one would need to describe what happened there, in order to understand what distinguishes the situation "after" so significantly from the situation "before".[51]

---

[49] She does not address the State of Israel as a theological reality as does Marquardt, however, her argument regarding the participation of others in the blessings of the firstborn suggests an uncomfortable closeness to Marquardt's "theology on the far side of God".

[50] Cf. also Metz 1980 and Metz 1972/1995. His approach to theology from the perspective of its victims has been evaluated in both feminist and in post-Holocaust theologies, cf. Maaßen 1993, 105ff. as well as Petersen [2]1998, 104f. and Reck 1998, 134ff.

[51] Reck 1998, 12.

Hence the Holocaust should not be used as a metaphor, but needs to describe a concrete historical context.[52] Jüngst takes the concreteness of the Holocaust seriously by referring to testimonies of survivors and their children about the impact of the Holocaust on their lives.[53] However, the concrete events which generate the trauma are not included in the reflection.

Jüngst uses the term "Shoah" consistently, but without explaining this choice of terminology over against other options for describing the events and experiences she refers to. This usage of terminology suggests a contradiction in her approach. On the one hand, she claims that non-Jewish Germans have banned the Holocaust from their memory and have chosen to suppress any experiences of the events in question. Consequently the transmission of Holocaust memory from one generation to the next in German society is disrupted. On the other hand, she suggests Shoah – not a well known word in Germany – as an appropriate and self-explanatory term. At the same time, Jüngst uses phrases such as Auschwitz and post-Holocaust theology. Consequently the reader is left with the task of relating the different terminologies to each other and building his/her own image of the events they refer to.

The rootedness of the term Shoah in Jewish and particularly Israeli discourses makes its application in German discourses problematic. Omer Bartov demonstrates the application of Shoah in modern Hebrew which is comparable to the extended use of Holocaust in English:

> Modern Hebrew uses the word *shoah*, that is, disaster, in many other contexts as well, such as "nuclear disaster" (*shoah gar'init*), "air disaster" (*shoah avirit*), "natural disaster" (*shoat teva*), and so forth. The term "Shoah" is an accurate description of the genocide of the Jews from a Jewish perspective, since it evokes the fact that this was indeed a disaster for the Jewish people.[54]

However, he continues to argue that

> At a second look, however, the very fact that it is often associated with natural disaster, or with spectacular man-made catastrophes, makes it particularly useful within the Israeli/Zionist context. Associating the Holocaust with a natural phenomenon such as the eruption of a volcano would mean that just as it is impossible to prevent the volcano from erupting but possible to move the house to a safer location, so too was it impossible to prevent the Nazis (or gentiles) from trying to kill the Jews but *was* possible to recreate a Jewish national existence that would have both hampered fulfilment of such aims, and made death more honorable, since it would have come only after organized military resistance [...] Hence while not a "holocaust" in the sacrificial sense, "Shoah" has an didactic aspect, in that it serves as a

---

[52] Cf. ibid. 13.

[53] Arguably survivor testimony does not include all aspects of the Holocaust, but rather privileges some experiences over against others (cf. for example the lack of testimony from places such as Belzec and Treblinka as well as Langer 1991 on "discourse of ruin").

[54] Bartov 1996, 59.

constant reminder that the Jews in the Diaspora, who lived on the edge of a volcano, had refused to heed the warnings of the Zionists and consequently perished.[55]

Reck explains why he chooses "Auschwitz" over against other available terms. He cautions against the application of Jewish terminology to German discourses since Jewish names for the Holocaust often have religious connotations expressing victim perspectives that cannot be assumed by a Christian theologian.[56]

Jüngst's explorations of the Holocaust concern the experiences of victims, perpetrators and their descendants during and after the events of the Holocaust. In this context she defines experiences with reference to Aristotle as follows:

> Experience, that was for Aristotle the memory of praxis. An event, the social, biographical, historical reality which surrounds me, becomes experience when it is admitted into one's memory, when it is interpreted against the background of previous experience and is assimilated into my self-understanding.[57]

Her definition of experience refers to a phenomenon similar to that described by memory. An event has to be acknowledged as important to one's self-understanding in order to enter the narratives which form the relevant memory of an individual or a community. To understand how the Holocaust has entered the self-understanding of Jews and Germans, Jüngst explores testimony of survivors and their children as well as that of the children of perpetrators. She cautions against the use of conceptualising, scientific terminology such as speaking about syndromes in connection with the psychological characteristics of survivors and their children.[58] According to Jüngst, this terminology facilitates on the one hand the process of distancing oneself from the experiences of the survivors which is necessary to be able to speak about these at all. On the other hand, she argues that this distancing also shifts the focus from the individual to a group and as such depersonalises the encounter with experiences of the Holocaust.

> Therefore I am attempting to let the male and female witnesses speak for themselves, as much as is possible and accessible to me, to "let them keep their word" (Kofman), because also Christian theology largely withholds their experiences.[59]

Jüngst gives space to extensive quotations from testimonies of survivors and their children in an attempt to recover what has hardly been noticed by Christian theology. Part of the experiences of Robert Antelme, a nameless survivor, and the parents of the film producer Tsipi Reibenbach are reported in the main text.[60] Jüngst argues that the experiences of the Holocaust can hardly be communicated in language. This has a

---

[55] Ibid. 60.
[56] Cf. Reck 1998, 24ff.
[57] Jüngst 1996, 128.
[58] Cf. ibid. 129.
[59] Ibid. 129.
[60] Cf. ibid. 130ff.

number of consequences: the inability to put their experiences into words protects what Jüngst calls "the secret knowledge of the victims", a suffering which cannot become experience, because it cannot be articulated.[61] It also protects against relativisation and comparison of these experiences and against forgetting. However, she argues that these mechanisms of protection should not lead to assigning to the Holocaust a sacred status which makes it impossible for the sufferings of other people to be heard and might even lead one to diminish other people's suffering.[62]

Children of survivors who have given interviews as part of research and psychoanalysis give voice to the transmission of the trauma their parents experienced as well. Jüngst does not comment here, she simply includes quotations from the children's own stories.[63]

From there she moves on to the impact of the Holocaust on Jewish religious thought which, according to Jüngst, was articulated in Germany first at the Protestant church congress 1979 in Nuremberg. She quotes from Marquardt's address on this occasion as follows:

> Yes, one dimension of our guilt, the most dreadful dimension, becomes visible only now: that we have not only made ourselves culpable with regard to the life of Israel, but also concerning their faith. However much we may have made the effort to transform from enemies of Israel into friends of Israel: we have done so without Israel's crisis with God, without having understood ourselves to be exposed to the same spiritual damnation in which the faith in the God of Abraham, Isaac and Jacob, who really is the father of our Lord Jesus Christ, has been thrown after Auschwitz.[64]

To understand the impact the Holocaust has on Jewish religious thought, Jüngst goes on to summarise the approaches Eliezer Berkovits, Ignaz Maybaum, Menachem Immanuel Hartom, Richard Rubenstein, Irving Greenberg, Michael Wyschogrod, Emil Fackenheim and the Jewish feminists Susannah Heschel, Judith Plaskow, Cynthia Ozick and Aviva Cantor have taken in their writings.[65] She concludes that "The experience of the Shoah is present and alive in theology and thought as much as in the daily experience of the survivors and their descendants."[66]

---

[61] Ibid. 129f.
[62] Cf. ibid. 130.
[63] Cf. ibid. 134ff.
[64] Marquardt 1980, 74. Cf. Jüngst 1996, 136.
[65] Cf. Jüngst 1996, 137-141. For other summaries cf. for example Brocke/Jochum (eds.) 1982; Amir ²1993 and Brocke 1980. Regarding Jewish feminist reflection on the Holocaust, it is important to bear in mind that unlike (male) Jewish Holocaust theologians, their writings do not centre on the Holocaust. Interestingly Jüngst includes also orthodox responses, but does not reflect on the variety of the approaches to the Holocaust she quotes.
[66] Jüngst 1996, 141.

Jüngst demonstrates the difference in remembering the history of NS with reference to the perception of the 1991 Gulf War in Israel and Germany, where reactions of the population and the decision making processes of politicians were guided by conscious and unconscious memories of World War II. Whereas Israelis felt threatened by what they interpreted as the possibility of a second Holocaust, Germans protested against the war because they did not want to be implicated in any war again and opted for pacifism without compromise. However, in doing so the peace movement overlooked the fact that Israelis interpreted their actions as a way of taking sides with Iraq.[67] Jüngst concludes that Christians in Germany had not internalised recent theological discoveries regarding the Christian-Jewish relationship, in particular after the Holocaust, as principles that guide their behaviour. She agrees with Marquardt who argues that

> Theological speech in favour of Israel is true only when it neither betrays nor sacrifices Israel, neither liquidates Israel spiritually nor theologically, but rather is an action in which the thought hastens to help Israel and supports it against the threat it receives from Christianity.[68]

And she concludes that at this moment "The threat from Christianity meant here: 'according to God's will war is not permitted'".[69] She gives priority to the experiences of survivors of the Holocaust to such an extent that their interpretation of the situation becomes normative. She argues that

> It is necessary to listen to the witness of the victims and: the male and female perpetrators and their descendants, the ones who have been spared, we need to ask about our own memories, traditions and experiences, we need to expose them away from all the denials and suppressions.[70]

However, the equation of experiences of survivors and their descendants with Israeli interpretations of a given situation, which results in the privileging of Israeli experiences and real fears, overlooks German experiences and real fears to the extent that the reality of their fears is denied. What has become clear in the evaluation of the exchange programmes of Germans and Jews is the need to gain an understanding of the other's perspective, as well as to understand one's own perspective through the eyes of the historical opposite. In doing so the distortions in one's own view of the other can be challenged and the other's interpretation can be taken seriously. Conflicting interpretations of a situation have to be acknowledged as real before they can be challenged. Both Germans and Israelis had learned lessons from the Holocaust which influenced their reaction to German involvement in the Gulf War. Whereas Israelis felt threatened by German refusal to protect their country against Iraqi missiles, Germans had learned never again to be involved in a war. Neither side was prepared to engage with the other's interpretation of their actions and the historical

---

[67] Cf. ibid. 142.
[68] Marquardt [2]1992, 110. Cf. Jüngst 1996, 142.
[69] Jüngst 1996, 142 note 61.
[70] Ibid. 143.

experiences which informed their behaviour. Whereas the demand is that Jews feel understood and safe in conversations with (Christian) Germans,[71] Germans also need to be able to trust Jews in the same way. Jüngst's interpretation of German pacifism as betrayal of Israel (and by implication of Jewry) denies Germans the safety demanded for Jews and thus acquiesces in the silencing of German experiences without giving them a proper hearing. That German inability or unwillingness to take Israeli perspectives on the Gulf War into account has the bypassing of Jewish Holocaust memory in German narratives of NS and the Holocaust as its background is undisputed. However, to expose German silence regarding Jewish experience, it is necessary to bring the conflicting narratives into contact with each other, rather than silence one by privileging the other. Describing a conflict between third generation students from Hildesheim and Haifa regarding Israeli policies towards Palestinians Andrew Bergerson concludes that

> Real differences of experience and power hinder this process [of understanding each other]. Unlike the third generation in Hildesheim, the Haifans have experienced war on an everyday basis. Unlike the Haifans, the Hildesheimers have been born to a nation with a murderous past. Remembrance and reconciliation requires Hildesheimers and Haifans to balance their sensitivity to the public ab/uses of history with a sensitivity to the fact that each group had two, very different relationships to the media, politics, and the war.[72]

Jüngst's aim is to explore possibilities for Christian-Jewish feminist conversations in contemporary post-Holocaust Germany. She notes that discourses on the memory of the Holocaust in Germany distance themselves from the experiences of the victims of the Holocaust.[73] She concludes that

> the Shoah has not entered the experience of its perpetrators and their descendants, has not been permitted to enter our memory, has not become part of our self-understanding.[74]

I would argue that this is only partially the case. While German narratives of NS and the war tend to omit the Holocaust and privilege memories of German suffering, it has also become clear that the Holocaust has entered German self-understandings. If this was not the case, public debates on the memory of the Holocaust would be inconceivable. These debates concern the place of the Holocaust in German history and collective memory and discuss the place of victim memory therein. Arguably the Holocaust has entered German self-understanding as an absence rather than as memories which recognise narratives of its victims as part of German history. However, the acknowledgement of absence in German public debates and private traumas surrounding the silences in victimiser narratives of NS and the war indicate the presence of the Holocaust in German self-understandings. What is not permitted in German memory are narratives relating experiences of victims and their

---

[71] Cf. ibid. 142.
[72] Bergerson 1997, 159.
[73] Cf. Jüngst 1996, 143f.
[74] Ibid. 144.

descendants which therefore do not inform German self-understandings. Hence, the claim that the Shoah has not entered German self-understanding is viable in the sense that Shoah names Jewish perspectives on the Holocaust and their transmission to subsequent generations.

Jüngst moves on to explore the testimonies of descendants of perpetrators and sympathisers (SympathisantInnen) because

> Considerations regarding the preconditions for a Jewish-Christian feminist conversation explicitly negate an identification with the experiences of Jewish men and women, rather they presuppose awareness of one's own history and tradition as well as self-awareness. [...] we will not be able and do not want to formulate a theology which disregards the murdered and the consequences of the Shoah for future generations. My life has to be examined from this perspective, it is a voluntary accompanying, a return to a place we do not yet know, where our experiences cease to be experiences and transform into hopes.[75]

To recover that part of experiences with NS which has not been confronted she focuses on literature concerning the second generation of Germans after the Holocaust. Material from interviews and studies conducted by Dan Bar-On, Peter Sichrovsky, Dörte von Westernhagen, Jürgen Müller-Hohagen and Gertrud Hardtmann is presented in detail so as to give a voice to memories which have thus far not been allowed entry to theological reflection.[76] Jüngst contends that

> If Christian-feminist theology reflects women's experiences, in the context of the FRG this reflection needs to include and theologically name the experiences which we have made as daughters, grandchildren, confidantes of male and female Nazi perpetrators and sympathisers. For our own sakes and the sakes of the victims we need to become aware of the experiences which have been suppressed; the experiences of the traumatised become the starting point for our theological thinking, to which I want to orient myself in listening and, as far as possible, in understanding. Thus also my own experiences and their characteristics will become clearer to me.[77]

Here Jüngst wishes to take a gendered approach and ask for the impact of NS on daughters and sons of male and female perpetrators and sympathisers. However, she is not in a position to analyse testimony of descendants of victimisers on the gendering of their experiences and how their memory of NS has influenced their self-understanding as men and women, because not enough source material is available as yet for such a study.[78] Jüngst suggests that there may be even greater taboos involved which to date prevent such studies, because their results might threaten to undermine dominant understandings of femininity.[79]

---

[75] Ibid. 14f.

[76] Cf. ibid 143ff.

[77] Jüngst 1996, 145f.

[78] Cf. ibid. 146.

[79] Cf. ibid. 147. Cf. also Ebbinghaus (ed.) 1996; Gravenhorst/Tatschmurat (eds.) 1990; Koonz 1987 and Owings 1995.

Interestingly, Jüngst does not express a similar need when reporting the experiences of survivors and their children. Questions of how one's gender influences the interpretation of Holocaust experiences and the construction of a post-Holocaust identity are surely no less important for feminist theological conversations in Germany after the Holocaust. Apparently Jüngst does not recognise the Holocaust as a gendered event which is experienced differently depending on one's gender, socialisation, religious or secular identity etc.[80] This lack of interest in the expression of gendered experiences of Holocaust survivors and their descendants is highlighted by the fact that she only reports male survivor testimony, apart from the brief description of Reibenbach's mother. And even then, Fruma Reibenbach is portrayed through a description of the way she organises her home and how much her behaviour in the present is interpreted as governed by experiences in the Holocaust she has never talked about.[81] Jüngst gives the power to develop categories about the destruction of what it means to be a human being and about the incommunicability of Holocaust experiences to Antelme.[82] A scholar and writer, he is more eloquent than Reibenbach, an Eastern European Yiddish-speaking woman. She has not been able to speak about any of her experiences during the Holocaust for the last fifty years. The film her daugther produced was the first time she dared to address these experiences verbally.[83]

Jüngst develops seven categories which describe aspects of generationally transmitted memory of NS and the Holocaust for second generation Germans: (1) silence in families suppresses the transmission of memories of failure during NS.[84] (2) Normality in everyday life is recalled as the predominant memory of life during NS, thus children are not enabled by their parents to take responsibility for failures in their own biography.[85] (3) Ambivalence towards fathers and breaking away from one's parental home demonstrate the difficulties in relating to contradictory aspects in the personality of one's father, which are solved either through solidarity with his own incomplete narrative of NS or by severing the ties with one's family completely.[86] (4) Choices in politics – job – religion of children of perpetrators show a preference for social professions, thus illustrating a need for restitution.[87] (5) In relation to Jewish men and women, many children of perpetrators show a need to identify with Jews and Jewish traditions in such a way that they are developing positive prejudices and idealisations.[88] Jüngst argues that

---

[80] As examples of a growing literature on women and the Holocaust cf. Bridenthal (ed.) 1984 and Rittner/Roth (eds.) 1993 as well as Linden 1993 and Ofer/Weitzman (eds.) 1998.
[81] Cf. Jüngst 1996, 133.
[82] Cf. ibid. 130ff.
[83] Cf. ibid. 132f.
[84] Cf. ibid. 149.
[85] Cf. ibid. 149f.
[86] Cf. ibid. 150-152.
[87] Cf. ibid. 152-154.
[88] Cf. ibid. 154f.

Such distancing as much as approaches to closeness are in danger of overrunning Jewish people, because both do not ask for Jewish self-understanding, but follow their own projections and the desires and needs which result from these. Jewish men and women become transfers of one's own imagination.[89]

(6) Psychological and psychosomatic consequences show similar symptoms as developed by children of survivors, so that

The distortions of reality among the perpetrators, their traumas, denials, suppressions, projections, defence mechanisms take revenge on the children and return as depressions, obsessional phantasies, anxieties, inhibitions of work, repressions of aggressions, anorexia, self-hatred, inhibitions of aggressions, sleeplessness ...[90]

Thus, the children of perpetrators relive part of the lives of their fathers. However, they understand themselves now to be in the role of the victims.[91] (7) The question of guilt haunts children of perpetrators in such a way that it develops into a constant feeling of guilt.[92] Jüngst concludes that

The evaluation of the interviews with children of perpetrators opens up a new dimension of women's experiences for Christian-feminist theology in the FRG: confused, suppressed, unconscious and unknown, nebulous, ambivalent experiences of guilt. The human face which has been destroyed forever is mirrored no longer only in the woman who struggles for her liberation. The dimension of guilt and responsibility, the suspicion of denial and suppression of NS history in the lives of women, the suspicion of inherited antisemitism, the flight from others and from oneself need to be integrated into the feminist formulation of women's experiences and their theological reflection.[93]

Jüngst addresses these needs in her reflections on the Christian-Jewish relationship from a feminist perspective.

2.2. The Christian-Jewish relationship

To enable Christian women in Germany to reflect on their own lives and experiences through the eyes of Jewish women, Jüngst argues that Christian women in Germany have to learn to name and acknowledge the tradition of the perpetrators into which they have been born.

Acknowledgement of one's own rootedness in the history of male and female perpetrators and sympathisers and the recognition of oneself therein is the precondition for assuming

---

[89] Ibid. 154.
[90] Ibid. 155f.
[91] Cf. ibid. 156.
[92] Cf. ibid. 157.
[93] Ibid. 158.

responsibility which includes an understanding that the children and grandchildren of the victims insist on a remembrance of the Shoah which protects their identity.[94]

According to the categories developed earlier to describe the consequences of generational transmission of NS memory between perpetrators and their children in German families, she argues for raising awareness about the mechanisms that hinder the confrontation with actions of the parents. Jüngst highlights how the second generation becomes complicit in silencing dangerous memory by acquiescing in the parents' construction of their biographies. As has been noted before regarding the relationship of Germans with Jews she maintains that

> Learning about Jewish history and contemporary life is indispensable, but it cannot substitute for the self-examination which asks what the preoccupation with Judaism means to me personally and what happens emotionally (and theologically) when I come into contact with real-life Jewish women. I believe that only in this way Christian feminists will be able to enter into a conversation.[95]

Thereby Jüngst's argument develops an understanding of guilt which intends to liberate through the acknowledgement of one's own complicity in traditions of guilt. She argues that the category of women's experience needs to be able to integrate the experiences of women who are implicated in a history of failure.[96]

Her concept of dialogue is oriented towards the philosophy of Emmanuel Lévinas. She argues that dialogue demands a complete acceptance and awareness of the Other in her Otherness.[97] According to her, Christian-Jewish encounters in Germany do not qualify as dialogues as yet, because Jews are in the minority and live in a social climate of antisemitism and xenophobia.[98] Thus the trust needed to be open for a dialogue is found neither on the Jewish nor the Christian side. Whereas antisemitism generates fear in the Jewish community, it suggests insecurity on the side of the part of the antisemitic culture as well which is unable to negotiate difference in a non-aggressive fashion. However, through learning about Jewish experiences without claiming them as one's own,[99] Christians in Christian-Jewish feminist conversations can contribute to the future possibility of dialogue. Jüngst argues that liberation can be achieved if the conversations enable Christian women to acknowledge that

---

[94] Ibid. 179.

[95] Ibid. 183.

[96] Cf. ibid. 187.

[97] Cf. ibid. 203. Cf. also Marquardt 1993, 184 and its critique in Kal 1998, 36ff. as well as Marquardt's response, Marquardt 1998c, 106ff. Cf. also Manemann 1997, 106ff. However, Susannah Heschel disputes this positive interpretation of Lévinas' concept of the Other for feminist thought. She argues that Lévinas' philosphy excludes women from an encounter with the Other and even denies that women can become "I" or "self", cf. Heschel 2000, 44.

[98] Cf. Jüngst 1996, 202f.

[99] Cf. ibid. 155: "Diese Identifizierung mit Juden und Jüdinnen als den Opfern ist letztlich Identitätsenteignung, je nachdem wie es dem eigenen Selbstbild dient. Projektionen bestimmen die Wahrnehmung der anderen und die Selbstwahrnehmung."

regarding the Holocaust they have inherited a perpetrator history, while at the same time enabling them to think theologically from the perspective of the victims of this perpetrator history. She envisages a community of solidarity of Jewish and Christian women which prioritises the perspective of the victims and keeps alive the memory of the tradition of the perpetrators.

As a pointer on the way towards such a community, Jüngst interprets the book of Ruth as a dialogue between Naomi and Ruth as two individuals who choose to share their fate with each other, although the circumstances do not support such a community. She compares the situation of adversity faced by this community of two women in a society dominated by men,[100] to the situation faced by Jewish and Christian women engaged in conversation in Germany.

> I think that Christian men and women, also in the FRG, are placed into this conversation [the Christian-Jewish] and are dependent on it, whether we like it or not and also when the facts speak against it.[101]

> It is the faithfulness of the same God which Jewish and Christian women rely on, "your God is my God" (Ruth 1:16); the sameness of the God of Israel and the God of Jesus Christ establish this interconnectedness of their lives.[102]

The story of Ruth and Naomi comes alive through reading it from both Ruth's and Naomi's perspectives. Jüngst develops an understanding of the social-historical context of these women's lives and offers a narrative which demonstrates how Ruth is able to subvert patriarchal tradition by using it for her own ends.[103] She argues that the personalised form of the biblical text helps to prevent the reader from stereotyping Naomi and Ruth as Jew and Gentile. Rather, the names of the two women make the story (primarily) a story about these two women to which other women are asked to relate their own stories and as such arrive at theological representations of their experiences.

> But Ruth and Naomi are not identical with Moab and Israel. The concreteness of their names, which runs consistently through the story from the beginning, prohibits their reduction to the *one* characteristic of being Jewish or non-Jewish. The subject is always a concrete relationship between two particular persons, which is, like love, always specific. I think that this indication given by the story is helpful. The interviews with children of perpetrators, namely, witness to a change of negative projections and prejudices about Jewish men and women into positive – projections and prejudices. These carry also a dehumanisation with them, because they hide the real-life people behind transfers of an imagined "type". Therefore implicit also in a Jewish-Christian feminist conversation is the risk of misinterpreting, for example, Judaism as the rescue from one's own patriarchal Christian tradition. This again presents a distortion, which renders the particular woman with her hopes directed at the

---

[100] Cf. ibid. 197.
[101] Ibid. 212.
[102] Ibid. 214.
[103] Cf. ibid. 216.

tradition and her difficulties with the tradition invisible behind the label "Jewish woman". Names and the story behind them protect from this distortion.[104]

According to Jüngst, the differences between Jewish and Christian women facilitate conversations, rather than hinder them. She argues that only the acknowledgement of one's own experiences and the ability to open up to someone else's experiences can lead to change and transformation in Christian-Jewish relations.[105]

> I think that the experience-oriented approach of feminist theologies can become significant for the crisis-wracked Jewish-Christian conversation in the FRG, because it supports the authenticity of speakers and listeners and helps to uncover and endure intra- and interpersonal contradictions as well as holding on to the vision of a liberation that can be shared.[106]

Jüngst's understanding of liberation wants to make positive use of differences between experiences while at the same time the idea of a shared essence in the experience of reality is presupposed. Thus, neither the experiences nor the reality these relate to can be different in such a way that they are mutually incomprehensible. Experiences and interpretations of a context can be different, and even contradictory or mutually exclusive, the context remains the territory accessible to all parties sharing in its interpretation.

As has been pointed out, challenges can be levelled against this interpretation of experiences, in particular from post-structuralist feminist theory. Yet, Jüngst's suggestions for further development in Christian-Jewish conversations present concrete opportunities for future growth and exploration of new areas for Christian-Jewish encounters in Germany.

3. Conclusion

Jüngst's book marks an important step in Christian reflection on Christian-Jewish relations broadening its context to include feminist perspectives as well as generational themes. She courageously introduces personal perspectives in the form of biographical narratives in the writing of theology, thus specifying the context and giving voice to the nature of the emotional relationship to the Holocaust of the participants in Christian-Jewish conversations. As such, Jüngst's inquiry into Christian theology after the Holocaust takes seriously the experiences of both Jews and Christians and moves Christian theological reflection onto a new level. In particular, the evaluation of the transmission of Holocaust and NS memory in descendants of victims and victimisers enables Jüngst to emphasise the differences in their relations to the history of the Holocaust and NS. Taking seriously these

---

[104] Ibid. 210.

[105] Cf. ibid. 216.

[106] Ibid. 216.

differences, and the distance between the communities of victims and victimisers, leads her to caution against Christian use of Jewish tradition in efforts to rewrite Christian theology after the Holocaust. Her theological approach appreciates the questions asked by Edna Brocke regarding Christian remembrance of Jews and the use of Jewish forms of memory:

> The question that can be addressed to many approaches concerns the possibility of whether culturally specific traditions can, so to speak, simply be "adopted" trans-culturally? Is it possible to "take over" remembrance outside of its specific and contingent context? Is it "legitimate" to appropriate traditions of remembrance – in the deeper sense of the word remembrance?[107]

However, in taking the presuppositions of post-Holocaust Christian theology for granted without questioning their applicability to a changing context of reflection, Jüngst limits the potential of her own inquiry. In simply restating the assumption of a Christian dependency on Jews common to post-Holocaust theology, in particular Marquardt's theology, to which Jüngst refers repeatedly, she refuses to challenge structures of post-Holocaust Christian theology in Germany. A closer examination of Christian reasons for claiming a dependency on contemporary Jews is needed. Stephen Haynes noted that biblical theology needs to argue for its claim that it is dependent on first century and emerging rabbinic Judaism, rather than simply assert that this is the case. I would suggest that the same argument needs to be made for the assertion that Christian faith is dependent on contemporary Jews. The fact that this assertion often implies ontological statements about the nature of a relationship between Jews and G-d which impact on the interpretation of Jewish identity, illustrates that Christian dependency in this context concerns more than the description of a historically contingent situation in Germany.

Furthermore, the approach chosen by Jüngst rests on the primacy of testimony of Holocaust survivors (and by extension, their descendants). This generates problems for the inclusion of the third generation of Germans (and Jews) in these conversations. I fully agree that a close examination of one's (family and) cultural background is necessary to gain a responsible perspective on one's own history and present situation. Hence the ability to name the guilt and failure of one's ancestors, as well as of oneself, is a precondition for building trust and establishing an honest conversation between Germans and Jews. However, the *a priori* privileging of survivor testimony and its inscription as normative hinders the recognition that the social-historical situation of the third generation differs from that of the first and second generation.

---

[107] Brocke 1998, 124. It would need to be explored whether her criticism addresses also the suggestions of Manemann and Metz, who both argue for an "anamnetic culture" which thinks from the perspective of the victims (of the Holocaust).

Reck's approach to the Holocaust takes Holocaust testimony as its starting point and assigns the authority to speak about the Holocaust to the people who have first hand experience. He differs from Jüngst in that his aim is to speak about the Holocaust itself theologically, rather than about its impact on post-Holocaust society. His theology is thus located one step prior to that of Jüngst – and other post-Holocaust theologians. Whereas post-Holocaust theology needs Holocaust testimony to locate changes in the understanding of humanity and Christian-Jewish relations, Reck aims to locate first of all the event itself. To do so he contends that the only reliable sources of information are testimonies from the Holocaust.

> Starting point for any theological reflection on Auschwitz are the voices of the victims. [...] The victims fundamentally remain an opposition; there is no commonality of experience – regarding their experiences of persecution and of the camps – which lends itself to a shared discourse; the only position towards them is that of listening.[108]

Hence, to privilege Holocaust testimony in this context has a different function from inscribing it as normative for theology itself. Reck's approach to Holocaust testimony is able to appreciate the fact that there are many situations impacting on the formulation of theology which cannot be informed by survivor testimony. While survivors of the Holocaust offer insights into human behaviour and experience which need to be acknowledged by theology, there are limits to their experience. Bartov argues that

> I believe that the experience and memories of survivors give them insight not only into the event itself, but also into some aspects of human behavior and psychology, into the potential of each of us and into the potential of human society to create hell on this earth. However, though it is difficult to say, I do not think that the experience of Auschwitz gives one moral superiority, both for the reasons raised by Levi (that is, that the survivors often belonged to the "privileged," and those were not necessarily morally superior to those who perished), and because in many other areas of human experience and creativity Auschwitz had absolutely nothing to teach us. Hence, while we must take into account what survivors tell us about human behavior, we must also remember that this is a partial view, formed under the most extreme conditions. It is a warning, but it is not a whole picture of human action and potential.[109]

To articulate the relevance of the memory of the Holocaust and NS in the context of Christian-Jewish conversations in Germany, it is necessary to take seriously the changing social-historical context of the FRG and the different influences on the identity of the participants in the conversations. Bergerson summarises the issues pertaining to NS and Holocaust memory in the context of a school exchange between Hildesheim and Haifa as follows:

> The students knew they had to remember, but they also still had to love and obey their grandparents, parents, and teachers; remember other traumatic personal experiences; negotiate

---

[108] Reck 1998, 131.
[109] Bartov 1996, 135.

national identities through discourse; make friends across a historical divide. A more critical awareness of these multiple, conflicting imperatives might have helped the students to determine, in their best judgment, which of these imperatives should take *pragmatic* priority. For the problematic of everyday life may not be reduced to an ideal distinction between politically correct vs. incorrect ways of "dealing with the past." The study of everyday life seeks to analyse how the tactical negotiations of multiple, conflicting imperatives contribute to historical reproduction and transformation *in spite of* resilient, uncompromising circumstances.[110]

Applied to Christian-Jewish relations in Germany, an awareness of the discourses on NS and Holocaust memory that shape German society, as well as the complexities of intergenerational transmission of Holocaust memory, is necessary so that the ways in which the third generation of Germans has learned to relate to the history of NS and the Holocaust can be addressed in conversations with Jews as well as in inner-Christian reflections. Literature addressing Christian-Jewish encounters on the level of local communities tends to focus on the lack of knowledge concerning Jews and Judaism among Germans and suggests ways in which knowledge about and sensitivity towards Jewish identities can be gained. However, this literature reflects German discourses on the Holocaust predominantly in the negative, pointing to their deficiencies and bemoaning their ignorance.[111] While noting deficiencies and ignorance among Germans regarding things Jewish is necessary, Jüngst rightly suggests that the other side of the coin is to reflect on the context of the third generation and its efforts at relating responsibly to NS and the Holocaust. Raising awareness of the structures of German Holocaust remembrance – even aside from cross-cultural encounters – allows insights into one's own society, community and family and can teach to appreciate as well as criticise what one has been taught.

---

[110] Bergerson 1997, 174f.

[111] Cf. for example Boschert-Kimmig 1992; Manemann 1997 and Boschki 1997.

Conclusion

The argument in this study followed German Protestant representations of the Holocaust and Jews in order to ascertain how these function in the construction of post-Holocaust theology in the social-historical context of the FRG. Except for Jüngst's work, the authors of the theologies considered belong to the second generation of Germans after the Holocaust. To understand how these theologies can enable the articulation of concerns particular to the third generation of Germans (and Jews) after the Holocaust, reflections on the generational transmission of NS and Holocaust memory were included.

Protestant theologians who address the Holocaust and Christian-Jewish relations are occupied with two issues. Firstly, they wish to reformulate Christian faith which has been challenged or exposed as immoral by Christian complicity in or tolerance of NS and the Holocaust. Secondly, they intend to reformulate Christian theology in such a way that it excludes antisemitism from the start and can never again be accused of supporting antisemitic beliefs and actions. In order to achieve these aims, theologians suggest a re-orientation of theology towards Jewish interpretations of biblical texts and responses to the Holocaust, assuming that in its core Jewish tradition has not been challenged by the Holocaust and that Jewish responses to the Holocaust can offer suggestions for a reorientation of Christian theology. Further, theologians inscribe a dependency of Christian faith on Jews in Christian theology and as such place thinking about Jews at the centre of Christian theological activity. The assumption is that, if Christian theology can only be formulated in orientation towards and dependence on Jews, antisemitism can be excluded and Christian faith (re)gain its morality.

The analysis of the three theological texts in chronological order shows a development from the Rhineland statement to Marquardt's dogmatic theology and a further broadening of the theological perspective with Jüngst's dissertation. Whereas the Rhineland statement attempts to include reflections on the social-historical context of Germany, it falls short of implementing its own presuppositions. Instead it roots its reflection on the Holocaust in theodicy and interprets Jews solely in biblical theological terms. However, the statement succeeded in paving the way for other member churches of the EKD to formulate their own theological statements. By inscribing the "reformist paradigm" of Christian interpretation of the Bible as official church teaching and practice, the EKiR initiated Jewish learning at church institutions in an effort to implement the need for Christian-Jewish conversations, to avoid antisemitism and better to understand Christian faith.

Marquardt sharpens the biblical theological presuppositions found in the Rhineland statement while at the same time focusing on the German context of his post-

Holocaust theology. He takes seriously the crisis he understands the Holocaust to be for the credibility of Christian faith and theology, to the extent of asking whether Christian faith and theology may not have become an impossibility after the Holocaust. As such he is the most radical of the three theologians examined, and also in the wider context of post-Holocaust theology in Germany he is alone in that respect. However, he does not stop his reflections with this possibility, although he understands this uncertainty of theology or statement of faith to be the background of the theological suggestions he makes. Whereas he sets out to consider the possibility that Christian theology may have become impossible or immoral after the Holocaust he appears unable to draw such radical conclusions. Rather, he continues to develop the dependency of Christians on Jews in all aspects of faith and theology as a suggestion for the future of Christian life, in particular, after the Holocaust. As such his theological representation of the Holocaust and Jews is problematic, given that his suggestion of Christian dependency on (religious) Jews implies an intrusion in the definition of Jewish self-understandings: Jews may only formulate their identities in relation to the needs of Christians. Hence he is unable to recognise Jewish tradition and, in particular, responses to the Holocaust in their own right. Given that his choices regarding the representation of events and witnesses of the Holocaust fail to capture the diversity of Jewish experiences and responses, his contribution to Holocaust memory in the context of Christian theology is ambiguous.

Jüngst bases her theological approach on the nature of the relationship between Christians and Jews as developed by Marquardt and broadens the inquiry to include insights from feminist theology and research on the generational transmission of NS and Holocaust memory. Hence, she is able to recognise the different traditions in which Jews and Germans after the Holocaust have learned about NS and the Holocaust and have come to develop their self-understanding in relation to this history in family and society. However, in remaining with second generation testimony of Jews and Germans she does not include the shift in German society from directly transmitted memories to culturally acquired narratives which begin to take hold with the third generation after the Holocaust. In listening to individual Jews and Germans, Jüngst avoids the emphasis on shared traditions of Christians and Jews which is common in post-Holocaust Christian theology. Although she treats the Christian-Jewish relationship as *sui generis* and implicitly relies on a "Judeo-Christian tradition" the emphasis on the social-historical distance of Germans and Jews rooted in the Holocaust, and preceded by centuries of antisemitism, which places Germans and Jews on opposite sides of the construction of memory of this history, makes an affirmation of supposedly shared traditions and hopes difficult if not impossible to Jüngst.

The direction of thought in the second generation can be characterised as moving too fast in its efforts to overcome the separation of Jewish and German memories after the Holocaust. The emphasis on shared traditions and hopes of Christians and Jews appears almost as a defence against the separation of tradition, memories and identities apparent in the absence of representations of Jews in German narratives of NS and in generationally transmitted memories of NS and the Holocaust. However, if Christoph Münz's observation regarding the separation of Jewish and Christian traditions is correct, theologies which rest on the assumption of a "Judeo-Christian tradition", need to be re-examined regarding their ability to address the current self-understandings of Christians in Germany.[1]

I would suggest that three strands of thought are particular to second generation German Protestant theologies which address the Holocaust. Firstly, all three texts wish to take Jews seriously in their self-understandings as Jews. However, the Rhineland statement and Marquardt fail to do so, because they do not pause to reflect on Jewish self-understandings in their own right – and sometimes in their opposition to and conflict with Christian self-understandings. Rather the concern appears to be the need to move the discussion forward to what is considered a shared heritage of Christians and Jews and which seems to promise a new start for Christian theology in friendship and learning from Jews. Portraying Jews in terms of "witness-people thinking" and casting Jews immediately in the role of teachers of Christians obscures Jewish self-understandings in their own right, because Jewish identities cannot be recognised beyond their role as witnesses to an exemplary human relationship with G-d and teachers of Christians. Hence the need of Christians to reconstruct their identities, after the Holocaust had shattered Christian self-understanding, is greater than the need to listen to the "Jewish other" and acknowledge their experiences and interpretations of the Holocaust – in particular where they challenge and oppose the Christian need for reassurance and reconstruction of faith and identity.

Secondly, the need directly to communicate with Jewish men and women and to share in each other's lives is expressed in all three theological texts. However, equally apparent is the widespread absence of such possibilities for encounter in German society. Aside from organised Christian Jewish encounters, "normal" social contact between Christians and Jews in Germany is limited and often conversations exclude memories of the Holocaust and Jewish self-understandings in German society.

Thirdly, the meaning of the Holocaust in these theologies is ambivalent. On the one hand, all three texts wish to take seriously and listen to what has happened to Jews in the Holocaust. On the other hand, the Holocaust becomes a paradigm for evil which is not examined in any detail and the experiences of which are reflected upon only in general terms of "crises for civilisation, culture, politics and religion"[2]. Related to this is the difficulty the theologies have in reflecting on the generational changes in the relation of Germans to the Holocaust. Because they do not reflect on the transmission of memory between the generations, neither the Rhineland synod nor Marquardt are

---

[1] Münz [2]1996, 470ff.
[2] Cf. EKiR (ed.) [2]1985, 13, 19.

able to analyse the identity forging narratives of German collective memory which often cast Germans in the role of victims of NS and exclude Jewish narratives from their memory. Hence their theologies hardly offer any suggestions regarding the recognition of Jewish memories as related to German memories. Dealing with the challenges posed by Jewish recollections of the Holocaust to German memories which have obliterated Jewish history is not part of the concerns of these theologies. Recognising obliteration of memory and falsification of history in German memories of NS which have been constructed by previous generations, and negotiating, challenging and overcoming a complicity in such obliteration and falsification in the third generation after the Holocaust can thus not be addressed in the context of the Rhineland statement and Marquardt.

However, the new perspectives of theological inquiry opened by Jüngst's approach indicate directions for Protestant thought in Germany. A deeper exploration of the social-historical contexts of German and Jewish lives as part of Christian-Jewish conversations may enable theologians of the third generation to address the changes in relation to NS and the Holocaust which have occurred in the past twenty years. Jüngst suggests, as a consequence of her examination of testimony of the second generation of both Jews and Germans, that the formulation of theology should facilitate the articulation of the inherited memories which have been influential in shaping the self-understandings of Germans and Jews in relation to the Holocaust.

This consequence also pertains to members of the third generation who have inherited discourses on the memory of the Holocaust in families and society which have been transmitted twice. Hence the challenges faced by the third generation do not only concern their self-understanding in relation to the Holocaust itself, but to the memories of the Holocaust they have inherited and which they have to appropriate to their situation.

The third generation has grown up with established post-Holocaust (Christian) German and Jewish identities. They have not experienced themselves the crisis NS and the Holocaust constituted for their parents' and grandparents' generations due to their temporal closeness to the events or their experience of these. Hence they cannot begin their theological journeys with the Holocaust, but need to start from their post-Holocaust context, in particular with the discourses on the Holocaust they inherited. As has been evident in the exchange programmes, challenges for Germans regarding their reception of the narratives of memory of their parents' and grandparents' generations occur in confrontation with Jewish narratives of the same time. The task for this generation is to recover what has been obliterated by previous constructions of memory. Bergerson argues that "Remembrance for the third generation is not the final destination, but the point of departure."[3] Theologically this would mean to

---

[3] Bergerson 1997, 147.

address the distortions in the representations of Jews in the efforts of German Protestants to reconstruct their identities after the Holocaust and, in confrontation with each other, to begin to gain a better understanding of themselves and the "Jewish other". Part of this evaluation of theology would need to be the challenging of the assumption that the Christian-Jewish relationship is *sui generis* and its consequences, such as the notion of Christian dependency on Jews and the portrayal of Jews as "witness-people." I would argue that only in establishing a viable Christian identity independent of Jews, will Christians be able to reflect theologically on Jewish traditions and identities in a non-imperialistic manner. As Victor Kal put it: "[...] a Christian who seeks an encounter [...] [with Jews] needs to stand *on his own* two feet."[4]

---

[4] Kal 1998, 31.

Bibliography

Adorno, Theodor W. 1959/1986, "What Does Coming to Terms with the Past Mean?" (1959), in: Hartman, ed., *Bitburg in Moral and Political Perspective*, 114-129.

Almog, Shmuel 1989, "What's in a Hyphen?", *Newsletter of the Vidal Sassoon International Centre for the Study of Antisemitism*, 1f.

American Jewish Committee 1978, *Americans Confront the Holocaust: A Study of Reactions to NBC-TV's Four-part Drama on the Nazi Era*, Institute of Human Relations, New York.

Améry, Jean 1980, *At the Mind's Limits: Contemplations by a Survivor on Auschwitz and Its Realities*, Indiana University Press, Bloomington.

Amir, Yehoshua [2]1993, "Jüdisch-theologische Positionen nach Auschwitz", in: Ginzel, ed., *Auschwitz als Herausforderung für Juden und Christen*, 439-455.

Antze, Paul/Lambek, Michael, eds. 1996, *Tense Past: Cultural Essays in Trauma and Memory*, Routledge, New York/London.

Aschheim, Steven E. 1996, *Culture and Catastrophe: German and Jewish Confrontations with National Socialism and Other Crises*, New York University Press, New York.

Aschheim, Steven E. 1997, "Archetypes and the German-Jewish Dialogue: Reflections Occasioned by the Goldhagen Affair", *German History* 15:2, 240-250.

Aschkenasy, Yehuda 1980, "Mein Weg nach Bad Neuenahr", in: Klappert/Starck, eds., *Umkehr und Erneuerung*, 1-4.

Ash, Mitchell G. 1997, "American and German Perspectives on the Goldhagen Debate: History, Identity, and the Media", *Holocaust and Genocide Studies* 7:3, 396-411.

Assmann, Jan 1988, "Kollektives Gedächtnis und kulturelle Identität", in: Assmann, Jan/Hölscher, Tonio, eds., *Kultur und Gedächtnis*, Suhrkamp, Frankfurt am Main, 9-19.

Assmann, Jan 1992, *Das kulturelle Gedächtnis: Schrift, Erinnerung und politische Identität in frühen Hochkulturen*, C.H. Beck, München.

Augstein, Rudolf et al. [3]1987, *"Historikerstreit": Eine Dokumentation der Kontroverse um die Einzigartigkeit der nationalsozialistischen Judenvernichtung*, Verlag Piper, München.

Baldwin, Peter, ed. 1990, *Reworking the Past: Hitler, the Holocaust, and the Historians' Debate*, Beacon Press, Boston.

Baldwin, Peter 1990, "The *Historikerstreit* in Context", in: Baldwin, ed., *Reworking the Past*, 3-37.

Barkenings, Hans-Joachim 1980, "Das eine Volk Gottes: Von der Substitutionstheorie zur Ökumene mit Israel", in: Klappert/Starck, eds., *Umkehr und Erneuerung*, 167-181.

Barkenings, Hans-Joachim 1986, "Erwägungen zur Änderung der rheinischen Kirchenordnung nach dem Synodalbeschluß zur Erneuerung des Verhältnisses von Christen und Juden", in: Brocke/Seim, eds., *Gottes Augapfel*, 147-158.

Barnouw, Dagmar 1996, *Germany 1945: Views of War and Violence*, Indiana University Press, Bloomington/Indianapolis.

Bar-On, Dan/Beiner, Friedhelm/Brusten, Manfred, eds. 1988, *Der Holocaust – Familiale und gesellschaftliche Folgen – Aufarbeitung in Wissenschaft und Erziehung? Ergebnisse eines Internationalen Forschungskolloquiums an der Bergischen Universität-Gesamthochschule Wuppertal 1988*, Druckerei der Bergischen Universität Wuppertal, Wuppertal.

Bar-On, Dan 1989, *The Legacy of Silence: Encounters with Children of the Third Reich*, Harvard University Press, Cambridge, Massachusetts/London, UK.

Bar-On, Dan/Brendler, Konrad/Hare, Paul A., eds. 1997, *"Da ist etwas kaputtgegangen an den Wurzeln ...": Identitätsformen deutscher und israelischer Jugendlicher im Schatten des Holocaust*, Campus Verlag, Frankfurt am Main/New York.

Bar-On, Dan 1995, *Fear and Hope: Three Generations of the Holocaust*, Harvard University Press, Cambridge, Massachusetts.

Bartov, Omer 1992, "Time Present and Time Past: The *Historikerstreit* and German Reunification", *New German Critique* 55, 173-190.

Bartov, Omer 1993, "Intellectuals on Auschwitz: Memory, History and Truth", *History and Memory* 5:1, 87-129.

Bartov, Omer 1996, *Murder in Our Midst: The Holocaust, Industrial Killing, and Representation*, Oxford University Press, New York/Oxford.

Bartov, Omer 1998, "Defining Enemies, Making Victims: Germans, Jews, and the Holocaust", *The American Historical Review* 103:3, 771-816.

Bartov, Omer 2000, "Germany as Victim", *New German Critique* 80, 29-40.

Baumann, Zygmunt 1989, *Modernity and the Holocaust*, Polity Press, Cambridge et al.

Ben-Amos, Dan/Weissberg, Liliane, eds. 1999, *Cultural Memory and the Construction of Identity*, Wayne State University Press, Detroit.

Benz, Wolfgang 1990, "Postwar Society and National Socialism: Remembrance, Amnesia, Rejection", *Dachau Review* 2, 156-167.

Benz, Wolfgang, ed. 1991, *Dimension des Völkermords: Die Zahl der jüdischen Opfer des Nationalsozialismus*, C.H. Beck, München.

Benz, Wolfgang 1994, "Auschwitz and the Germans: The Remembrance of Genocide", *Holocaust and Genocide Studies* 8:1, 94-106.

Benz, Wolfgang 1995, "Zum Umgang mit nationalsozialistischer Vergangenheit in der Bundesrepublik", in: Danyel, Jürgen, ed., *Die geteilte Vergangenheit: Zum Umgang mit Nationalsozialismus und Widerstand in beiden deutschen Staaten*, Zeithistorische Studien 4, Akademie Verlag, Berlin, 47-60.

Benz, Wolfgang 1999, *The Holocaust: A German Historian Examines the Genocide*, Columbia University Press, New York.

Berg, Nicolas/Jochimsen, Jess/Stiegler, Bernd, eds. 1996, *Shoah: Formen der Erinnerung. Geschichte, Philosophie, Literatur, Kunst*, Wilhelm Funk Verlag, München.

Berg, Nicolas 1996, "'Auschwitz' und die Geschichtswissenschaft – Überlegungen zu Kontroversen der letzten Jahre", in: Berg/Jochimsen/Stiegler, eds., *Shoah: Formen der Erinnerung*, 31-52.

Bergerson, Andrew Stuart 1997, "In the Shadow of the Towers: An Ethnography of a German-Israeli Student Exchange Program", *New German Critique* 71, 141-176.

Bergmann, Martin S./Jucovy, Milton E., eds. 1982, *Generations of the Holocaust*, Basic Books, New York.

Bergmann, Martin S./Jucovy, Milton E. 1982, "Prelude", in: Bergmann/Jucovy, eds., *Generations of the Holocaust*, 3-29.

Bergmann, Werner 1995, "Die Bitburg-Affäre in der deutschen Presse: Rechtskonservative und linksliberale Interpretationen", in: Bergmann/Erb/Lichtblau, eds., *Schwieriges Erbe: Der Umgang mit Nationalsozialismus und Antisemitismus in Österreich, der DDR und der Bundesrepublik Deutschland*, Schriftenreihe des Zentrums für Antisemitismusforschung Berlin 3, Campus Verlag, Frankfurt/New York, 408-428.

Berkovits, Eliezer 1973, *Faith after the Holocaust*, KTAV, New York.

Bethge, Eberhard 1980, "Der Holocaust als Wendepunkt" in: Klappert /Starck, eds., *Umkehr und Erneuerung*, 89-100.

Biale, David 1986, *Power and Powerlessness in Jewish History: The Jewish Tradition and the Myth of Passivity*, Schocken Books, New York.

Bodemann, Y. Michal, ed. 1996, *Jews, Germans, Memory: Reconstructions of Jewish Life in Germany*, Social History, Popular Culture and Politics in Germany, The University of Michigan Press, Ann Arbor.

Bodemann, Y. Michal 1996a, "'How can one stand to live there as a Jew ...': Paradoxes of Jewish Existence in Germany", in: Bodemann, ed., *Jews, Germans, Memory*, 19-46.

Bodemann, Y. Michal 1996b, *Gedächtnistheater: Die jüdische Gemeinschaft und ihre deutsche Erfindung*, Rotbuch Verlag, Hamburg.

Borneman, John/Peck, Jeffrey M. 1995, *Sojourners: The Return of German Jews and the Question of Identity*, Texts and Contexts 16, University of Nebraska Press, Lincoln/London.

Boschert-Kimmig, Reinhold 1992, "Erziehung nach Auschwitz: Zur praktischen Dimension des christlich-jüdischen Dialogs", *Kirche und Israel* 7:1, 83-91.

Boschki, Reinhold/Konrad, Franz-Michael, eds. 1997, *Ist die Vergangenheit noch ein Argument? Aspekte einer Erziehung nach Auschwitz*, Attempto Verlag, Tübingen.

Boschki, Reinhold 1997, "Das Schweigen Gottes in Auschwitz: Religiöse Erziehung nach der Shoah", in: Boschki/Konrad, eds., *Ist die Vergangenheit noch ein Argument?* 119-160.

Braham, Randolph L., ed. 1986, *The Origins of the Holocaust: Christian Anti-Semitism*, East European Monographs No CCIV, Columbia University Press, New York.

Braybrooke, Marcus 1991, *Children of the One God: A History of the Council of Christians and Jews*, Valentine Mitchell, London.

Brendler, Konrad 1997, "Die NS-Geschichte als Sozialisationsfaktor und Identitätsballast der Enkelgeneration", in: Bar-On/Brendler/Hare, eds. 1997, *"Da ist etwas kaputtgegangen an den Wurzeln ..."*, 53-104.

Brenner, Michael 1983, *Am Beispiel Weiden: Jüdischer Alltag im Nationalsozialismus*, Arena Verlag, Würzburg.

Brenner, Michael 1997, *After the Holocaust: Rebuilding Jewish Lives in Postwar Germany*, Princeton University Press, Princeton, New Jersey.

Bridenthal, Renate, ed. 1984, *When Biology Became Destingy: Women in Weimar and Nazi Germany*, Monthly Review Press, New York.

Brocke, Edna/Seim, Jürgen, eds. 1986, *Gottes Augapfel: Beiträge zur Erneuerung des Verhältnisses von Christen und Juden*, Neukirchener Verlag, Neukirchen-Vluyn.

Brocke, Edna 1980, "Der Holocaust als Wendepunkt?" in: Klappert/Starck, eds., *Umkehr und Erneuerung*, 101-110.

Brocke, Edna 1992, "Im Tode sind alle gleich – Sind im Tode alle gleich?", in: Loewy, ed., *Holocaust: Die Grenzen des Verstehens*, 71-82.

Brocke, Edna 1998, "Anonymisierung der Opfer in einem 'gemeinsamen' Gedenken: Ein jüdisches Votum", in: Staffa/Spielmann, eds., *Nachträgliche Wirksamkeit*, 113-133.

Brocke, Michael/Jochum, Herbert, eds. 1982, *Wolkensäule und Feuerschein: Jüdische Theologie des Holocaust*, Chr. Kaiser Verlag, München.

Brockway, Allan et al. 1988, *The Theology of the Churches and the Jewish People: Statements of the World Council of Churches and its member churches*, WCC Publications, Geneva.

Broder, Henryk M./Lang, Michel R. et al. 1979, *Fremd im eigenen Land: Juden in der Bundesrepublik Deutschland*, Fischer Taschenbuch Verlag, Frankfurt am Main.

Broszat, Martin 1990, "A Plea for the Historicization of National Socialism", in: Baldwin, ed., *Reworking the Past*, 77-87.

Broszat, Martin/Friedländer, Saul 1990, "A Controversy about the Historicization of National Socialism", in: Baldwin, ed., *Reworking the Past*, 102-134.

Browning, Christopher 1992, *Ordinary Men: Reserve Police Battalion 101 and the Final Solution in Poland*, Harper Collins, New York.

Browning, Christopher R. [3]1996, "German Memory, Judicial Interrogation, and Historical Reconstruction: Writing Perpetrator History from Postwar Testimony", in: Friedlander, ed., *Probing the Limits of Representation*, 22-36.

Brumlik, Micha/Kiesel, Doron/Kugelmann, Cilly/Schoeps, Julius H., eds. 1986, *Jüdisches Leben in Deutschland seit 1945*, Athenäum, Frankfurt am Main.

Brumlik, Micha/Kunik, Petra, eds. [2]1988, *Reichspogromnacht: Vergangenheitsbewältigung aus jüdischer Sicht*, Brandes & Apsel Verlag, Frankfurt am Main.

Brumlik, Micha/Funke, Hajo/Rensmann, Lars 2000, *Umkämpftes Vergessen: Walser-Debatte, Holocaust-Mahnmal und neuere deutsche Geschichtspolitik*, Schriftenreihe Politik und Kultur 3, Das Arabische Buch, Berlin.

Brumlik, Micha, ed. 1998, *Zuhause, keine Heimat? Junge Juden und ihre Zukunft in Deutschland*, Bleicher Verlag, Gerlingen.

Brumlik, Micha 1998a, "Momentaufnahmen und Selbstbildnisse", in: Brumlik, ed., *Zuhause, keine Heimat?*, 7-23.

Brumlik, Micha 1998b, "Konkrete Freundschaft: Friedrich-Wilhelm Marquardt zu Ehren", in: Hennecke/Weinrich, eds., *"Abirren"*, 183-188.

Buren, Paul M. van 1981/1987/1988, *A Theology of the Jewish-Christian Reality – Part I: Discerning the Way; Part II: A Christian Theology of the People Israel; Part III: Christ in Context*, Harper & Row, San Francisco.

Burgauer, Erica 1993, *Zwischen Erinnerung und Verdrängung – Juden in Deutschland nach 1945*, Rowohlt Taschenbuch Verlag, Reinbek bei Hamburg.

Burke, Peter 1989, "History as Social Memory", in: Butler, Thomas (ed.), *Memory: History, Culture and the Mind*, Wolfson College Lectures, Blackwell, Oxford, 97-113.

Buruma, Ian 1994, *The Wages of Guilt: Memories of War in Germany and Japan*, Jonathan Cape/Random House, London.

Cady, Linell Elizabeth 1997, "Identity, Feminist Theory, and Theology", in: Chopp, Rebecca S./Davaney, Sheila Greeve, eds., *Horizons in Feminist Theology: Identity, Tradition and Norms*, Fortress Press, Minneapolis, 17-32.

Confino, Alon 1997, *The Nation as a Local Metaphor: Württemberg, Imperial Germany, and National Memory, 1871-1918*, The University of North Carolina Press, Chapel Hill/London.

Confino, Alon 1998, "Edgar Reitz's *Heimat* and German Nationhood: Film, Memory, and Understandings of the Past", *German History* 16:2, 185-208.

Connerton, Paul 1989, *How societies remember*, Cambridge University Press, Cambridge et al.

Croner, Helga, ed. 1985, *More Stepping Stones to Jewish-Christian Relations: An Unabridged Collection of Christian Documents*, Studies in Judaism and Christianity, Paulist Press, New York et al.

Cullen, Michael S., ed. 1999, *Das Holocaust-Mahnmal: Dokumentation einer Debatte*, Pendo Verlag, Zürich/München.

Czaplicka, John 1995, "History, Aesthetics, and Contemporary Commemorative Practice in Berlin", *New German Critique* 56, 155-187.

Davies, Alan T., ed. 1979, *Antisemitism and the Foundations of Christianity*, Paulist Press, New York et al.

Dawidowicz, Lucy S. [6]1993, *The Holocaust and the Historians*, Harvard University Press, Cambridge, Massachusetts/London, UK.

D'Costa, Gavin 1990, "One Covenant or Many Covenants?", *Journal of Ecumenical Studies* 27:3, 441-452.

Diner, Dan, ed. 1987, *Ist der Nationalsozialismus Geschichte? Zu Historisierung und Historikerstreit*, Fischer Taschenbuch Verlag, Frankfurt am Main.

Diner, Dan 1990, "Negative Symbiosis: Germans and Jews After Auschwitz", in: Baldwin, ed., *Reworking the Past*, 251-261.

Diner, Dan 1995, *Kreisläufe: Nationalsozialismus und Gedächtnis*, Berlin Verlag, Berlin.

Diner, Dan 1996a, "On the Ideology of Antifascism", *New German Critique* 67, 123-132.

Diner, Dan 1996b, "Ereignis und Erinnerung: Über Variationen historischen Gedächtnisses", in: Berg/Jochimsen/Stiegler, eds., *Shoah: Formen der Erinnerung*, 13-30.

Domansky, Elisabeth 1992, "'Kristallnacht,' the Holocaust and German Unity: The Meaning of November 9 as an Anniversary in Germany", *History and Memory* 4:1, 60-94.

Domansky, Elisabeth 1997, "A Lost War: World War II in Postwar German Memory", in: Rosenfeld, Alvin H., ed., *Thinking about the Holocaust After Half a Century*, Jewish Literature and Culture, Indiana University Press, Bloomington/Indiana, 233-272.

Doneson, Judith E. 1987, *The Holocaust in American Film*, Jewish Publication Society, Philadelphia.

Ebbinghaus, Angelika, ed. 1996, *Opfer und Täterinnen: Frauenbiographien des Nationalsozialismus*, Die Frau in der Gesellschaft, Fischer Taschenbuch Verlag, Frankfurt am Main.

Ebeling, Gerhard 1975, "Die Klage über das Erfahrungsdefizit in der Theologie als Frage nach ihrer Sache", in: Ebeling, Gerhard, *Wort und Glaube III: Beiträge zur Fundamentaltheologie, Soteriologie und Ekklesiologie*, J.C.B. Mohr, Tübingen, 3-28.

Ebeling, Gerhard 1978, "Schrift und Erfahrung als Quelle theologischer Aussagen", *Zeitschrift für Theologie und Kirche* 75, 99-116.

Eckardt, A. Roy/Eckardt, Alice L. [2]1988, *Long Night's Journey Into Day: A Revised Retrospective on the Holocaust*, Wayne State University Press, Detroit.

Ehlers, Hella 1994, "A Second Chance to Mourn", in: Ehlers, Hella/Crick, Joyce, eds., *The Trauma of the Past: Remembering and Working through*, Lecture series organised by the Goethe-Institut London in January 1993, Goethe-Institut, London, 9-35.

Ellis, Marc H. 1990, *Beyond Innocence and Redemption: Confronting the Holocaust and Israeli Power. Creating a Moral Future for the Jewish People*, Harper & Row, San Francisco et al.

Ellis, Marc H. 1994, *Ending Auschwitz: The Future of Jewish and Christian Life*, Westminster/John Knox Press, Louisville, Kentucky.

Ellis, Marc H. 1997, *Unholy Alliance: Religion and Atrocity in Our Time*, SCM Press, London.

Elsaesser, Thomas 1992, "The New German Cinema's Historical Imaginary", in: Murray/Wickham, (eds., *Framing the Past*, 280-307.

Epstein, Helen 1979, *Children of the Holocaust: Conversations with Sons and Daughters of Survivors*, G.P. Putnam's, New York.

Ericksen, Robert P./Heschel, Susannah, eds. 1999, *Betrayal: German Churches and the Holocaust*, Fortress Press, Minneapolis.

Evangelische Kirche im Rheinland, ed. [2]1985, *Zur Erneuerung des Verhältnisses von Christen und Juden*, Handreichung Nr. 39, [2]1985 C. Blech. *EKiR (ed.) [2]1985*

Evangelische Kirche im Rheinland, ed. 1993, *Kirche und Israel: Zur Erneuerung des Verhältnisses von Christen und Juden. Proponendum zur Änderung des Grundartikels der Kirchenordnung*, Handreichung Nr. 45, C. Blech, Düsseldorf. *EKiR (ed.) 1993*

Evans, Richard 1989, *In Hitler's Shadow: West German Historians and the Attempt to Escape from the Nazi Past*, Tauris & Co. Publishers, London.

Feinberg, Anat 1997, "Abiding in a Haunted Land: The Issue of Heimat in Contemporary German-Jewish Writing", *New German Critique* 70, 161-181.

Fisher, Eugene J./Klenicki, Leon, eds. 1990, *In Our Time: The Flowering of Jewish-Catholic Dialogue*, Studies in Judaism and Christianity, Paulist Press, New York et al.

Fisher, Eugene J./Klenicki, Leon, eds. 1996, *Pope John Paul II: Spiritual Pilgrimage. Texts on Jews and Judaism 1979-1995*, Crossroad/ADL B'nai B'rith, New York.

Fisher, Eugene J. 1999, *Catholic-Jewish Relations: Documents from the Holy See*, Catholic Truth Society, London.

Flannery, Austin OP, ed. [9]1992, *Vatican Council II: The Conciliar and Post Conciliar Documents*, Dominican Publications, Dublin.

Fleischmann, Lea [5]1996, *Dies ist nicht mein Land: Eine Jüdin verläßt die Bundesrepublik*, Wilhelm Heyne Verlag, München.

Fleischner, Eva, ed. 1977, *Auschwitz: Beginning of a New Era? Reflections on the Holocaust*, KTAV, New York.

Fox, Thomas L. 1999, *Stated Memory: East Germany and the Holocaust*, Studies in German Literature, Linguistics and Culture, Camden House, Rochester, NY/Woodbridge, UK.

Frei, Norbert [2]1997, *Vergangenheitspolitik: Die Anfänge der Bundesrepublik und die NS-Vergangenheit*, C.H. Beck, München.

Freud, Sigmund 1912-1913, *Totem and Taboo*, The Standard Edition of the Complete Psychoanalytical Works of Sigmund Freud, Volume 13, The Hogarth Press, London (1953-1974).

Friedlander, Albert 1990, *A Thread of Gold: Journeys towards Reconciliation*, SCM Press Ltd./Trinity Press International, London/Philadelphia.

Friedlander, Saul 1993, *Memory, History, and the Extermination of the Jews of Europe*, Indiana University Press, Bloomington/Indianapolis.

Friedlander, Saul 1994, "Trauma, Memory, and Transference", in: Hartman, ed., *Holocaust Remembrance*, 252-263.

Friedlander, Saul, ed. [3]1996, *Probing the Limits of Representation: Nazism and the "Final Solution"*, Harvard University Press, Cambridge, Massachusetts/London, UK.

Fuchs, Ottmar 1997, "Kontextuelle Christologie im Horizont unbedingter Solidarität: Für die generative Dimensionierung der jüdisch-christlichen Beziehung", in: Görg, Manfred/Langer, Michael, eds., *Als Gott weinte: Theologie nach Auschwitz*, Verlag Friedrich Pustet, Regensburg, 162-202.

Fulbrook, Mary 1999, *German National Identity after the Holocaust*, Polity Press, Cambridge.

Funke, Andreas 1991, "Umkehr und Teilnahme: Zur Form von Friedrich-Wilhelm Marquardts Dogmatik", *Kirche und Israel* 6:1, 75-86.

Gager, John G. 1983, *The Origins of Anti-Semitism: Attitudes Toward Judaism in Pagan and Christian Antiquity*, Oxford University Press, New York et al.

Galinski, Dieter/Herbert, Ulrich/Lachauer, Ulla, eds. 1982, *Nazis und Nachbarn: Schüler erforschen den Alltag im Nationalsozialismus*, Rowohlt, Reinbek.

Geisler, Michael E. 1992, "The Disposal of Memory: Fascism and the Holocaust on West German Television", in: Murray/Wickham, eds., *Framing the Past*, 220-260.

Geyer, Michael/Hansen Miriam 1994, "German-Jewish Memory and National Consciousness", in: Hartman, ed., *Holocaust Remembrance*, 175-190.

Geyer, Michael 1996, "The Politics of Memory in Contemporary Germany", in: Copjec, Joan, ed., *Radical Evil*, Verso, London/New York, 169-200.

Geyer, Michael 1997, "The Place of the Second World War in German Memory and History", *New German Critique* 71, 5-40.

Gilcher-Holtey, Ingrid 1998, "The Mentality of the perpetrators", in: Shandley, ed., *Unwilling Germans?* 105-108.

Gilman, Sander L. 1991, *Inscribing the Other*, Texts and Contexts 1, University of Nebraska Press, Lincoln/London.

Ginsburg, Hans Jakob 1986, "Politik danach – Jüdische Interessenvertretung in der Bundesrepublik", in: Brumlik/Kiesel/Kugelmann/Schoeps, eds., *Jüdisches Leben in Deutschland seit 1945*, 108-118.

Ginzel, Günther Bernd, ed. ²1993, *Auschwitz als Herausforderung für Juden und Christen*, Schneider, Gerlingen.

Ginzel, Günther Bernd ²1993, "Christen und Juden nach Auschwitz" in: Ginzel, ed., *Auschwitz als Herausforderung für Juden und Christen*, 234-274.

Giordano, Ralph ²1990, *Die zweite Schuld oder Von der Last Deutscher zu sein*, Knaur, München.

Glotz, Peter 1997, "Nation der Killer?", in: Schoeps, ed., *Ein Volk von Mördern?* 125-129.

Goldberg, David Theo/Krausz, Michael, eds. 1993, *Jewish Identity*, Temple University Press, Philadelphia.

Goldhagen, Daniel Jonah 1996a, *Hitler's Willing Executioners: Ordinary Germans and the Holocaust*, Little, Brown and Company, London.

Goldhagen, Daniel Jonah 1996b, *Hitlers willige Vollstrecker: Ganz gewöhnliche Deutsche und der Holocaust*, Siedler, Berlin.

Goldhagen, Daniel Jonah 1997, *Briefe an Goldhagen*, Siedler Verlag, Berlin.

Goldhagen, Daniel Jonah 1998a, "The Failure of the Critics", in: Shandley, ed., *Unwilling Germans?* 129-150.

Goldhagen, Daniel Jonah 1998b, "*Modell Bundesrepublik*: National History, Democracy, and Internationalization in Germany", in: Shandley, ed., *Unwilling Germans?* 275-285.

Gravenhorst, Lerke/Tatschmurat, Carmen, eds. 1990, *Töchter-Fragen: NS-Frauen-Geschichte*, Forum Frauenforschung 5, Kore, Verlag Traute Hensch, Freiburg.

Greiffenhagen, Martin/Greiffenhagen, Sylvia, eds. 1981, *Ein schwieriges Vaterland: Zur politischen Kultur Deutschlands*, Fischer Taschenbuch Verlag, Frankfurt am Main.

Grosser, Alfred 1990, *Ermordung der Menschheit: Der Genozid im Gedächtnis der Völker*, Carl Hanser Verlag, München/Wien.

Grözinger, Yael 1995, "Oh, You're Jewish? That's Okay", in: Stern, ed., *Speaking Out*, 116-125.

Gutman, Yisrael/Berenbaum, Michael, eds. 1994, *Anatomy of the Auschwitz Death Camp*, Indiana Uinversity Press, Bloomington/Indianapolis.

Haacker, Klaus 1986, "Der Holocaust als Datum der Theologiegeschichte", in: Brocke/Seim, eds., *Gottes Augapfel*, 137-145.

Haas, Peter J. 1988, *Morality After Auschwitz: The Radical Challenge of the Nazi Ethic*, Fortress Press, Philadelphia.

Habermas, Jürgen 1993, "A Kind of Settlement of Damages: The Apologetic Tendencies in German History Writing", in: Knowlton/Cates, eds., *Forever in the Shadow of Hitler?* 34-44.

Halbwachs, Maurice 1980, *The Collective Memory*, Harper & Row, New York.

Hamburger Institut für Sozialforschung, ed. 1998, *Besucher einer Ausstellung: Die Ausstellung "Vernichtungskrieg. Verbrechen der Wehrmacht 1941 bis 1944" in Interview und Gespräch*, Hamburger Edition, Hamburg.

Hardtmann, Gertrud 1988, "Von unerträglicher Schuld zu erträglichem Schuldgefühl?", in: Bar-On/Beiner/Brusten, eds., *Der Holocaust – Familiale und gesellschaftliche Folgen*, 56-61.

Hardtmann, Gertrud 1997, "Auf der Suche nach einer unbeschädigten Identität: Die dritte Generation in Deutschland", in: Bar-On/Brendler/Hare, eds., *"Da ist etwas kaputtgegangen an den Wurzeln ..."*, 105-136.

Hartman, Geoffrey H., ed. 1986, *Bitburg in Moral and Perspective*, Indiana University Press, Bloomington.

Hartman, Geoffrey H., ed. 1994, *Holocaust Remembrance: The Shapes of Memory*, Blackwell, Oxford, UK/Cambridge, USA.

Hass, Aron 1990, *In the Shadow of the Holocaust: The Second Generation*, Cambridge University Press, Cambridge et al..

Hass, Aron 1995, *The Aftermath: Living with the Holocaust*, Cambridge University Press, Cambridge.

Haynes, Stephen R. 1991, *Prospects for Post-Holocaust Theology*, American Academy of Religion Academy Series 77, Scholars Press, Atlanta, Georgia.

Haynes, Stephen R. 1995a, *Jews and the Christian Imagination: Reluctant Witnesses*, Studies in Literature and Religion, Macmillan Press, Basingstoke/London et al.

Haynes, Stephen R. 1995b, "Changing Paradigms: Reformist, Radical, and Rejectionist Approaches to the Relationship between Christianity and Antisemitism", *Journal of Ecumenical Studies* 32:1, 63-88.

Haynes, Stephen R. 1996, "Christianity, Anti-Semitism, and Post-Holocaust Theology: Old Questions, Changing Paradigms", in: Millen/Bennett et al., eds., *New Perspectives on the Holocaust*, 294-318.

Hecker, Margarete 1993, "Family Reconstruction in Germany: An Attempt to Confront the Past", in: Heimannsberg, Barbara/Schmidt, Christoph J., eds., *The Collective Silence: German Identity and the Legacy of Shame*, Jossey-Bass Publishers, San Francisco, 73-94.

Heil, Johannes/Erb, Rainer, eds. 1998, *Geschichtswissenschaft und Öffentlichkeit: Der Streit um Daniel J. Goldhagen*, Fisher Taschenbuch Verlag, Frankfurt am Main.

Heil, Johannes/Erb, Rainer 1998, "Klage und Analyse im Widerstreit: Eine Einführung", in: Heil/Erb, eds., *Geschichtswissenschaft und Öffentlichkeit*, 16-24.

Hennecke, Susanne/Weinrich, Michael, eds. 1998, *"Abirren": Niederländische und deutsche Beiträge von und für Friedrich-Wilhelm Marquardt*, Erev-Rav, Wittingen.

Henningsen, Manfred 1988, "The Politics of Symbolic Evasion: Germany and the Aftermath of the Holocaust", in: Rosenberg, Alan/Myers, Gerald, eds., *Echoes from the Holocaust: Philosophical Reflections on a Dark Time*, Temple University Press, Philadelphia, 396-411.

Henrix, Hans Hermann 1989, "Vom Dialog zur Dogmatik: Zu Friedrich-Wilhelm Marquardt, Von Elend und Heimsuchung der Theologie. Prolegomena zur Dogmatik", *Kirche und Israel* 4:1, 66-72.

Henrix, Hans Hermann 1993, "'Israel ist seinem Wesen nach formale Christologie': Die Bedeutung H.U. von Balthasars für F.-W. Marquardts Christologie", *Berliner Theologische Zeitschrift* 10, 135-153.

Herbert, Ulrich 1993, "Der Holocaust in der Geschichtsschreibung der Bundesrepublik Deutschland", in: Moltmann/Kiesel/Kugelmann/Loewy/Neuhaus, eds., *Erinnerung*, 31-45.

Herf, Jeffrey 1986, "The 'Holocaust' Reception in West Germany: Right, Center, and Left", in: Rabinbach/Zipes, eds., *Germans and Jews since the Holocaust: The Changing Situation in West Germany*, Holmes & Meier, New York/London, 208-233.

Herf, Jeffrey 1997, *Divided Memory: The Nazi Past in the Two Germanys*, Harvard University Press, Cambridge, Massachusetts/London, England.

Heschel, Susannah 2000, "Emmanuel Lévinas in feministischer Perspektive", *Kirche und Israel* 15:1, 41-46.

Heyl, Matthias 1995, "Jews are no metaphors, oder: Die Kontextualisierung des Holocaust in Deutschland", in: Schreier/Heyl, eds., *"Daß Auschwitz nicht noch einmal sei ... "*, 27-62.

Heyl, Matthias 1996, "Education after Auschwitz: Teaching the Holocaust in Germany", in: Millen/Bennett et al., eds., *New Perspectives on the Holocaust*, 275-286.

Hillgruber, Andreas 1986, *Zweierlei Untergang: Die Zerschlagung des deutschen Reiches und das Ende des europäischen Judentums*, Corso bei Siedler, Berlin.

Hilton, Michael 1994, *The Christian Effect on Jewish Life*, SCM, London.

Hobsbawm, Eric/Ranger, Terence, eds. 1983, *The Invention of Tradition*, Past and Present Publications, Cambridge University Press, Cambridge et al.

Honecker, Martin 1998, "'Mit Israel in der Wurzel verbunden': Zur Auseinandersetzung über den Grundartikel der rheinischen Kirche", in: Kriener/Schmidt, eds., *Gottes Treue – Hoffnung von Christen und Juden*, 195-206.

Hutton, Patrick H. 1993, *History as an Art of Memory*, University Press of New England, Hanover/London.

Huyssen, Andreas 1995, *Twilight Memories: Marking Time in a Culture of Amnesia*, Routledge, New York/London.

Interview with Daniel Jonah Goldhagen by Rudolf Augstein 1998, "What were the Murderers Thinking?", in: Shandley, ed., *Unwilling Germans?* 151-162.

Irwin-Zarecka, Iwona 1994, *Frames of Remembrance: The Dynamics of Collective Memory*, Transaction Publishers, New Brunswick, USA/London, UK.

Jacobs, Stephen L., ed. 1993a, *Contemporary Jewish Religious Responses to the Shoah*, Studies in the Shoah V, University Press of America, Lanham.

Jacobs, Stephen L., ed. 1993b, *Contemporary Christian Religious Responses to the Shoah*, Studies in the Shoah VI, University Press of America, Lanham.

Jacoby, Jessica/Schoppmann, Claudia/Zena-Henry, Wendy, eds. 1994, *Nach der Shoah geboren: Jüdische Frauen in Deutschland*, Elefanten Press, Berlin.

Jochum, Herbert 1986, "Von den 'bösen' zu den 'frommen' Juden: Anmerkungen zur christlichen Konstruktion jüdischer Wirklichkeit", in: Brocke, Edna/Barkenings, Hans-Joachim, eds., *"Wer Tora vermehrt, mehrt Leben"*, FS Heinz Kremers zum 60. Geburtstag, Neukirchener Verlag, Neukirchen-Vluyn, 33-47.

Jodice, David A. 1991, *United Germany and Jewish Concerns: Attitudes Toward Jews, Israel, and the Holocaust*, Working Papers on Anti-Semitism, The American Jewish Committee, New York.

Joffe, Josef 1987, "The Battle of the Historians: A Report from Germany", *Encounter* 69:1, 72-77.

Jüngst, Britta 1996, *Auf der Seite des Todes das Leben: Auf dem Weg zu einer christlich-feministischen Theologie nach der Shoah*, Chr. Kaiser/Gütersloher Verlagshaus, Gütersloh.

Jurgovsky, Manfred 1998, "Nachträgliche Wirksamkeit. Was bedeutet: Aufarbeitung der Gegenwart?", in: Staffa/Spielmann, eds., *Nachträgliche Wirksamkeit*, 23-29.

Kaes, Anton 1989, *From* Hitler *to* Heimat, Harvard University Press, Cambridge, Massachusetts/London, UK.

Kaes, Anton 1992, "History and Film: Public Memory in the Age of Electric Dissemination", in: Murray/Wickham, eds., *Framing the Past*, 308-323.

Kal, Victor 1998, "Eine universale Halacha? Marquardt, Lévinas und der jüdische Partikularismus", in: Hennecke/Weinrich, ds., *"Abirren"*, 23-38.

Kampe, Norbert 1987, "Normalizing the Holocaust? The Recent Historians' Debate in the Federal Republic of Germany", *Holocaust and Genocide Studies* 2:1, 61-80.

Kampen, Wilhem van, ed. 1978, *Holocaust: Materialien zu einer amerikanischen Fernsehserie über die Judenverfolgung im "Dritten Reich"*, Landeszentrale für politische Bildung, Düsseldorf.

Kellenbach, Katharina von 1994, *Anti-Judaism in Feminist Religious Writings*, American Academy of Religion Cultural Criticism Series 1, Scholars Press, Atlanta, Georgia.

Kemp, Sandra/Squires, Judith, eds. 1997, *Feminisms*, Oxford Readers, Oxford University Press, Oxford/New York.

Kestenberg, Judith S./Kestenberg, Milton 1982, "1. The Background of the Study", in: Bergmann/Jucovy, eds., *Generations of the Holocaust*, 33-45.

Kestenberg, Judith S. 1982, "Introduction to Part III: The Persecutors' Children", in: Bergmann/Jucovy, eds., *Generations of the Holocaust*, 161-166.

Kirchberg, Julie 1996, "Jüngst, Britta: Auf der Seite des Todes das Leben", book review, *Kirche und Israel* 11:2, 186-188.

Klappert, Bertold/Starck, Helmut, eds. 1980, *Umkehr und Erneuerung: Erläuterungen zum Synodalbeschluß der Rheinischen Landessynode 1980 "Zur Erneuerung des Verhältnisses von Christen und Juden"*, Neukirchener Verlag, Neukirchen-Vluyn.

Klappert, Bertold/Gollwitzer, Helmut/Bethge, Eberhard/Lapide, Pinchas, eds. 1980, *Kritische Stellungnahmen zu einem Bonner Theologenpapier über das Verhältnis von Juden und Christen*, epd Dokumentation 42, epd, Frankfurt am Main.

Klappert, Bertold 1980a, *Israel und die Kirche: Erwägungen zur Israellehre Karl Barths*, Theologische Existenz heute 207, Chr. Kaiser, München.

Klappert, Bertold 1980b, "Die Wurzel trägt dich: Einführung in den Synodalbeschluß der Rheinischen Landessynode", in: Klappert/Starck, eds., *Umkehr und Erneuerung*, 23-54.

Klappert, Bertold 1980c, "Zeichen der Treue Gottes", in: Klappert/Starck, eds., *Umkehr und Erneuerung*, 73-88.

Klappert, Bertold [2]1993, "Die Juden in einer christlichen Theologie nach Auschwitz", in: Ginzel, ed., *Auschwitz als Herausforderung für Juden und Christen*, 481-512.

Klappert, Bertold 1994, "Jesus als König, Priester und Prophet: Eine Wiederholung der Wege und des Berufs Israels. Versuch einer Würdigung der Christologie Friedrich-Wilhelm Marquardts", *Berliner Theologische Zeitschrift* 11:1, 25-41.

Knowlton, James/Cates, Truett, eds. 1993, *Forever in the Shadow of Hitler? Original Documents of the Historikerstreit, The Controversy Concerning the Singularity of the Holocaust*, Humanities Press, New Jersey.

Kohlstruck, Michael 1997, *Zwischen Erinnerung und Geschichte: Der Nationalsozialismus und die jungen Deutschen*, Dokumente, Texte, Materialien 22, Metropol Verlag, Berlin.

Kohn, Johanna 1986, *Haschoah: Christlich-jüdische Verständigung nach Auschwitz*, Fundamentaltheologische Studien 13, Chr. Kaiser/Grünewald, München/Mainz.

Koonz, Claudia 1987, *Mothers in the Fatherland: Women, the Family, and Nazi Politics*, Jonathan Cape, London.

Koonz, Claudia 1994a, "Between Memory and Oblivion: Concentration Camps in German Memory", in: Gillis, John R., ed., *Commemorations: The Politics of National Identity*, Princeton University Press, Princeton, New Jersey, 258-280.

Koonz, Claudia 1994b, "Germany's Buchenwald: Whose Shrine? Whose Memory?" in: Young, James E., ed., *The Art of Memory: Holocaust Memorials in History*, Prestel Verlag, Munich/New York, 111-119.

Kremers, Heinz 1980, "Der Weg der rheinischen Kirche von 1945 bis zur Landessynode 1980" in: Klappert/Starck, eds., *Umkehr und Erneuerung*, 5-11.

Kriener, Katja/Schmidt, Johann Michael, eds. 1998, *Gottes Treue – Hoffnung von Christen und Juden: Die Auseinandersetzung um die Ergänzung des Grundartikels der Kirchenordnung der Evangelischen Kirche im Rheinland*, Neukirchener Verlag, Neukirchen-Vluyn.

Kriener, Tobias 1999, "Landverheißung und Zionismus in der Theologie Friedrich-Wilhelm Marquardts – eine Problemanzeige", in: Lehming/Liß-Walther/Loebroks/Veg, eds., *Wendung nach Jerusalem*, 217-226.

Krondorfer, Björn/Schmidt, Jon, eds. 1990, *A Journal of a German/American Student Exchange Program: "Encountering the Holocaust as a Third Generation", July 31 – August 28, 1989*, Dokumentation 73/90, Evangelische Akademie Berlin [West], Berlin.

Krondorfer, Björn 1991, "Gefühle der Schuld und der Abwehr: Begegnungen zwischen Nachkriegs-Deutschen und Juden der Nach-Schoah", *Tribüne* 30:119, 130-139.

Krondorfer, Björn 1995, *Remembrance and Reconciliation: Encounters between Young Jews and Germans*, Yale University Press, New Haven et al.

Krondorfer, Björn 1997, *Third-Generation Jews and Germans: History, Memory, and Memorialization*, Working Papers of the Volkswagen-Foundation Program in Post-War German History 7, Washington D.C.

Krondorfer, Björn 1998, "Biographische Arbeit in deutsch/jüdischen Begegnungsgruppen nach der Shoah", in: Bundesministerium für Bildung, Wissenschaft, Forschung und Technologie, ed., *Biographische Arbeit in der Erwachsenenbildung: Beispiele aus der Praxis*, bmf+t, Berlin, 19-42.

Kugelmann, Cilly [2]1988, "Die gespaltene Erinnerung: Zur Genese von Gedenktagen an den Holocaust", in: Brumlik/Kunik, eds., *Reichspogromnacht*, 11-17.

LaCapra, Dominick 1998, *History and Memory after Auschwitz*, Cornell University Press, Ithaca/London.

Langer, Lawrence 1991, *Holocaust Testimonies: The Ruins of Memory*, Yale University Press, New Haven.

Langer, Lawrence 1995, *Admitting the Holocaust: Collected Essays*, Oxford University Press, New York/Oxford.

Langmuir, Gavin I. 1990, *Toward a Definition of Antisemitism*, University of California Press, Berkeley et al.

Lehming, Hannah/Liß-Walther, Joachim/Loebroks, Matthias/Veg, Rien van der, eds. 1999, *Wendung nach Jerusalem: Friedrich-Wilhelm Marquardts Theologie im Gespräch*, Chr. Kaiser/Gütersloher Verlagshaus, Gütersloh.

Levi, Primo 1988, *The Drowned and the Saved*, Michael Joseph, New York.

Levinson, Nathan Peter 1980, "Antwort und Anfrage", in: Klappert/Starck, eds., *Umkehr und Erneuerung*, 231-235.

Levkov, Ilya, ed. 1987, *Bitburg and Beyond: Encounters in American, German and Jewish History*, Shapolsky Publishers, New York.

Libeskind, Daniel 1999, *Jüdisches Museum Berlin: Zwischen den Linien*, Prestel Verlag, München et al.

Liebster, Wolfram 1980, "Umkehr und Erneuerung im Verhältnis von Christen und Juden", in: Klappert/Starck, eds., *Umkehr und Erneuerung*, 55-65.

Linden, Robin Ruth 1993, *Making Stories, Making Selves: Feminist Reflections on the Holocaust*, Ohio State University Press, Columbus.

Linke, Uli 1995, "Murderous Fantasies: Violence, Memory, and Selfhood in Germany", *New German Critique* 64, 37-59.

Liß-Walther, Joachim 1999, "Denken aus der Umkehr heraus: Eine Einführung in die Dogmatik Friedrich-Wilhelm Marquardts", in: Lehming/Liß-Walther/Loebroks/Veg, eds., *Wendung nach Jerusalem*, 13-52.

Littell, Franklin H./Locke, Hubert G., eds. 1974, *The German Church Struggle and the Holocaust*, Wayne State University Press, Detroit.

Littell, Franklin H. ²1988, *The Crucifixion of the Jews: The Failure of Christians to Understand the Jewish Experience*, Mercer University Press, Macon.

Littell, Franklin H., ed. 1997, *Hyping the Holocaust: Scholars Answer Goldhagen*, Merion Westfield Press International, Merion Station.

Loewy, Hanno, ed. 1992, *Holocaust: Die Grenzen des Verstehens. Eine Debatte über die Besetzung der Geschichte*, Rowohlt Taschenbuch Verlag, Reinbek bei Hamburg.

Loewy, Hanno 1995, "Im deutschen Bewußtsein gibt es keinen 'Holocaust' – über Mißverständnisse und andere Formen des Gedenkens", in: Schreier/Heyl, eds., *"Daß Auschwitz nicht noch einmal sei ...": Zur Erziehung nach Auschwitz*, Krämer, Hamburg, 317-334.

Loshitzky, Yosefa, ed. 1997, *Spielberg's Holocaust: Critical Perspectives on Schindler's List*, Indiana University Press, Bloomington/Indianapolis.

Lozowick, Yaacov/Millen, Rochelle L. 1996, "Pitfalls of Memory: Israeli-German Dialogues on the Shoah", in: Millen/Bennett et al., eds., *New Perspectives on the Holocaust*, 265-274.

Lowenthal, David 1985, *The Past is a foreign country*, Cambridge University Press, Cambridge et al.

Lutz, Felix Philipp 1993, "Verantwortungsbewußtsein und Wohlstandschauvinismus: Die Bedeutung historisch-politischer Einstellungen der Deutschen nach der Einheit", in: Weidenfeld, Werner, ed., *Deutschland, Eine Nation – doppelte Geschichte: Materialien zum deutschen Selbstverständnis*, Band 5 der Arbeitsergebnisse der Studiengruppe Deutschlandforschung, Verlag Wissenschaft und Politik, Köln, 157-173.

Maaßen, Monika 1993, *Biographie und Erfahrung von Frauen: Ein feministisch-theologischer Beitrag zur Relevanz der Biographieforschung für die Wiedergewinnung der Kategorie der Erfahrung*, Frauenforschung 2, Morgana Frauenbuchverlag, Münster.

Magnus, Uwe 1979, "Die Einschaltquoten und Sehbeteiligungen", in: Märtesheimer, Peter/Frenzel, Ivo, eds., *Im Kreuzfeuer: Der Fernsehfilm "Holocaust": Eine Nation ist betroffen*, Fischer Taschenbuch Verlag, Frankfurt am Main, 221-224.

Maier, Charles S. ⁶1994, *The Unmasterable Past: History, Holocaust, and German National Identity*, Harvard University Press, Cambridge, Massachusetts/London, UK.

Manemann, Jürgen 1997, "Wider das Vergessen: Entwurf einer Kritischen Theorie des Eingedenkens aus politisch-theologischer Sicht", in: Boschki/Konrad, eds., *Ist die Vergangenheit noch ein Argument?* 88-118.

Mannheim, Karl 1952, "The Problem of Generations", in: Mannheim, Karl, *Essays on the Sociology of Knowledge*, edited by Paul Kecskemeti, Routledge and Kegan Paul Ltd., London, 276-320.

Marcuse, Harold 2001, *Legacies of Dachau: The Uses and Abuses of a Concentration Camp, 1933-2001*, Cambridge University Press, Cambridge et al.

Markovits, Andrei S./Hayden, Rebecca S. 1986, "'Holocaust' before and after the Event: Reactions in West Germany and Austria", in: Rabinbach/Zipes, eds., *Germans and Jews since the Holocaust*, 234-257.

Markovits, Andrei S. 1998, "Discomposure in History's Final Resting Place", in: Shandley, ed., *Unwilling Germans?* 119-128.

Marquardt, Friedrich-Wilhelm 1976, *Die Entdeckung des Judentums für die christliche Theologie: Israel im Denken Karl Barths*, Abhandlungen zum christlich-jüdischen Dialog 1, Chr. Kaiser Verlag, München.

Marquardt, Friedrich-Wilhelm 1979, "Kann man nach Auschwitz noch von Gott reden?", *Reformatio* 28, 276-288.

Marquardt, Friedrich-Wilhelm 1980, "Christsein nach Auschwitz", in: Osten-Sacken, Peter von der/Stöhr, Martin, eds., *Glaube und Hoffnung nach Auschwitz: Jüdisch-christliche Dialoge, Vorträge, Diskussionen*, Institut Kirche und Judentum, Berlin, 62-76.

Marquardt, Friedrich-Wilhelm 1981, "'Rabbinische' und 'dogmatische' Struktur theologischer Aussage", in: Stöhr, Martin, ed., *Jüdische Existenz und die Erneuerung der christlichen Theologie: Versuch einer Bilanz des christlich-jüdischen Dialogs für die Systematische Theologie*, Abhandlungen zum christlich-jüdischen Dialog 11, Chr. Kaiser, München, 163-181.

Marquardt, Friedrich-Wilhelm 1983, *Die Gegenwart des Auferstandenen bei seinem Volk Israel: Ein dogmatische Experiment*, Abhandlungen zum christlich-jüdischen Dialog 15, Chr. Kaiser Verlag, München.

Marquardt, Friedrich-Wilhelm 1986, "Treue und Zeichen: Zum Sinn dieser Begriffe im theologischen Verhältnis zu Israel", in: Brocke/Seim, eds., *Gottes Augapfel*, 121-135.

Marquardt, Friedrich-Wilhelm [2]1992, *Von Elend und Heimsuchung der Theologie: Prolegomena zur Dogmatik*, Chr. Kaiser, München. [1]1988

Marquardt, Friedrich-Wilhelm 1990/1991, *Das christliche Bekenntnis zu Jesus, dem Juden: Eine Christologie*, Band 1+2, Chr. Kaiser, München.

Marquardt, Friedrich-Wilhelm , 1993/1994/1996 *Was dürfen wir hoffen, wenn wir hoffen dürften? Eine Eschatologie*, Band 1-3, Chr. Kaiser/Gütersloher Verlagshaus, Gütersloh.

Marquardt, Friedrich-Wilhelm 1997, *Eia, wärn wir da – eine theologische Utopie*, Chr. Kaiser/Gütersloher Verlagshaus, Gütersloh.

Marquardt, Friedrich-Wilhelm 1998a, "Amsterdamer Werkstattbericht", in: Hennecke/Weinrich, eds., *"Abirren"*, 79-94.

Marquardt, Friedrich-Wilhelm 1998b, "Zwischen Amsterdam und Berlin", in: Hennecke/Weinrich, eds., *"Abirren"*, 97-147.

Marquardt, Friedrich-Wilhelm 1998c, "'Abirren': Zu Erscheinungsformen den Häretischen in meiner Theologie", in: Hennecke/Weinrich, eds., *"Abirren"*, 151-174.

Marrus, Michael R. 1987, *The Holocaust in History*, University Press of New England, London et al.

McClintock Fulkerson, Mary 1994, *Changing the Subject: Women's Discourses and Feminist Theology*, Fortress Press, Minneapolis.

Metz, Johann Baptist 1980, *Faith in History and Society: Toward a Practical Fundamental Theology*, Burns and Oates, London.

Metz, Johann Baptist 1984, "Facing the Jews: Christian Theology after Auschwitz", in: Schüssler Fiorenza/Tracy, eds., *The Holocaust as Interruption*, 26-33.

Metz, Johann Baptist 1972/1995, "The Future in the Memory of Suffering" (1972), in: Metz, Johann Baptist/Moltmann, Jürgen, *Faith in the Future: Essays on Theology, Solidarity, and Modernity*, Concilium Series, Orbis Books, Maryknoll, New York, 3-16.

Middleton, David/Edwards, Derek, eds. 1990, *Collective Remembering*, Inquiries in Social Construction, Sage Publications, London et al.

Millen, Rochelle L./Bennett, Timothy A. et al., eds. 1996, *New Perspectives on the Holocaust: A Guide for Teachers and Scholars*, New York University Press, New York/London.

Miller, Judith 1990, *One, by One, by One: Facing the Holocaust*, Weidenfeld & Nicholson, London.

Mitscherlich, Alexander/Mitscherlich, Margarete 1968, *Die Unfähigkeit zu trauern: Grundlagen kollektiven Verhaltens*, R. Piper & Co. Verlag, München.

Moeller, Robert G. 1996, "War Stories: The Search for a Usable Past in the Federal Republic of Germany", *The American Historical Review* 101:4, 1008-1048.

Moltmann, Bernhard/Kiesel, Doron/Kugelmann, Cilly/Loewy, Hanno/Neuhaus, Dietrich, eds. 1993, *Erinnerung: Zur Gegenwart des Holocaust in Deutschland-West und Deutschland-Ost*, Arnoldshainer Texte 79, Haag und Herchen, Frankfurt am Main.

Moses, A.D. 1998, "Structure and Agency in the Holocaust: Daniel J. Goldhagen and his Critics", *History and Theory* 37:2, 195-219.

Müller-Hohagen, Jürgen 1988, *Verleugnet, verdrängt, verschwiegen: Die seelischen Auswirkungen der Nazizeit*, Kösel Verlag, München.

Münz, Christoph [2]1996, *Der Welt ein Gedächtnis geben: Geschichtstheologisches Denken im Judentum nach Auschwitz*, Chr. Kaiser/Gütersloher Verlagshaus, Gütersloh.

Murray, Bruce A./Wickham, Christopher J., eds. 1992, *Framing the Past: The Historiography of German Cinema and Television*, Southern Illinois University Press, Carbondale/Edwardsville.

Ne'eman Arad, Gulie, ed. 1992, *Passing into History: Nazism and the Holocaust beyond Memory*, In Honor of Saul Friedländer on His Sixty-Fifth Birthday, *History and Memory* 9:1/2, Indiana University Press, Bloomington.

Neusner, Jacob 1991, *Jews and Christians: The Myth of a Common Tradition*, SCM/Trinity Press International, London/Philadelphia.

Niederland, William G. 1968, "Clinical Observations on the 'Survivor Syndrome': Symposium on Psychic Traumatization through Social Catastrophe", *International Journal of Psychoanalysis* 49, 313-315.

Niethammer, Lutz, ed. [2]1985, *Lebenserfahrung und kollektives Gedächtnis: Die Praxis der Oral History*, Suhrkamp, Frankfurt.

Nolan, Mary 1988, "The *Historikerstreit* and Social History", *New German Critique* 44, 51-80.

Nolte, Ernst 1993a, "Between Historical Legend and Revisionism? The Third Reich in the Perspective of 1980", in: Knowlton/Cates, eds., *Forever in the Shadow of Hitler?* 1-15.

Nolte, Ernst 1993b, "The Past That Will Not Pass: A Speech That Could Be Written but Not Delivered", in: Knowlton/Cates, eds., *Forever in the Shadow of Hitler?* 18-23.

Nora, Pierre 1996, *Realms of Memory*, Columbia University Press, New York.

Ofer, Dalia/Weitzman, Leonore J., eds. 1998, *Women and the Holocaust*, Yale University Press, New Haven/London.

Olick, Jeffrey K./Robbins, Joyce 1998, "Social Memory Studies: From 'Collective Memory' to the Historical Sociology of Mnemonic Practices", *Annual Reviews in Sociology* 24, 105-140.

Owings, Alison 1995, *Frauen: German Women Recall the Third Reich*, Penguin, London.

Papademetriou, George C. 1990, *Essays on Orthodox Christian-Jewish Relations*, Wyndham Hall Press, Bristol, Indiana.

Parkes, James 1948, *Judaism and Christianity*, Victor Gollancz Ltd., London.

Pätzold, Kurt 1998, "On the Broad Trial of the German Perpetrators", in: Shandley, ed., *Unwilling Germans?* 163-166.

Petersen, Birte [2]1998, *Theologie nach Auschwitz? Jüdische und christliche Versuche einer Antwort*, Veröffentlichungen aus dem Institut Kirche und Judentum 24, Institut Kirche und Judentum, Berlin.

Petrie, Jon 2000, "The secular word HOLOCAUST: scholarly myths, history, and 20th century meanings", *Journal of Genocide Research* 2:1, 31-63.

Petzel, Paul 1994, *Was uns an Gott fehlt, wenn uns die Juden fehlen: Eine fundamentaltheologische Studie*, Matthias-Grünewald-Verlag, Mainz.

Pfisterer, Rudolf 1992, "Land und Volk Israel in der Sicht eines evangelischen Theologen", in: Schoeps, Julius H., ed., *Aus zweier Zeugen Mund*, FS Pnina Navé Levinson und Nathan Peter Levinson, Bleicher Verlag, Gerlingen, 83-100.

Pollefeyt, Didier, ed. 1997, *Jews and Christians: Rivals or Partners for the Kingdom of God? In Search for an Alternative for the Theology of Substitution*, Louvain Theological and Pastoral Monographs 21, Peters Press/W.B. Eerdmans, Louvain.

Rabinbach, Anson/Zipes, Jack, eds. 1986, *Germans and Jews since the Holocaust: The Changing Situation in West Germany*, Holmes & Meier, New York/London.

Rabinbach, Anson 1988, "The Jewish Question in the German Question", *New German Critique* 44, 159-192.

Rapaport, Lynn 1997, *Jews in Germany after the Holocaust: Memory, identity and Jewish-German relations*, Cambridge University Press, Cambridge.

Reck, Norbert 1998, *Im Angesicht der Zeugen: Eine Theologie nach Auschwitz*, Matthias-Grünewald-Verlag, Mainz.

Reemtsma, Jan Philipp 1998, "Turning Away from Denial: *Hitler's Willing Executioners* as a Counterforce to 'Historical Explanation'", in: Shandley, ed., *Unwilling Germans?* 255-262.

Reemtsma, Jan Philipp 1999, "Die einzige Lösung", *Die Zeit* 25, 19 June.

Reichel, Peter 1995, *Politik mit der Erinnerung: Gedächtnisorte im Streit um die nationalsozialistische Vergangenheit*, Carl Hanser Verlag, München/Wien.

Reinharz, Jehuda, ed. 1987, *Living with Antisemitism: Modern Jewish Responses*, University Press of New England, London et al.

Reitz, Edgar 1984, *Liebe zum Kino: Utopien und Gedanken zm Autorenfilm 1962-1983*, Verlag Köln 78, Köln.

Rendtorff, Rolf/Henrix, Hans Hermann, eds. [2]1989, *Die Kirchen und das Judentum: Dokumente von 1945 bis 1985*, Verlag Bonifatius-Druckerei/Chr. Kaiser, Paderborn/München.

Rendtorff, Rolf 1989a, "Der Dialog hat erst begonnen", in: Görg, Manfred et al., *Christen und Juden im Gespräch: Eine Bilanz nach 40 Jahren Staat Israel*, Verlag Friedrich Pustet, Regensburg, 39-55.

Rendtorff, Rolf 1989b, *Hat denn Gott sein Volk verstoßen? Die evangelische Kirche und das Judentum seit 1945. Ein Kommentar*, Abhandlungen zum christlich-jüdischen Dialog 18, Chr. Kaiser, München.

Rendtorff, Rolf 1991, "Ist Dialog möglich? Ansätze zum christlich-jüdischen Gespräch nach der Schoah", in: Marcus, Marcel/Stegemann, Ekkehard W./Zenger, Erich, eds., *Israel und Kirche heute: Beiträge zum christlich-jüdischen Dialog*, FS Ernst Ludwig Ehrlich zum 70. Geburtstag, Herder Verlag, Freiburg et al., 123-134.

Richarz, Monika 1986, "Juden in der Bundesrepublik Deutschland und in der Deutschen Demokratischen Republik seit 1945", in: Brumlik/Kiesel/Kugelmann/Schoeps, eds., *Jüdisches Leben in Deutschland seit 1945*, 13-30.

Richter 1992, Horst-Eberhard, "Erinnerungsarbeit und Zukunftserwartung der Deutschen", in: Hardtmann, Gertrud, ed., *Spuren der Verfolgung: Seelische Auswirkungen des Holocaust auf die Opfer und ihre Kinder*, Bleicher Verlag, Gerlingen, 222-234.

Rittner, Carol/Roth, John K., eds. 1991, *Memory Offended: The Auschwitz Convent Controversy*, Praeger Publishers, New York et al.

Rittner, Carol/Roth, John K., eds. 1993, *Different Voices: Women and the Holocaust*, Paragon House, New York.

Roberts, Ulla 1998, *Spuren der NS-Zeit im Leben der Kinder und Enkel: Drei Generationen im Gespräch*, Kösel Verlag, München.

Rommelspacher, Birgit 1994, *Schuldlos – Schuldig? Wie sich junge Frauen mit Antisemitismus auseinandersetzen*, Konkret Literatur Verlag, Hamburg.

Roseman, Mark 1999, "Surviving Memory: Truth and Inaccuracy in Holocaust Testimony", *Journal of Holocaust Education* 8:1, 1-20.

Rosenberg, Bernhard H., ed. 1992, *Theological and Halakhic Responses to the Holocaust*, KTAV, Hoboken, NJ.

Rosenfeld, Alvin 1994, "Jean Améry as Witness", in: Hartman, ed., *Holocaust Remembrance*, 59-69.

Rosenfeld, Sidney 1980, "Afterword", in: Améry, *At the Mind's Limits*, 104-111.

Rosenthal, Gabriele, ed. 1998, *The Holocaust in Three Generations: Families of Victims and Perpetrators of the Nazi Regime*, Cassell, London/Washington.

Rosenthal, Gabriele 1998a, "Similarities and differences in family dialogue", in: Rosenthal, ed., *The Holocaust in Three Generations*, 8-13.

Rosenthal, Gabriele 1998b, "National Socialism and antisemitism in intergerenational dialogue", in: Rosenthal, ed., *The Holocaust in Three Generations*, 240-248.

Roth, John K./Berenbaum, Michael, eds. 1989, *Holocaust, Religious and Philosophical Implications*, Paragon House, New York.

Rothschild, Fritz A., ed. 1996, *Jewish Perspectives on Christianity: Leo Baeck, Martin Buber, Franz Rosenzweig, Will Herberg and Abraham J. Heschel*, Continuum, New York.

Ruether, Rosemary Radford 1974, *Faith and Fratricide: The Theological Roots of Anti-Semitism*, Seabury Press, New York.

Rüter, Gregor/Westhoff, Rainer 1985, *Geschichte und Schicksal der Telgter Juden, 1933-1945*, Stadt Telgte, Telgte.

Santner, Eric L. 1992, "On the Difficulty of Saying 'We': The Historians' Debate and Reitz's *Heimat*", in: Murray/Wickham, eds., *Framing the Past*, 261-279.

Santner, Eric L. [3]1996, "History beyond the Pleasure Principle: Some Thoughts on the Representation of Trauma", in: Friedlander, ed., *Probing the Limits of Representation*, 143-154.

Schellong, Dieter 1998, "Eigentümlichkeiten und Banalitäten im kirchlichen Gedenken", in: Staffa/Spielmann, eds., *Nachträgliche Wirksamkeit*, 95-112.

Schindler, Pesach 1973, "The Holocaust and Kiddush HaShem in Hassidic Thought", *Tradition* 13/14, 88-104.

Schneider, Richard Chaim 1997, *Fetisch Holocaust: Die Judenvernichtung – verdrängt und vermarktet*, Kindler Verlag, München.

Schneider, Richard Chaim 2000, *Wir sind da! Die Geschichte der Juden in Deutschland von 1945 bis heute*, Ullstein Verlag, Berlin.

Schoeps, Julius H., ed. 1997, *Ein Volk von Mördern? Die Dokumentation zur Goldhagen-Kontroverse um die Rolle der Deutschen im Holocaust*, Hoffman & Campe, Hamburg.

Schoeps, Julius H. 1990, *Leiden an Deutschland: Vom antisemitischen Wahn und der Last der Erinnerung*, Piper, München/Zürich.

Scholem, Gerschom 1976, "Against the Myth of German-Jewish Dialogue" (1964), in: Scholem, Gershom, *On Jews and Judaism in Crisis: Selected Essays*, ed. Werner J. Dannhauser, Schocken Books, New York, 61-64.

Schreier, Helmut/Heyl, Matthias, eds. 1992 *Das Echo des Holocaust: Pädagogische Aspekte des Erinnerns*, Krämer, Hamburg.

Schreier, Helmut/Heyl, Matthias, eds. 1995, *"Daß Auschwitz nicht noch einmal sei ...": Zur Erziehung nach Auschwitz*, Krämer, Hamburg.

Schuman, Howard/Scott, Jacqueline 1989, "Generations and Collective Memory", *American Sociological Review* 54, 359-381.

Schüssler Fiorenza, Elisabeth/Tracy, David, eds. 1984, *The Holocaust as Interruption*, Concilium 175, T & T Clark LTD, Edinburgh.

Secretariat for Ecumenical and Interreligious Affairs/National Conference of Catholic Bishops, eds. 1998, *Catholics Remember the Holocaust*, United States Catholic Conference, Washington, DC.

Seebass, Horst 1998, "Zur Entscheidung der Landessynode 1996 über das Proponendum 'Kirche und Israel'", in: Kriener/Schmidt, eds., *Gottes Treue – Hoffnung von Christen und Juden*, 171-179.

Segev, Tom 1993, *The Seventh Million: The Israelis and the Holocaust*, Hill and Wang, New York.

Seim, Jürgen 1980, "Die gemeinsame Bibel", in: Klappert/Starck, eds., *Umkehr und Erneuerung*, 111-127.

Seim, Jürgen 1998, "Muß Israel in der Kirchenordnung stehen?", in: Kriener/Schmidt, eds., *Gottes Treue – Hoffnung von Christen und Juden*, 283-295.

Senders, Stefan 1996, "Laws of Belonging: Legal Dimensions of National Inclusion in Germany", *New German Critique* 67, 147-176.

Shandler, Jeffrey 1999, *While America Watches: Televising the Holocaust*, Oxford University Press, New York/Oxford.

Shandley, Robert R., ed. 1998, *Unwilling Germans? The Goldhagen Debate*, University of Minnesota Press, Minneapolis/London.

Shandley, Robert R. 1998, "Introduction", in: Shandley, ed., *Unwilling Germans?* 1-30.

Sichrovsky, Peter 1986, *Strangers in their own Land: Young Jews in Germany and Austria*, I.B. Tauris & Co. Ltd., London.

Sichrovsky, Peter 1987, *Schuldig geboren: Kinder aus Nazifamilien*, Kiepenheuer & Witsch, Köln.

Siegele-Wenschkewitz, Leonore, ed. 1988, *Verdrängte Vergangenheit, die uns bedrängt: Feministische Theologie in der Verantwortung für die Geschichte*, Chr. Kaiser, München.

Siegele-Wenschkewitz, Leonore, ed. 1994, *Christlicher Antijudaismus und Antisemitismus: Theologische und kirchliche Programme Deutscher Christen*, Arnoldshainer Texte 85, Haag & Herchen, Frankfurt am Main.

Siegele-Wenschkewitz, Leonore 1988, "Zur Einführung", in: Siegele-Wenschkewitz, ed., *Verdrängte Vergangenheit, die uns bedrängt*, 7-53.

Staffa, Christian/Krondorfer, Björn, eds. 1992, *The third generation after the Shoah: between remembering, repressing and commemorating, attempts of a common time in Philadelphia, Berlin, Auschwitz, American/Jewish and East/West German student exchange program, July 25th – August 22nd, 1991*, Dokumentation 88/92, Evangelische Akademie Berlin [West], Berlin.

Staffa, Christian/Krondorfer, Björn/Jurgovsky, Manfred, eds. 1994, *Living in a Post-Shoah World: Reflections of American, German, Jewish and Christian Students, 3rd summerprogram on the Holocaust, July 21 – August 19, 1993*, Nachlese 5/94, Evangelische Akademie Berlin-Brandenburg, Berlin.

Staffa, Christian/Krondorfer, Björn, eds. 1997, *Living in a Post-Shoah World: Reflections of American, German, Jewish and Christian Students, 4th summerprogram on the Holocaust, July 24th – August 16th, 1995*, Nachlese 1/97, Evangelische Akademie Berlin-Brandenburg, Berlin.

Staffa, Christian/Spielmann, Jochen, eds. 1998, *Nachträgliche Wirksamkeit: Vom Aufheben der Taten im Gedenken*, Schriftenreihe des Instituts für vergleichende Geschichtswissenschaften Berlin 1, Institut für vergleichende Geschichtswissenschaften, Berlin.

Starck, Helmut 1980, "Der Weg des Ausschusses", in: Klappert/Starck, eds., *Umkehr und Erneuerung*, 12-23.

Steiner, George 1959/1985, "The Hollow Miracle" (1959), in: Steiner, George, *Language and Silence: Essays 1958-1966*, faber and faber, London/Boston, 117-132.

Stendahl, Krister 1986, "Die nächste Generation in den jüdisch-christlichen Beziehungen", *Kirche und Israel* 1:1, 11-15.

Stern, Frank 1992, *The Whitewashing of the Yellow Badge: Antisemitism and Philosemitism in Postwar Germany*, Studies in Antisemitism, Pergamon Press, Oxford et al.

Stern, Susan, ed. 1995, *Speaking Out: Jewish Voices from United Germany*, edition q, Chicago et al.

Stiftung für die Rechte zukünftiger Generationen, ed. 1999, *Was bleibt von der Vergangenheit? Die junge Generation im Dialog über den Holocaust*, Ch. Links Verlag,.

Stransky, Thomas F. CSP [2]1995, "Holy Diplomacy: Making the Impossible Possible", in: Brooks, Roger, ed., *Unanswered Questions: Theological Views of Jewish-Catholic Relations*, University of Notre Dame Press, Notre Dame, Indiana, 51-69.

Tal, Uriel 1989, "On the Study of the Holocaust and Genocide", in: Marrus, Michael R., ed., *The Nazi Holocaust: Historical Articles on the Destruction of European Jewry, Volume 1. Perspectives on the Holocaust*, Meckler, Westport/London, 179-224.

Thiele, Hans-Günther, ed. 1997, *Die Wehrmachtsausstellung: Dokumentation einer Kontroverse*, Bundeszentrale für politische Bildung, Bonn.

Thierfelder, Jörg/Wölfing, Willi, eds. 1996, *Für ein neues Miteinander von Juden und Christen*, Schriftenreihe der Pädagogischen Hochschule Heidelberg 27, Deutscher Studien Verlag, Weinheim.

Torpey, John 1988, "Introduction: Habermas and the Historians", *New German Critique* 44, 5-24.

Traverso, Enzo 1995, *The Jews and Germany: From the "Judeo-German Symbiosis" to the Memory of Auschwitz*, Texts and Contexts 14, University of Nebraska Press, Lincoln/London.

Ullrich, Volker 1998, "A Triumphal Procession: Goldhagen and the Germans", in: Shandley, ed., *Unwilling Germans?* 197-202.

Vogt, Rolf and Barbara 1997, "Goldhagen und die Deutschen: Psychoanalytische Reflexionen über die Resonanz auf ein Buch und seinen Autor in der deutschen Öffentlichkeit", *Psyche* 51:6, 494-569.

Wardi, Dina 1992, *Memorial Candles: Children of the Holocaust*, Tavistock/Routlegde, London et al.

Webber, Jonathan, ed. 1994, *Jewish Identities in the New Europe*, Littman Library of Jewish Civilization, London/Washington.

Webber, Jonathan 1994, "Introduction", in: Webber, ed., *Jewish Identities in the New Europe*, 1-32.

Wehler, Hans-Ulrich 1988, *Entsorgung der deutschen Vergangenheit? Ein polemischer Essay zum "Historikerstreit"*, Verlag C.H. Beck, München.

Wehler, Hans-Ulrich 1998, "Like a Thorn in the Flesh", in: Shandley, ed., *Unwilling Germans?* 93-104.

Weissberg-Bob, Nea, ed. 1996, *Als man den Juden alles, sogar das Leben raubte ...: Von den Nachwirkungen nationalsozialistischer Zerstörung. Gespräche mit den Nachkommen der Täter und der Opfer*, Lichtiger Verlag, Berlin.

Wessel, Coen 1998, "Einführung in Marquardts Dogmatik", in: Hennecke/Weinrich, eds., *"Abirren"*, 11-22.

Westernhagen, Dörte von 1987, *Die Kinder der Täter: Das Dritte Reich und die Generation danach*, Kösel Verlag, München.

White, Hayden [3]1996, "Historical Emplotment and the Problem of Truth", in: Friedlander, ed., *Probing the Limits of Representation*, 37-53.

Wiedmer, Caroline 1999, *The Claims of Memory: Representations of the Holocaust in Contemporary Germany and France*, Cornell University Press, Ithaca/London.

Wiesel, Elie 1978, "Trivialising the Holocaust: Semi-Fact and Semi-Fiction", *New York Times*, 16 April.

Winkelmann, Bernd 1988, "Einstellung heutiger Jugendlicher zum Holocaust: Zum historischen Bewußtsein 16-21-jähriger", in: Bar-On/Beiner/Brusten, eds., *Der Holocaust – Familiale und gesellschaftliche Folgen*, 194-213.

Wollaston, Isabel 1995, "Religious Language after the Holocaust", in: Young, Frances, ed., *Dare We Speak of God in Public? The Edward Cadbury Lectures 1993-94*, Mowbray, London, 81-87.

Wollaston, Isabel 1996, *A War Against Memory? The Future of Holocaust Remembrance*, SPCK, London.

Yahil, Leni 1990, *The Holocaust: The Fate of European Jewry, 1932-1945*, Oxford University Press, New York.

Yerushalmi, Yosef Hayim 1989, *Zakhor: Jewish History and Jewish Memory*, Schocken Books, New York.

Young, James E. 1986, "Memory and Monument", in: Hartman, ed., *Bitburg in Moral and Political Perspective*, 103-113.

Young, James E. 1988, *Writing and Rewriting the Holocaust: Narrative and the Consequences of Interpretation*, Indiana University Press, Bloomington/Indianapolis.

Young, James E. 1996, "Jom Hashoah: Die Gestaltung eines Gedenktages", in: Berg/Jochimsen/Stiegler, eds., *Shoah: Formen der Erinnerung*, 53-76.

Young, James E. 1997, "Toward a Received History of the Holocaust", *History and Theory* 36:4, 21-43.

Young, James E. 2000, *At Memory's Edge: After-Images of the Holocaust in Contemporary Art and Architecture*, Yale University Press, New Haven/London.

Zielinski, Siegfried 1986, "History as Entertainment and Provocation: The TV Series 'Holocaust' in West Germany", in: Rabinbach/Zipes, eds., *Germans and Jews since the Holocaust*, 258-283.

The Holy Bible: New Revised Standard Version, Catholic Edition, Geoffrey Chapman, London, 1993.

TANAKH: A New Translation of the Holy Scriptures According to the Traditional Hebrew Text, The Jewish Publication Society, Philadelphia/Jerusalem, 1985.

Websites

http://www.toreflectandtrust.org
http://www.secondgeneration.org

Religion – Geschichte – Gesellschaft
Fundamentaltheologische Studien
herausgegeben von Johann Baptist Metz (Münster / Wien),
Johann Reikerstorfer (Wien) und Jürgen Werbick (Münster)

Johann Baptist Metz; Johann Reikerstorfer;
Jürgen Werbick
Gottesrede
Wie ist nach der Botschaft vom "Tod Gottes"
nicht nur erneut von Religion, sondern von Gott,
vom Gott der biblischen Tradition zu reden? Welche Sprache hat die Theologie für "Gott in dieser
Zeit", die von Katastrophen wie der von Auschwitz gezeichnet ist? Solchen "fundamentalen"
Fragen der christlichen Gottesrede stellen sich die
drei Herausgeber der Reihe in diesem Band:
Johann Baptist Metz, der die "schwachen" Kategorien der Gottesrede in der "Zeit der Gotteskrise"
entfaltet ("Im Eingedenken fremden Leids. Zu
einer Basiskategorie christlicher Gottesrede"),
Johann Reikerstorfer, dem es vor allem um eine
Auseinandersetzung mit Letztbegründungsabsich-
ten in der Theologie/Religionsphilosophie geht,
("Leiddurchkreuzt – Zum Logos christlicher Got-
tesrede") und
Jürgen Werbick, der anhand der Problematik des
Bittgebets die heutige "Schwierigkeit, ja zu sa-
gen" untersucht ("Was das Beten der Theologie zu
denken gibt").
Bd. 1, 2. erw. Aufl. Herbst 2001, 104 S., 19,80 DM, br.,
ISBN 3-8258-2470-5

Jürgen Manemann
"Weil es nicht nur Geschichte ist"
Die Begründung der Notwendigkeit einer
fragmentarischen Historiographie des Nationalsozialismus aus politisch-theologischer
Sicht
Der Blick auf die Katastrophe Auschwitz verweist die Theologie *radikal* auf Geschichte und
Gesellschaft. Aber nicht nur die Theologie ist
durch Auschwitz systematisch herausgefordert und
gezwungen, ihre Denkvoraussetzungen kritisch zu
überprüfen. Auch die Geschichtswissenschaft muß
sich der genannten Herausforderung stellen, denn
auch ihr geht es um eine Kultur der Erinnerung,
die wider die Apologetik und Relativierung das
Recht der Opfer und die Schuld der Täter fest-
stellen und festhalten will. Das Nachdenken über
diese Erinnerungskultur und der Streit über sie
verbinden die historische und die theologische
Vernunft. Diese produktive und konfliktreiche
Spannung drängt einen interdisziplinären Vergleich
und Austausch geradezu auf. Die vorliegende
Arbeit verknüpft die historische Erinnerung mit
einem sich dem theologischen Denken verdan-
kenden Eingedenken und entwirft von dort aus

einen Umgang mit dem Nationalsozialismus, der
der intellektuellen Komplizenschaft mit den Tätern
entgeht.
Bd. 2, 1995, 320 S., 58,80 DM, gb., ISBN 3-8258-2345-8

José A. Zamora
Krise – Kritik – Erinnerung
Ein politisch-theologischer Versuch über das
Denken Adornos im Horizont der Krise der
Moderne
José A. Zamora nimmt in seiner großangelegten
Untersuchung Habermas' Vorschlag eines Rück-
gangs hinter die *Dialektik der Aufklärung* auf,
jedoch mit gegenläufiger Intention: Er untersucht
Adornos Frühwerk in der Absicht, die Genesis
eines 'anamnetischen Denkens' nachzuzeichnen,
das Adorno in der Auseinandersetzung mit der
Krise der kulturellen Moderne und der histori-
schen Erfahrung in den 30er Jahren formuliert
hat und das eine 'Halbierung der Rationalität'
dokumentiert und kritisiert, auf die man sich heute
weiterhin besinnen muß. Adornos 'konstellative
Methode' versagt sich Theorie-Lösungen und ver-
weilt bei den Aporien der Moderne, um das in ihr
Unsichtbar-Gewordene, das vergangene Leid und
das Andere des Bestehenden, sichtbar zu machen.
Denn es ist die zunehmende Amnesie, die das
Projekt der Moderne in eine 'Sackgasse' geführt
hat.
Bd. 3, 1995, 512 S., 78,80 DM, gb., ISBN 3-8258-2389-X

Martha Zechmeister
Gottes-Nacht
Erich Przywaras Weg negativer Theologie
Gegenüber einer Auslegung des Werks Przywaras
(1889 – 1972) als niveauvolle, aber im Grunde
überholte Erneuerung scholastischer Ontologie ist
die These der Arbeit, daß sich in ihm die Züge
einer Gott-Rede enthüllen, die der Radikalität
heutiger "Gotteskrise" zu entsprechen vermag:
In erlittener Nicht-Identität, in den geschichtlichen Katastrophen, im Sich-Wundreiben an der
Andersheit des konkret anderen mitmenschlichen
Subjekts beginnt die Selbstbezogenheit und Selbst-
genügsamkeit des Gott-Suchers aufzubrechen für
den "Ganz-Anderen", für den je größeren Gott.
Damit gibt sich aber auch der Zentralbegriff der
Theologie Erich Przywaras, die analogia entis,
gegen jedes Mißverständnis als Gott und Mensch
zusammenzwingende Formel als das Wort, das
einerseits das verzweifelte Ringen Przywaras um
eine lebbare Einheit in einer auseinanderbersten-
den Moderne und andererseits den Widerstand
gegen eine Vereinnahmung Gottes vom Menschen
her bezeichnet: analogia entis als Einweisung in
die negative Theologie.
"In einer Zeit, in der – wie zum Beispiel im
französischen und deutschen Sprachraum – die

LIT Verlag Münster – Hamburg – Berlin – London
Bestellungen über:
Grevener Str. 179 48159 Münster
Tel.: 0251 – 23 50 91 – Fax: 0251 – 23 19 72
e-Mail: lit@lit-verlag.de – http://www.lit-verlag.de

Preise: unv. PE

Negative Theologie und ihre Traditionen neue Aufmerksamkeit gewinnen, ist eine Arbeit über Erich Przywara, die ihn als einen der Höhepunkte dieser Tradition liest ("Gottes-Nacht"), von eminenter Bedeutung." (J. B. Metz)
Bd. 4, 2. Aufl. 2000, 344 S., 49,80 DM, br., ISBN 3-8258-3105-1

Gabriele Grunden
Fremde Freiheit
Jüdische Stimmen als Herausforderung an den Logos christlicher Theologie
Die Verurteilung des Antijudaismus gehört mittlerweile zum guten Ton christlicher Theologie. Doch damit ist noch lange nicht ein christliches Selbstverständnis erreicht, das von antijüdischen Zügen frei wäre. Die vorliegende Studie geht hier einen wichtigen Schritt weiter: Sie faßt nicht nur den aktuellen Stand jüdischer Jesusforschung zusammen, sondern erhellt auch das theologische und religiöse Selbstverständnis maßgeblicher jüdischer Philosophen der Gegenwart (Cohen, Rosenzweig, Lévinas). So werden Konturen einer "Exilshermeneutik" sichtbar, die je aktuell die angemessene Treue zur Tradition sucht. Sie belegen, daß christliche Behauptungen einer notwendigen Überbietung des Judentums der Grundlage entbehren: Stattdessen stellt die Autorin die Strukturanalogie zwischen der Bindung an die Thora und dem Bekenntnis zu Christus heraus. Bei der Bewährung dieser These in Auseinandersetzung mit heutigen Ansätzen christlicher Theologie (Metz, Pröpper) weiß sich die Autorin dem Auftrag Adornos verpflichtet, "den besseren Zustand zu denken, in dem man ohne Angst verschieden sein kann".
Bd. 5, 1996, 276 S., 58,80 DM, gb., ISBN 3-8258-2572-8

Ottmar John
"... und dieser Feind hat zu siegen nicht aufgehört" (W. Benjamin)
Die Bedeutung Walter Benjamins für eine Theologie nach Auschwitz
Bd. 6, Herbst 2001, 480 S., 58,80 DM, br., ISBN 3-8258-2705-4

Hans-Gerd Janßen
Dem Leiden widerstehen
Aufsätze zur Grundlage einer praktischen Theodizee
Die Theodizeefrage, also die Frage nach der Wirklichkeit Gottes angesichts der Erfahrung abgrundtiefen Leidens, ist zur Kernfrage einer heute möglichen Rede von Gott, von Erlösung und Heil geworden. Die unterschiedlichen Antwortversuche – von den klassischen Theodizeesystemen bis hin zur Theologie des "leidenden Gottes" – überzeugen nicht. Auf diese Unmöglichkeit einer theoretisch formulierbaren Antwort reflektiert die "praktische Theodizee". Sie fragt danach, wie Menschen in ihrem Handeln den Herausforderungen dieser Frage, also den Herausforderungen durch Gott und durch das Leiden, standhalten können – ohne den Aporien in purem Aktionismus auszuweichen. Die Theorie solcher Praxis weiß um die Grenzen menschlichen Handelns, das gleichwohl der Ort ist, von dem her eine mögliche Rede von Gott angesichts des Leidens sich begründen läßt.
Bd. 7, 1996, 112 S., 24,80 DM, br., ISBN 3-8258-3012-8

Dieter Henrich; Johann Baptist Metz; Bernd Jochen Hilberath; R. J. Zwi Werblowsky
Die Gottrede von Juden und Christen unter den Herausforderungen der säkularen Welt
Symposion des Gesprächskreises "Juden und Christen" beim Zentralkomitee der deutschen Katholiken am 22./23. November 1995 in der Katholischen Akademie Berlin
Angesichts der konfliktträchtigen Auslegungsgeschichte der gemeinsamen Hebräischen Bibel durch Juden und Christen, die noch ihre Wirkung im Nachhall des säkular-nationalistischen Judenhasses gefunden hat, standen beim Berliner Symposion vor allem folgende Fragen im Raum: Lesen Juden und Christen wirklich dieselbe Bibel? Gestattet das Verbot, sich von Gott – aber auch vom Menschen und vom Sinn der Geschichte – ein Bild zu machen, überhaupt eine theologisch-philosophische Rede über Gott? Aber wie ist ohne sie im Ernst eine Rede zu Gott, im persönlichen Gebet wie in der Liturgie verantwortbar? Verstärken nicht zusätzlich der wissenschaftliche Diskurs seit der Aufklärung sowie die Konfrontation mit den Weltreligionen die Notwendigkeit einer intellektuell redlichen Vergewisserung, was Gottrede in Wahrheit meine? Wie ist mit dem Paradox umzugehen, daß Juden und Christen so wenig darüber sagen können, wer Gott ist, wohl aber so klar und eindeutig, was sein Wille sei: das unabdingbare Gebot der Liebe? Von welchen existentiellen Erfahrungen in den Tiefenschichten des säkularen Menschen und unserer gottvergessenen Zeit kann die Gottrede so ihren Ausgang nehmen, daß sie über den "Zirkel der Eingeweihten" hinaus verstehbar und wirksam wird?
Bd. 8, 1997, 104 S., 24,80 DM, br., ISBN 3-8258-3192-2

Ulrich Engel
Umgrenzte Leere
Zur Praxis einer politisch-theologischen Ästhetik im Anschluß an Peter Weiss' Romantrilogie "Die Ästhetik des Widerstands"

LIT Verlag Münster – Hamburg – Berlin – London
Bestellungen über:
Grevener Str. 179 48159 Münster
Tel.: 0251 – 23 50 91 – Fax: 0251 – 23 19 72
e-Mail: lit@lit-verlag.de – http://www.lit-verlag.de
Preise: unv. PE

In kritische Auseinandersetzung mit Hans Urs von Balthasar und gestützt durch eine Relecture der einschlägigen philosophischen Theoriekonstrukte Walter Benjamins und Theodor W. Adornos optiert die Untersuchung zu Peter Weiss' Romantrilogie "Die Ästhetik des Widerstands" eindringlich für eine praktisch verfaßte Ästhetikfigur, die in ihrem Kern als negative Theorie zu denken ist.

Vor diesem Hintergrund entfaltet die vorliegende Studie eine Ansatz theologischer Ästhetik als eine materialistisch fundierte Theorie widerständig-hoffenden Handelns. Als Wahrnehmungslehre schärft sie den Blick für die Katastrophen der Geschichte und die unabgegoltenen Leiden der Opfer, zugleich aber auch für das messianische Kommen des abwesenden Gottes. Beharrlich weigert sie sich, das eschatologisch noch Ausstehende vorschnell zu affirmieren: In ihrer ästhetischen wie auch in ihrer theologischen Gestalt ist sie "umgrenzte Leere".

Bd. 9, 1998, 472 S., 79,80 DM, gb., ISBN 3-8258-3444-1

Reinhold Boschki; Dagmar Mensink (Hrsg.)
Kultur allein ist nicht genug
Das Werk von Elie Wiesel – Herausforderung für Religion und Gesellschaft
"Wir müssen uns darüber im klaren sein, daß es möglich ist, eine Kultur … in ein Instrument der Unmenschlichkeit zu verwandeln. Deshalb bin ich überzeugt: Kultur allein ist nicht genug." sagt Elie Wiesel – Auschwitz-Überlebender, jüdischer Schriftsteller und Friedensnobelpreisträger. Er weiß, daß nur gelebte Mitmenschlichkeit den Ausbruch von Haß und Menschenverachtung inmitten einer modernen Gesellschaft verhindern kann.
Es setzt dabei auf die verändernde Kraft des Erzählens. Sein Buch *Nacht* und seine Erzählungen und Romane aus der Welt der Bibel, des Talmud und des Schtetl sind durchdrungen von bohrenden Fragen: Was ist der Mensch, daß er tötet um des Tötens willen? Wo war Gott in Auschwitz?
Dieses Buch lotet die Bedeutung von Wiesels Zeugnis für Wissenschaft, Religion und gesellschaftliche Praxis aus. Unter den Beiträgen von SchülerInnen und Freunden sind erstmals auch maßgebliche amerikanische Stimmen in deutscher Sprache zugänglich. Ein Vortrag von Elie Wiesel und eine ausführliche Bibliographie ergänzen die kenntnisreichen Studien zum Werk des Autors, der am 30. September 1998 siebzig Jahre alt wurde.
Mit Beiträgen von: Irving Abrahamson, Alan L. Berger, Joel Berger, Ruth Bergida, Reinhold Boschki, Gundula van den Berg, Micha Brumlik, Harry James Cargas, Alice L. Eckardt, A. Roy Eckardt, Anat Feinberg, Albert H. Friedlander, Martha Hauptman, Joseph A. Kanofsky, Volkhard Knigge, Karl-Josef Kuschel, Lawrence L. Langer,

Verena Lenzen, Dagmar Mensink, Johann Baptist Metz, Christoph Münz, Nehemia Polen, Rolf Rendtorff, John K. Roth, Alan Rosen, Janet Schenk McCord, Werner Schneider, Dorothee Sölle, Jean-François Thomas und Elie Wiesel.

Bd. 10, 1998, 432 S., 69,80 DM, br., ISBN 3-8258-3576-6

Johann Reikerstorfer (Hrsg.)
Vom Wagnis der Nichtidentität
Johann Baptist Metz zu Ehren
Die Autoren dieser "Festgabe" möchten J. B. Metz anläßlich seines 70. Geburtstags ein Stück seiner Geschichte, die sich vor allem mit Wien, dem philosophischen Institut der Universität und dem Institut für Fundamentaltheologie verbindet, in Erinnerung rufen und als eine produktive Begegnung dokumentieren. Als Leitmotiv dient ihnen die Interpretation der neuen Politischen Theologie als "negative Theologie", um sie unter dieser Hinsicht im heutigen theologischen Grundlagendiskurs als Angebot für eine kommunikative Gottesrede zu erfragen, die sich der "Nichtidentität" aussetzt und verpflichtet weiß. J. Reikerstorfer zeigt, daß in der denkgeschichtlichen Entwicklung dieses Konzepts die kritisch-produktive Kraft der Negativität zuletzt mit der Frage nach der "Zeit", ihrer Eigenart und dem darin gelegenen Sinn von "Alterität" ihre volle Schärfe gewinnt und entfaltet. In Auseinandersetzung mit dem Karsamstagsmotiv bei H. U. v. Balthasar und E. Przywara erörtert M. Zechmeister die Metzsche "Leidenserinnerung" als Basis für eine "Theologie des Gottvermissens". Die Universalität dieser Gottesrede sucht P. Zeillinger gegenüber der Kritik an universalistischen Ansprüchen über die "schwachen Kategorien" der Erinnerung und der Anerkennung der Anderen in ihrem Anderssein zu entwickeln, während B. Taubald den Einbruch des Nichtidentischen in die neue Politische Theologie im Spiegel ihres Erinnerungsbegriffs aufspürt und die Erinnerung selbst in ihrer Intention als leidempfindliche Vergegenwärtigung des "Unsagbaren" interpretiert. Schließlich bringt W. Klaghofer literarische Motive bei F. Werfel in eine Nähe zu J. B. Metz, indem er die messianische Hoffnung auf das Ende der Zeiten als Widerstand gegen das menschliche Unrecht politischer Gewalt- und Unterdrückungsgeschichten ins Blickfeld rückt.

Bd. 11, 1998, 184 S., 34,80 DM, br., ISBN 3-8258-3767-x

Jürgen Manemann;
Johann Baptist Metz (Hrsg.)
Christologie nach Auschwitz
Stellungnahmen im Anschluß an Thesen von Tiemo Rainer Peters
Der vorliegende Band präsentiert zehn Thesen zur "Christologie nach Auschwitz" von *Tiemo Rainer Peters* und versammelt dazu Stellungnahmen, zu-

LIT Verlag Münster – Hamburg – Berlin – London
Bestellungen über:
Grevener Str. 179 48159 Münster
Tel.: 0251 – 23 50 91 – Fax: 0251 – 23 19 72
e-Mail: lit@lit-verlag.de – http://www.lit-verlag.de
Preise: unv. PE

stimmende, weiterführende, kritisch rückfragende Kurzkommentare – von Schülern und Freunden, von Sympathisanten und auch von kritischen Begleitern einer Politischen Theologie, für die die Katastrophe von Auschwitz zur inneren Situation der christlichen Gottesrede gehört, so daß ihr der Rückzug auf eine situationsblinde Heilsmetaphysik oder auf einen menschenleeren Geschichtsidealismus angesichts dieser Katastrophe verwehrt ist.
Beiträger sind:
Reinhold Boschki, Edna Brocke, Ulrich Engel, Paulus Engelhardt, Hans-Gerd Janßen, Ottmar John, Maureen Junker-Kenny, Bertil Langenohl, Jürgen Manemann, Friedrich-Wilhelm Marquardt, Reyes Mate, Johann Baptist Metz, Jürgen Moltmann, Otto Hermann Pesch, Birte Petersen, Thomas Pröpper, Johann Reikerstorfer, Jürgen Werbick
Die zweite Auflage ist erweitert um eine Erwiderung von Tiemo Rainer Peters.

Bd. 12, 2. Aufl. 2001, 192 S., 29,90 DM, br., ISBN 3-8258-3979-9

Karl Rahner Akademie (Hrsg.)
Geschichte denken
Mit Beiträgen von H. M. Baumgartner, K. Flasch, J. Maier, J. B. Metz, A. Schmidt, H. Schnädelbach und H. Schweppenhäuser
Das Nachdenken über Geschichte hat mit der Publikation von Francis Fukuyama "Das Ende der Geschichte" kein Ende gefunden, wohl eher einen neuen Impuls bekommen. Zweifellos: Philosophie, die beansprucht, einen objektiven Sinn der Geschichte aufzeigen zu können, ist nicht ohne Grund in Verruf geraten. Aber sollte man deshalb gleich für den "Abschied von der Geschichtsphilosophie"(O. Marquard) plädieren? Wer sich in der Wirklichkeit, so wie sie geworden ist, nicht bloß einrichten will, der wird auf geschichtsphilosophische Erkenntnis nicht verzichten wollen, der wird auch nach dem propagierten "Ende der Geschichte" weiterhin "Geschichte denken".

Bd. 13, 1999, 128 S., 29,80 DM, br., ISBN 3-8258-4176-6

Johann Reikerstorfer (Hrsg.)
Zum gesellschaftlichen Schicksal der Theologie
Ein Wiener Symposium zu Ehren von Johann Baptist Metz (November 1998). Mit Beiträgen von E. Jüngel, J. B. Metz u. a.
Tiefgreifende Wandlungen im gesellschaftlichen Bewußtsein sind mittlerweile auch zu neuen Herausforderungen der theologischen Fakultäten geworden. Die religiös pluralistische Situation, die schwindende Akzeptanz unserer Kirchen mit ihren Konkordaten, der wachsende Integrationsprozeß der europäischen Länder, die keine Universitätstheologie nach deutschsprachigem Modell kennen, nicht zuletzt aber auch Entwicklungen im modernen Wissenschaftsverständnis machen grundsätzlich Überlegungen zum Status des universitären Theologiebetriebs unausweichlich.
Der vorliegende Band dokumentiert ein "Wiener Symposion zum gesellschaftlichen Schicksal der Theologie", das die Katholisch-Theologische Fakultät der Universität Wien anläßlich des 70. Geburtstags von Johann Baptist Metz am 27./28. November 1998 veranstaltete. Der offene interdisziplinäre Disput vereint ein breites Spektrum an Perspektiven und Kompetenzen und versucht Chancen und Verpflichtungen in der modernen Wissenschaftswelt im Blick auf eine gesellschaftlich angefragte und herausgeforderte Theologie zu erkunden. Leitende Gesichtspunkte des Kolloquiums stammen aus den Bereichen der Gesellschafts- und Universitätspolitik, des Staatskirchenrechts, sowie der Philosophie und der systematischen Theologie. Hierfür schärfte die Politische Theologie von J. B. Metz nicht nur die Aufmerksamkeit für entsprechende Problemstellungen, sie war im Rahmen des Symposions auch vielfach "Motor" und immer wieder gesuchter "Ansprechpartner" in den Beiträgen und Stellungnahmen.
Mit Beiträgen von H. J. Vogel u. E. Busek (Politik), L. Nagl (Philosophie), E. Jüngel u. U. Körtner (ev. Theologie), P. M. Zulehner u. J. Reikerstorfer (kath. Theologie), R. Potz (Staatskirchenrecht), G. Luf (Rechtsphilosophie) und Weihbischof H. Krätzl, sowie Auszügen aus der Diskussion mit J. B. Metz.

Bd. 14, 1999, 176 S., 39,80 DM, br., ISBN 3-8258-4175-8

Ulrich Willers
Nietzsches Jesus
Bd. 15, Herbst 2001, 128 S., 29,80 DM, br., ISBN 3-8258-4925-2

Barbara Nichtweiß (Hrsg.)
Vom Ende der Zeit
Geschichtstheologie und Eschatologie bei Erik Peterson. Symposium Mainz 2000. Mit Beiträgen von Klaus Berger, Ferdinand Hahn, Karl Lehmann, Eduard Lohse, Hans Maier, Christoph Markschies u. a.
Das spannungsreiche Verhältnis von Geschichte und Christentum bestimmte die Theologie Erik Petersons (1890–1960): Trotz der Entdeckung der biblischen Eschatologie und ihrer kritischen Implikationen blieb er als Historiker der Geschichte in reflektierter Erforschung verpflichtet. Theologen und Historiker diskutieren nun seine – z. T. noch unveröffentlichten – Beiträge zu Religionsgeschichte (C. Markschies), Exegese (F. Hahn, E. Lohse, K. Scholtissek, K. Berger), systematischer Theologie (Th. Ervens, S. Dückers, G. Unbarri, K. Anglet) und politischer Zeitgeschichte (W. Löser,

LIT Verlag Münster – Hamburg – Berlin – London
Bestellungen über:
Grevener Str. 179 48159 Münster
Tel.: 0251 – 23 50 91 – Fax: 0251 – 23 19 72
e-Mail: lit@lit-verlag.de – http://www.lit-verlag.de
Preise: unv. PE

H. *Maier)* sowie Aspekte eines wechselvollen Lebens *(K. Lehmann, G. Caronello, B. Nichtweiß).*
Bd. 16, 2001, 344 S., 49,80 DM, gb., ISBN 3-8258-4926-0

Maureen Junker-Kenny (ed.)
Memory, Narrativity, Self and the Challenge to Think God
The Reception within Theology of the Recent Work of Paul Ricoeur
The idea behind the book is explore the usefulness of major categories of Paul Ricoeur's work, such as "memory", "narrativity". and his conception of self, within different theological disciplines, such as Systematic Theology, Theological Ethics, and Practical Theology. Experts from different cultural and language traditions were invited in order to highlight the variations in the reception of Ricoeur's work in the North American, British, German and Scandinavian contexts with their different philosophical and theological heritages. While Ricoeur has been a continuous dialogue partner for theology in North America, it is only now that philosophical and theological interest is resurging in Germany; this is evident in the number of conference invitations, books and PhD themes as well as interviews such as the one in DIE ZEIT where he is portrayed as the doyen of French philosophy. The focus of his theological reception is in Christian Ethics where his categories are seen as most fruitful in conceptualizing relationships between biographical, moral and religious identity. The concept of narrativity as mediating between the normative ethics of the Kantian tradition and the ethics of striving or virtue ethics of the Neoaristotelians, Hille Haker's contribution explores this theme. In Systematic Theology, Werner Jeanrond and Janet Soskice discuss Ricoeur in the context of the hermeneutics of revelation and of prior attempts of "naming God" by Christian thinkers such as Augustine. Christoph Mandry shows from the perspective of Philosophical or Foundational Theology how Ricoeur is inclined to deny the challenge not simply to proclaim God but also to think the concept of God in the history of the dialectic between the human self and God within Continental European philosophy. In Practical Theology, John van den Hengel outlines Ricoeur's contribution to a theory of Christian praxis. Paul Ricoeur's responses to the papers and at the Roundtable discussion are immediate and clarifying with regard to misconceptions of his position, changes within his thinking and his self-understanding as a philosopher in dialogue with professional interpreters of the Christian tradition. In this sense, I believe that the different perspectives on his work would cohere as a book since they complement each other with regard to the evolution of his thinking, the value of his mediating position in so many contemporary modern/postmodern debates, spanning Aristotle, Kant, Derrida and Levinas, and the usefulness of his categories for foundational questions in different theological disciplines. Its coherence does not lie in shared points of departure between the authors but rather in converging insights from different language and thought traditions.
Bd. 17, Herbst 2001, ca. 200 S., ca. 39,80 DM, pb., ISBN 3-8258-4930-9

Benjamin Taubald
Anamnetische Vernunft
Untersuchungen zu einem Begriff der neuen Politischen Theologie
"Ein wichtiger Beitrag zur Theoriegestalt der neuen Politischen Theologie und zur Erläuterung ihrer Basiskategorie, der *memoria passionis,* im philosophisch-theologischen Grundlagendiskurs."
Johann Baptist Metz
Bd. 18, 2001, 208 S., 39,80 DM, br., ISBN 3-8258-5151-6

Detlef Schneider-Stengel
Christentum und Postmoderne
Zu einer Neubewertung von Theologie und Metaphysik
Christliche Theologie und philosophische Ansätze der Postmoderne stehen, so scheint es, in einem schwierigen, wenn nicht konträren Verhältnis zueinander. Wenn man aber genauer hinsieht, dann haben beide mehr gemeinsam, als sie selbst voneinander glauben. Denn die Postmoderne, so die These von Leslie Fiedler, ist genuin religiös. Die vorliegende Arbeit hat sich zum Ziel gesetzt, mit Hilfe der Religionsphilosophie anhand moderner Mythos- und Metapherntheorien einen Dialog zu initiieren, der für beide Seiten sehr fruchtbar wäre. Die aufgezeigten und entwickelten Dialogmodelle könnten dann als hermeneutische Gesprächshilfen dienen.
Bd. 19, Herbst 2001, 296 S., 49,80 DM, br., ISBN 3-8258-5011-0

Jürgen Werbick
Gebetsglaube und Gotteszweifel
Ist der Zweifel nur ein Glaubensdefizit, so daß der Glaube ihn eigentlich überwinden müßte? Die Studien dieses Bandes versuchen, zu einer anderen Bestimmung des Verhältnisses von Glauben und Zweifeln zu kommen. Ihre gemeinsame Intention ist die Entfaltung einer Gebetstheologie, die sich von den Grundvollzügen des Betens zu denken geben läßt. Zentrale Themen dieser Theologie des Betens sind u. a.: Gewißheit und Zweifel, Gebet als Gottsuche, die Krise des Bittgebets und der Glaube an den allmächti-

LIT Verlag Münster – Hamburg – Berlin – London
Bestellungen über:
Grevener Str. 179 48159 Münster
Tel.: 0251 – 23 50 91 – Fax: 0251 – 23 19 72
e-Mail: lit@lit-verlag.de – http://www.lit-verlag.de
Preise: unv. PE

gen Gott, die Bitte um Erlösung, Doxologie und Trinitätslehre, Dogma – Symbol – Gebet.
Bd. 20, Herbst 2001, 288 S., 39,80 DM, gb., ISBN 3-8258-5379-9

Paulus Budi Kleden
Christologie in Fragmenten
Die Rede von Jesus Christus im Spannungsfeld von Hoffnungs- und Leidensgeschichte bei Johann Baptist Metz
Wer den Namen Johann Baptist Metz hört, dem fällt wohl zuerst die Theodizeefrage ein, da es dieses Thema ist, um welches das Schaffen von Metz unermüdlich kreist. Indem Metz aber auf der geschichtlichen Unbeantwortbarkeit der Theodizeefrage beharrt, setzt er sich dem Vorwurf auf, die Heilsbedeutung des Christusereignisses nicht hinreichend zu berücksichtigen. Indem aber nach den impliziten Voraussetzungen dieser Theologie gefragt wird, zeigen sich die darin enthaltenen christologischen Gehalte auf, die das zunächst augenscheinliche christologische Defizit zumindest teilweise auszugleichen imstande sind.
Bd. 21, 2001, 448 S., 79,80 DM, br., ISBN 3-8258-5198-2

Bernhard Nitsche
Göttliche Universalität in konkreter Geschichte
Eine transzendental-geschichtlichen Vergewisserung der Christologie in Auseinandersetzung mit Richard Schaeffler und Karl Rahner
Die Kritik am christlichen Absolutheitsanspruchs und am idealistischen Geschichtsdenken ist Anlaß, nach einer philosophisch vergewisserten Methode zu fragen, welche die Einmaligkeit menschlicher Freiheitsgeschichte und das bleibende Verwiesensein der freien Menschen aufeinander sowie die Ansprechbarkeit für Gott und seine mögliche Offenbarung in der Geschichte angemessen reflektieren kann. Richard Schaeffler und Karl Rahner stehen von religionsphilosophischer bzw. theologischer Seite für ein Freiheitsdenken, welches den geschichtlichen Charakter der transzendentalen Bedingungen des menschlichen Weltverhaltens hervorhebt. In kritischer Auseinandersetzung mit ihren Optionen kann plausibilisiert werden, daß die singuläre Geschichte des konkreten Menschen Jesus für alle Menschen Bedeutung gewinnen kann, ohne die Situation des Leidens und der Ungerechtigkeit auszublenden, die bleibende Berufung Israels zu enteignen oder die Marginalisierung von Frauen im Christentum zu überspielen. Inhaltlich wird die geschichtsbewußte und das Leiden und Unabgegoltene der Menschen erinnernde Gestalt transzendentalen Denkens in einer futurisch-eschatologischen Konzeption des (er-)wartenden Christus zentriert, welche als positionell christliche Wahrheitsantizipation des Ganzen in den Dialog der jeweils perspektivischen Weltanschauungen und Religionen eingebracht wird.
Bd. 22, 2001, 562 S., 79,80 DM, gb., ISBN 3-8258-5136-2

Klaus Kienzler; Josef Reiter; Ludwig Wenzler (Hrsg.)
Das Heilige im Denken
Ansätze und Konturen einer Philosophie der Religion. Zu Ehren von Bernhard Casper
Die Fülle der geschichtlichen Religionen ist unüberschaubar. Doch ihnen allen ist gemeinsam die Beziehung auf das Heilige. Deutung des Phänomens des Heiligen wie Klärung seines Begriffs bilden deshalb den Ansatz für jede Philosophie der Religion. "Erst aus dem Wesen des Heiligen ist das Wesen von Gottheit zu denken.´´(Martin Heidegger). Wie das Heilige erscheint und erfahren wird, ist jedoch entscheidend mitbestimmt durch Denkweisen und Denkformen, in denen es sich zeigt. Die Phänomenologie des Heiligen entfaltet sich somit als Korrelationsforschung. Denkvollzug und Denkinhalt bestimmen sich gegenseitig. Unter dieser methodischen Hinsicht sind die Beiträge des Bandes erarbeitet. Exemplarisch zeigen sie auf, in welchen "Gestalten´´ sich das Heilige in seiner Begegnung mit unterschiedlichen Weisen des Denkens manifestiert. So werden die Dimensionen einer phänomenologisch-hermeneutischen Religionsphilosophie sichtbar.
Bd. 23, Herbst 2001, 454 S., 89,80 DM, br., ISBN 3-8258-5533-3

Ulrich Willers; Gotthard Fuchs (Hrsg.)
Theodizee im Zeichen von Dionysos
Mit Beiträgen von Johann Figl, Hans Gerald Hödl, Magnus Striet, Christoph Türcke u. a.
Bd. 25, Herbst 2001, 208 S., 39,80 DM, br., ISBN 3-8258-5561-9

Ansgar Koschel (Hrsg.)
Katholische Kirche und Judentum im 20. Jahrhundert
Mit Beiträgen von Herbert Bettelheim, Ernst-Ludwig Ehrlich, Mehachem Kanafi, Gerhard Riegner, Herbert Smolinsky und Erich Zenger
Bd. 26, Herbst 2001, 168 S., 34,80 DM, br., ISBN 3-8258-5507-4

Lydia Bendel-Maidl
Tradition und Innovation
Zur Dialektik von historischer und systematischer Perspektive in der Theologie am Beispiel der Transformationen in der

LIT Verlag Münster – Hamburg – Berlin – London
Bestellungen über:
Grevener Str. 179 48159 Münster
Tel.: 0251 – 23 50 91 – Fax: 0251 – 23 19 72
e-Mail: lit@lit-verlag.de – http://www.lit-verlag.de

Preise: unv. PE

Rezeption des Thomas von Aquin im
20. Jahrhundert
Bd. 27, Herbst 2001, 504 S., 89,90 DM, br.,
ISBN 3-8258-5589-9

Jahrbuch Politische Theologie

herausgegeben von Torsten Habbel,
Hans-Gerd Janßen, Ottmar John,
Jürgen Manemann, Michael J. Rainer,
Claus Urban, Bernd Wacker und José A. Zamora

Jürgen Manemann (Hrsg.)
Demokratiefähigkeit
Mit Statements von E. W. Böcken-
förde, E. Brocke, F. Duve, P. Hintze,
W. Kretschmann, J. Moltmann, D. Sölle
und Beiträgen von T. R. Peters, J. B.
Metz, O. John, M. J. Rainer, W. Oelmüller,
J. Manemann u. a.
Den vorliegenden Band I "Demokratiefähigkeit"
eröffnen Statements zur Frage "Was heißt eigent-
lich politisch?" Beteiligt sind der Verfassungs-
richter *Ernst-Wolfgang Böckenförde*, die Politiker
Peter Hintze (CDU), *Freimut Duve* (SPD) und
Winfried Kretschmann (Bündnis 90/Die Grünen)
sowie mit theologischer Perspektive *Jürgen Molt-
mann*, *Dorothee Sölle* und *Edna Brocke*.
Beiträge von *Tiemo R. Peters, Johann Baptist
Metz, Ottmar John, Michael J. Rainer, Willi Oelmüller, Jürgen Manemann, Edmund Arens, Kuno
Füssel* und *Michael Ramminger* vertiefen den
grundlegenden Zusammenhang zwischen Monotheismus, Theodizee und moderner demokratischer
Gesellschaft. *Debatte* – diesmal um die "Politik
der Anerkennung der Anderen" (mit Thesen von
Günter P. Suess und Kommentaren von Walter
Lesch, Matthias Möhring-Hesse und Peter Rott-
länder), *Rezensionen* (zur aktuellen C. Schmitt-
Diskussion) und Portraits einschlägiger *Institu-
te/Projekte* (Fritz Bauer Institut, Frankfurt a. M.;
Institut für Theologie und Politik, Münster) zeigen
weitere Dimensionen politisch-theologischer Ar-
beit.
Bd. 1/1996, 2. Aufl. 2000, 240 S., 34,80 DM, br.,
ISBN 3-8258-2227-3

Michael J. Rainer; Hans-Gerd Janßen (Hrsg.)
Bilderverbot
Das Jahrbuch Politische Theologie Band II stellt
mit "Bilderverbot" ein ungewöhnliches, aber
theologisch zentrales Thema in den Mittelpunkt.
Im Blick auf häufig undurchschaute Querverbin-
dungen z. B. in Kunst und Medien, verweist das
Jahrbuch auf neue und alte "unsichtbare Mächte".
Es untersucht fragwürdige Profile politischer
Ästhetik und kritisiert mitunter verdeckte

Ansprüche auf universale Gültigkeit seitens
bildloser Machtsysteme. Die ursprünglich in den
Religionen gestellte Problem der "Abbildbarkeit
des Unvorstellbaren" gewinnt über die aktuelle
Denkmaldebatte neue Brisanz.
Bd. 2/1997, 1997, 344 S., 39,80 DM, br., ISBN 3-8258-2795-x

Jürgen Manemann (Hrsg.)
Befristete Zeit
In Band 3 wird der Zeitindex der Theologie dis-
kursorisch herausgearbeitet: "Wer christlich zu
denken glaubt und dies ohne Frist zu denken
glaubt, ist schwachsinnig." (J. Taubes). Zeit als
Frist denken – das ist der Theologie aufgege-
ben. Eine apokalyptisch angeschärfte Gottesrede
verweigert sich der bloßen Faktizität, indem sie
ihren Herrschaftscharakter zu enthüllen und einen
Horizont aufzubrechen versucht, von dem aus
Geschichte in ihrer Herrschafts- und Unterwer-
fungsstruktur entlarvt und in ihrer subjekthaft
erfahrenen Leidens- und Hoffnungsstruktur er-
kennbar wird. Ein solcher Entwurf provoziert
eine kontroverse Diskussion im Zeitalter der Be-
schleunigungen und der Zeitvergessenheit. Zu
dieser Diskussion im Konzert mit anderen Dis-
ziplinen (Soziologie, Philosophie, Politologie,
Ästhetik u. a.) herauszufordern, ist die Aufgabe
des 3. Bandes.
Bd. 3, 1999, 280 S., 39,80 DM, br., ISBN 3-8258-3957-5

Jürgen Manemann (Hrsg.)
Monotheismus
Der 4. Band des Jahrbuchs Politische Theolo-
gie schaltet sich in den gegenwärtigen Diskurs
über den Monotheismus ein. Ansetzend mit der
Frage nach dem Zusammenhang von Ethik und
Monotheismus wird die Kritik des ethischen
Monotheismus im ausgehenden 20. Jahrhundert fo-
kussiert. Der Band enthält Analysen gegenwärtiger
Anti-Monotheismen in der (post-)modernen Ge-
sellschaft und in christlichen trinitätstheologischen
Auslegungen. Zur Debatte steht im besonderen
das Monotheismusverständnis, das Jan Assmann
in seinen Studien entworfen hat .und sein Versuch,
die dem Monotheismus inhärenten Feindbilder,
nämlich Ägypten und den Polytheismus, zu reha-
bilitieren.
Autoren dieses Bandes sind u. a.: J. Assmann, R.
Faber, T. Freyer, D. Krochmalnik, J. Manemann,
G. Neuhaus, D. Patterson, M.-T. Wacker.
Bd. 4, Herbst 2001, 280 S., 39,80 DM, br.,
ISBN 3-8258-4426-9

LIT Verlag Münster – Hamburg – Berlin – London
Bestellungen über:
Grevener Str. 179 48159 Münster
Tel.: 0251 – 23 50 91 – Fax: 0251 – 23 19 72
e-Mail: lit@lit-verlag.de – http://www.lit-verlag.de
Preise: unv. PE